Hockey NOW!

FIFTH EDITION

Hockey NOW!

FIFTH EDITION

MIKE LEONETTI

FIREFLY BOOKS

A FIREFLY BOOK

Published by Firefly Books Ltd. 2008

First printing

Publisher Cataloging-in-Publication Data (U.S.)
Leonetti, Mike, 1958-
    Hockey now! / Mike Leonetti.
5th ed.
[ ] p. : col. photos. ; cm.
Includes index.
ISBN-13: 978-1-55407-339-9 (pbk.)
ISBN-10: 1-55407-339-1 (pbk.)
1. National Hockey League -- Biography. 2. Hockey players --
Biography. I. Title.
796.962/092 dc22   GV848.5 A1L45 2008

Library and Archives Canada Cataloguing in Publication
Leonetti, Mike, 1958-
    Hockey now! / Mike Leonetti. -- 5th ed.
Includes index.
ISBN-13: 978-1-55407-339-9 (pbk.)
ISBN-10: 1-55407-339-1 (pbk.)
1. Hockey players--Biography. 2. National Hockey League--
Biography. 3. Hockey players--Pictorial works. 4. National Hockey
League--Pictorial works. I. Title.
GV848.5.A1L455 2008   796.962092'2   C2008-901126-0

Published in the United States by
Firefly Books (U.S.) Inc.
P.O. Box 1338, Ellicott Station
Buffalo, New York 14205

Published in Canada by
Firefly Books Ltd.
66 Leek Crescent
Richmond Hill, Ontario L4B 1H1

Cover and interior design by Kimberley Young

Printed in China

The publisher gratefully acknowledges the financial support for our publishing program by the Government of Canada through the Book Publishing Industry Development Program.

PHOTO CREDITS

Graig Abel/NHL 12, 30, 34, 36, 106, 114, 115, 140; Claus Andersen 46; Scott Audette/NHL 18, 35, 38, 60, 72(back), 74, 92, 93, 96, 108, 112 (front) 130; Brian Babineau/NHL 28, 76; Steve Babineau/NHL 116; Bruce Bennett 20, 23, 37, 51, 90, 121, 122, 125; Scott Cunningham/NHL 8 (front), 10, 11, 16, 31, 112 (back), 120, 141, 146 (front), 149; Andy Devlin 4, 45, 49, 56, 97, 155; Stephen Dunn 83; Steve Dykes 89; Gregg Forwerck/NHL 9; Jeff Gross 58; Norm Hall/NHL 61, 129; Jed Jacobsohn 100; Glenn James/NHL 102; Robert Laberge 146 (back), 167; Ronald Martinez 103, 145; Phillip MacCallum 117; Dale MacMillan 66; Andy Marlin/NHL 163; Jim McIsaac 32, 64, 65, 85, 113, 132, 148, 157, 165; Juan Ocampo/NHL 43; Christian Petersen 33, 41, 101, 143; Len Redkoles/NHL 8 (back),19, 22, 39, 75, 80, 81, 153, 171; Dave Reginek/NHL 40 (front), 48, 54, 59, 71, 72 (front), 94, 110, 127, 136, 142, 144, 147; Andre Ringuette/NHL14, 29, 87, 98, 107, 123, 124, 131; Debora Robinson/NHL 42; John Russell/NHL 40 (back), 44, 50, 57, 63, 78, 104, 111, 126, 128, 138, 173, 175; Jamie Sabau 2, 139, 151, 159, 161; Dave Sandford 68, 95, 99, 118, 135; Dave Sandford/NHL 21, 27, 133; Bill Smith/NHL 47; Don Smith/NHL 67, 119; Mike Stobe /NHL 13, 24, 25, 26, 73, 82, 84, 109; Gerry Thomas/NHL 62, 137; Jeff Vinnick/NHL 52, 53, 70, 88, 105; Brad Watson/NHL 169; Bill Wippert/NHL 15, 77, 86, 134

Front Cover: Scott Audette/NHL (Vincent Lecavalier); Kevin C. Cox (Sidney Crosby); Michael Martin/NHL (Jarome Iginla); Jim McIsaac (Alex Ovechkin); Debora Robinson/NHL (Chris Pronger)

Back Cover: Graig Abel/NHL (Vesa Toskala); Dale MacMillan (Joe Thornton); Andre Ringuette/NHL (Jason Spezza)

DEDICATION

The fifth edition of *Hockey Now!* is dedicated to the new youth of the NHL — the players who are securing the future of the game.

CONTENTS

The NHL has become younger, faster and more exciting than ever. Young guns now dot every NHL roster as each club tries to keep up with the demands of the game. Make no mistake, some teams have been better at this transition to a more youthful league since the post-lockout rules than others, but the wave of the future is undeniable. The shift to young legs also makes it clear the NHL is in good hands for years to come as the league is filled with some of the most promising emerging stars in all of sport.

For the fifth edition of *Hockey Now!* we have parted ways with some of the NHL's old guard. A few of them like Mike Modano, Joe Sakic and Brendan Shanahan, may still be playing in the NHL but it is pretty clear that their influence is on the wane with their careers on the verge of ending. In their place are the stars like Alex Ovechkin, Sidney Crosby, Dion Phaneuf, Henrik Zetterberg and Pavel Datsyuk — the NHL's new elite. What is even more exciting are fresh faces like Evgeni Malkin, Jonathan Toews, Mike Richards, Ryan Getzlaff, Corey Perry, Jason Spezza, Paul Statsny and Zach Parise, who have risen to prominence.

Many of the stars profiled in this edition represent the best of the new wave of NHLers. In addition to their youth, these players possess an abundance of offensive flair. They can shoot effectively, be very physical when needed and are highly skilled and ready to leap into the attack — many were ready to jump into the league

shortly after their draft day! Teams like Montreal, Pittsburgh and Washington all thrived in 2007–08 with a highly skilled style that stressed offense. Other young studs making waves today include players like Patrick Kane, Nicklas Backstrom, Carey Price, Jordan Staal, Anze Kopitar, Jack Johnson and Steve Stamkos, among others. Once these players get a little more experience, it is almost certain they'll be in the pages of the next *Hockey Now!*.

Every protégé needs a mentor and the youth of the NHL have many veterans in the prime of their career to observe. Players like Vincent Lecavalier, Jarome Iginla, Nicklas Lidstrom, Martin Brodeur and Joe Thornton are all of all-star caliber. Their skill, veteran grit and various paths to prominence make them great leaders. They

all took their time and earned the recognition of being players who make significant contributions.

The 2008 Stanley Cup final between the Pittsburgh Penguins and Detroit Red Wings proved to be an interesting contrast between youthful exuberance and veteran savvy. The Penguins ripped through the Eastern Conference in the playoffs and it looked like the surging Pittsburgh club led by Crosby, Malkin and Marc-Andre Fluery was set to win the championship. However the veteran poise of the Red Wings proved to be too much for the less-experienced Penguins and it was over in six games. Perhaps the real lesson is that all teams need a mix of youth and experience if they are to win hockey's ultimate prize.

INTRODUCTION

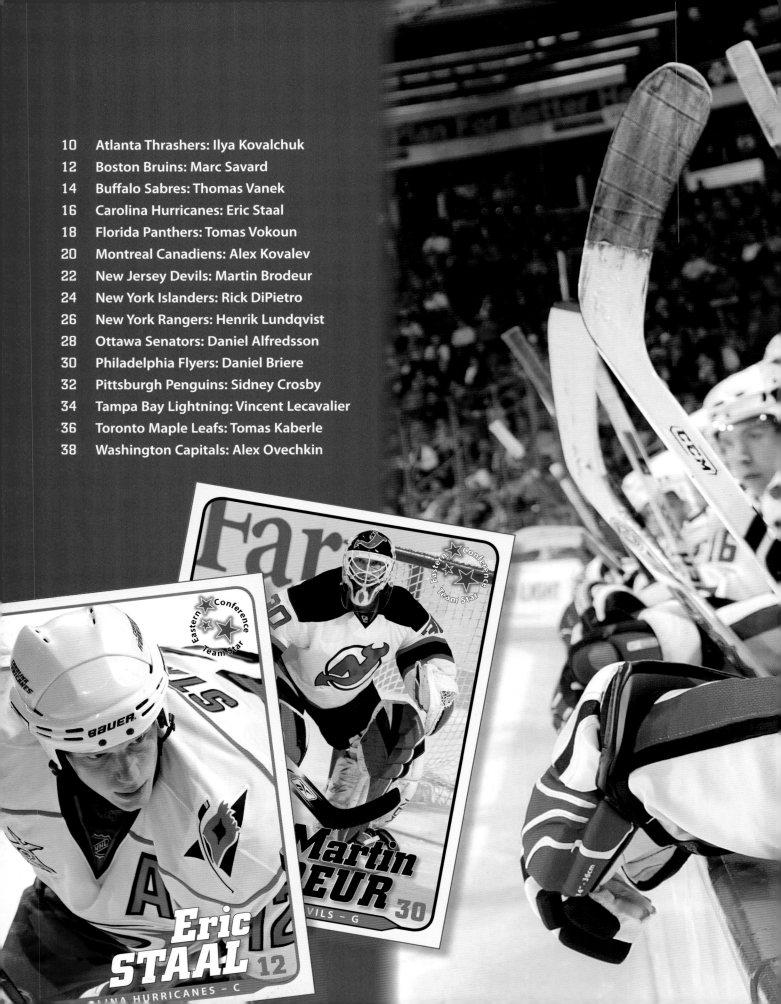

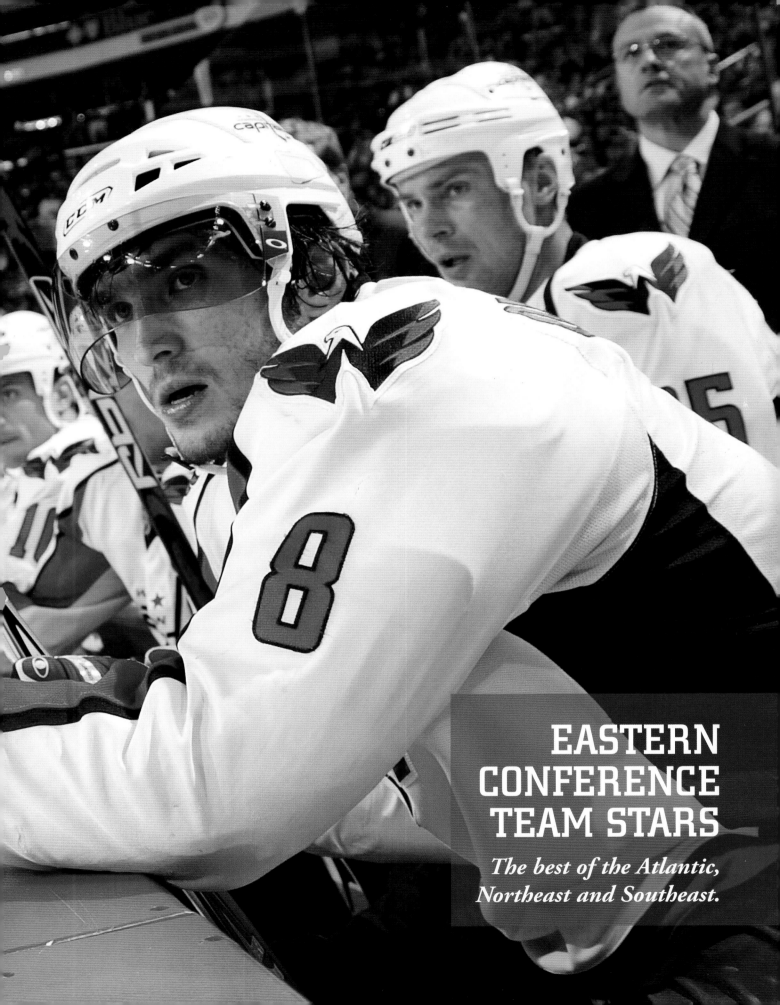

EASTERN CONFERENCE TEAM STARS

The best of the Atlantic, Northeast and Southeast.

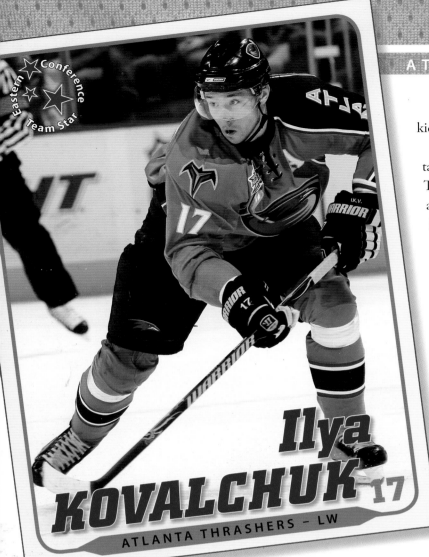

Eastern Conference Team Star

Ilya KOVALCHUK 17

ATLANTA THRASHERS – LW

There is a thin line between confidence and cockiness, and Ilya Kovalchuk has been known to cross it. But then again, the Atlanta Thrasher superstar has plenty of reasons to be self-assured. North Americans first saw a display of the youngster's brashness at the 2001 World Junior Championship, when Kovalchuk scored an empty-net goal against Canada and skated down the ice pumping his fist. In a game against Edmonton in his rookie year, Kovalchuk was caught using an illegal stick. The Oilers didn't score on the power play, but Kovalchuk stormed out of the penalty box to take a pass with a stick he had borrowed from a teammate and scored the game-winning goal. He then enraged the Oilers by skating by their bench and pretending to check his stick for faults. No doubt this kid was different than the average player.

Kovalchuk become the first Russian ever to be taken No. 1 overall at the NHL draft when the Thrashers called his name in 2001. Four months after his draft day, the big winger was lining up with fellow rookie Dany Heatley on what would become the Thrashers' top line. It was a perfect match, both in Thrasher uniforms and in street clothes. Off the ice, the two franchise cornerstones clicked from the moment they met. They had lockers next to each other, roomed together on the road and Heatley helped Kovalchuk learn English. On the ice, Kovalchuk led all NHL rookies in 2001–02 with 29 goals and Heatley led in assists. Heatley finished first in rookie scoring and Kovalchuk was second despite missing 15 games with an injury. That was the same order they finished in the voting for the Calder Trophy, awarded to the NHL's top rookie performer. The Thrashers didn't have much else to go along with their two fab freshmen, however, and finished 2001–02 with just 54 points. Kovalchuk and Heatley combined for a whopping 30 percent of the club's 187 goals.

Kovalchuk not only avoided the sophomore jinx, he also improved his numbers by scoring 38 goals and adding 29 assists. His defensive game still left a lot to be desired as he was a horrid minus-24, but given their lack of talent the Thrashers really had no option but to live with defensive shortcomings. The next season, 2003–04, saw Kovalchuk tie Jarome Iginla and Rick Nash for the league lead in goals with 41. That got him a share of the Maurice Richard Trophy. Still, the Thrashers missed the post-season and then started 2005–06 without Heatley, who was traded to Ottawa after missing most of the previous season following a car accident. Kovalchuk was now being counted on more than ever and he responded with a career-best 98 points. The right winger also became a respectable defensive player.

Kovalchuk's play is defined by speed, puck possession and using his sturdy 6-foot-1, 220-pound frame to drive to the net. He has huge forearms and incredibly strong wrists, which allow him to fire pucks quickly on net with plenty of juice behind each drive. Kovalchuk's great shot first developed as a youngster when he practiced hitting targets his father set up for him. Slapshots were not allowed because he might break a stick and replacements were not readily available. He became adept at hitting the corners of the net because his father stressed to him that it was better to miss the net than put the puck right into the goalie. The Thrashers know they have a pure goal-scorer, but sometimes face a challenge in getting Kovalchuk, who's minus-73 in his career, to increase his attention to defense while not cramping his spectacular offensive style.

Over the last three years, Kovalchuk has remained one of the great pure goal-scorers of this era, scoring 52, 42 and 52 goals. However, the Thrashers have made the playoffs only once over that time and their star player remains frustrated at the team's lack of success when it matters most.

What Kovalchuk can actually do when surrounded by talent was shown during the 2008 World Championship when he scored the winning goal for the Russians to beat the host Canadians in overtime of the championship game. His reaction to scoring the gold medal marker also told everyone how much he wants to win. The Atlanta club will be relying heavily on Kovalchuk's enormous talent, but they need to help out their star if they are to rise in the standings.

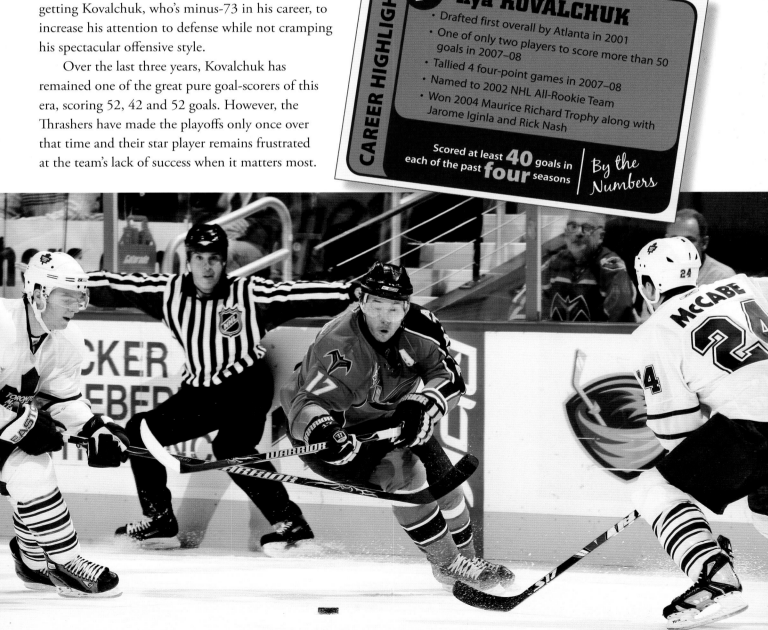

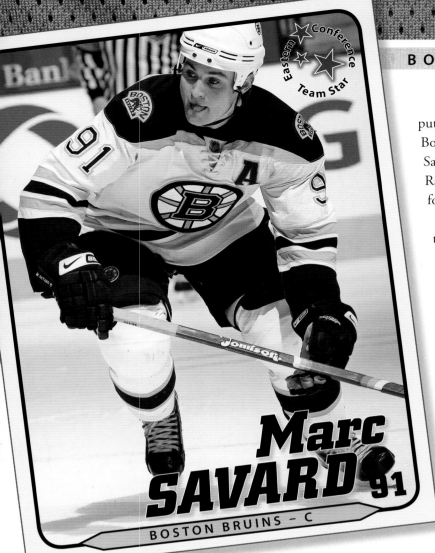

Marc SAVARD 91
BOSTON BRUINS – C

putting players like Eric Lindros and the incomparable Bobby Orr in the NHL! Despite the great numbers, Savard was selected 91st overall by the New York Rangers in 1995. It was clear sign of things to come for the talented youngster.

Savard did make the Rangers team right out of training camp in 1997, but lasted just 28 games on Broadway before he was sent to the minors for the rest of the 1997–98 season, notching 74 points in 58 games for Hartford of the American Hockey League. His good performance got him into 70 games for New York the following year, recording a respectable 45 points. However, the Rangers sent the 5-foot-10, 196-pound Savard (plus their 1999 first round pick) to Calgary in a deal to acquire Jan Hlavac and the Flames 1999 first and third-round picks. Savard was a Flame for the next three-plus seasons, recording 53 and 65 points, respectively, in his first two seasons in the western Canadian city. However, his third year saw him notch just 33 points in 56 games as he didn't exactly see eye-to-eye with Calgary coach Greg Gilbert. The bench boss did not make it through the next season, but neither did Savard, who was dealt to Atlanta just ten games into the 2002–03 campaign. The move afforded Savard an opportunity to re-start his career with the young Thrashers team.

Injuries slowed Savard during his first couple of years in Georgia, but he had a major break through in his third season as a Thrasher. The crafty set-up man racked up 97 points in 2005–06, good for ninth in league scoring. It was perfect timing for Savard, who was becoming a free agent. He pitched his services to the Maple Leafs, but Toronto was not interested. However, the struggling Boston Bruins stepped up and offered Savard a deal that paid him $5 million a season. The Beantowners had another wretched season in 2006–07, but Savard once again finished among the league's top scorers with a 96-point effort. Such a performance usually gains a player almost instant recognition as one

Marc Savard seems to be the National Hockey League's answer to the late comedian Rodney Dangerfield — he simply gets no respect! The small but slick center has always played the game with a high degree of skill, even dating back to his junior days. The native of Ottawa, Ontario first came to prominence when he recorded 99 points in 36 games while playing for the Metcalfe Jets as a Jr. B player in 1992–93. He then joined the Oshawa Generals for the next four seasons and tore up the Ontario Hockey League with his tremendous offensive production. Twice he led the OHL in scoring (139 points in 1994–95 and 130 points in 1996–97) and ended his junior days with 413 points in 238 games. He still holds the Generals team record for most career points and the Oshawa club is famous for

of the best point-producers in the game, but that is not the case for the multi-talented Savard. His minus-19 rating in 2006–07 is the main knock against the offensive talent's game. To truly be a star, Savard will need to be effective in both ends of the rink.

Savard's game is built around his great skill at dishing the puck off to teammates. He is a master of disguise when he has the puck, rarely showing what he will do until the last second. Like all great passers, Savard's vision on the ice allows him to make a pass in any situation and he can make a difficult cross-ice feed look very easy. He is not a gifted skater, but knows how to carry the puck to the spots he seeks out. Once inside the attacking zone, he is extremely dangerous and can make defenders guess wildly as to where the black disk is going.

In 2007–08, the Bruins' new head coach, Claude Julien, made the club more responsible defensively and Savard was called upon to be more of a leader than he has been in the past. He responded to the challenge by posting a plus/minus rating of plus-3 and recording 63 assists (third-

best mark in the NHL) and he finally received a call to play in the NHL All-Star Game. Savard also experienced another first: playoff hockey. The Bruins grabbed the Eastern Conference's final invitation to the spring dance and although they exited in Round 1, it was still another milestone for Savard, who had never played an NHL post-season game.

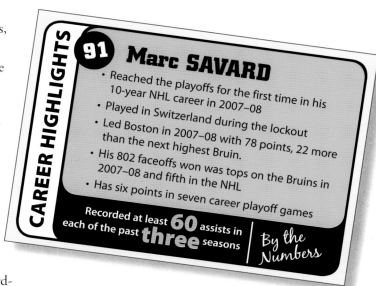

CAREER HIGHLIGHTS

91 Marc SAVARD

- Reached the playoffs for the first time in his 10-year NHL career in 2007–08
- Played in Switzerland during the lockout
- Led Boston in 2007–08 with 78 points, 22 more than the next highest Bruin.
- His 802 faceoffs won was tops on the Bruins in 2007–08 and fifth in the NHL
- Has six points in seven career playoff games

Recorded at least **60** assists in each of the past **three** seasons | By the Numbers

Thomas
VANEK 26

BUFFALO SABRES – LW

the end, the Sabres knew they had to match the offer and announced at a press conference that Vanek was not going anywhere. The real question was, would the Sabres one day regret matching the contract and not taking the picks? It's a debate that won't be answered for years to come, but if the 2007–08 season is a fair measuring point, Buffalo management made the right choice.

Vanek's route to the NHL was by no means conventional. He was born in Austria and grew up in the capital city of Vienna, where his father played hockey. Young Thomas hung out at the rink with his father and would try to catch some NHL hockey on television, although not much was available to him. He did have NHL heroes like Mario Lemieux and Jaromir Jagr, and was soon playing organized hockey, which had him traveling to tournaments all over Europe. Vanek also got to North America on one occasion to play in Quebec and immediately thought about moving to Canada to pursue a hockey career. His father received a job offer to work in Alberta when Vanek was 14 years old and that settled the issue. Being in a hockey environment (he started out playing in Edmonton) was all Vanek needed to get himself ready for a professional career and it also helped him develop his English skills rapidly.

He was recruited to play hockey for South Dakota's Sioux Falls Stampede of the United States Hockey League and recorded 91 points in 53 games during the 2001–02 campaign. His strong play and all-star nominations got him into the University of Minnesota. He scored 57 goals over his two-year stint as a Golden Gopher and earned the honor of being named MVP of the 2003 NCAA Tournament. NHL scouts took note of the developing star, and Buffalo, a team renowned for its great scouting and drafting record, grabbed Vanek fifth overall at the 2003 entry draft. He joined the American Hockey League's Rochester Americans for the 2004–05 season and quickly established himself with 42 goals and 68 points in 74 games. The NHL lockout ended prior to

When it came time to make a decision on Thomas Vanek, what choice did the Buffalo Sabres really have? It was the summer of 2007 and they had just lost star centers Chris Drury (New York Rangers) and Daniel Briere (Philadelphia Flyers) as free agents without getting anything in return. Now, the Edmonton Oilers were attempting to poach one of their restricted free agents — second team all-star left winger Thomas Vanek — with an offer sheet worth $50-million over seven years. Within the confines of the collective bargaining agreement, Buffalo had two choices: match the Oilers' offer, or take four first round draft choices and say goodbye to a 43-goal scorer. Chances are that the already fragile Buffalo fan base would not react well to losing the 6-foot-3, 203-pound Vanek. In the start of the next season and Vanek looked ready to meet the challenge of making the Sabres.

Buffalo was one of the few teams ready for the new-look NHL in the 2005–06 season with its emphasis on speed and skill. Vanek fit right in and scored a very respectable 25 goals and added 23 assists. His plus/minus ranking was not impressive at minus-11, but that can be explained in part by a lack of experience. No one was anticipating a 43-goal, 84-point season in 2006–07, but that's exactly what Vanek gave the Sabres, a team that won the Presidents' Trophy for having the most regular season points in the NHL. Vanek's plus/minus mark jumped to a remarkable plus-47 and his great play was recognized with second team all-star selection. His only struggles, thus far, have come in the playoffs. Whether such a short NHL career was worthy of the contract offer he received from the Oilers is a point all hockey fans will argue over, but there was no doubt Vanek was going to take it.

26 Thomas VANEK

ICE CHIPS

Thomas Vanek recorded four hat tricks in 2007–08, including a natural hat trick (three consecutive goals) against the Tampa Bay Lightning on March 19.

CAREER HIGHLIGHTS

- First European to play for the University of Minnesota Golden Gophers
- Named to AHL All-Rookie Team in 2005
- Led Sabres with 36 goals in 2007–08
- Ranked second in the NHL with 19 power play goals in 2007–08
- Tied for third in the league in 2007–08 with nine game-winning goals

Living up to the contract made life difficult for Vanek in the early going of 2007–08 (only 13 goals in his first 50 games), but he got better as the season wore on, scoring 36 goals. The Sabres missed the playoffs, but Vanek showed he was still a feared sniper with a great set of hands and a shot that should keep his name prominent among the leading goal-scorers for years to come.

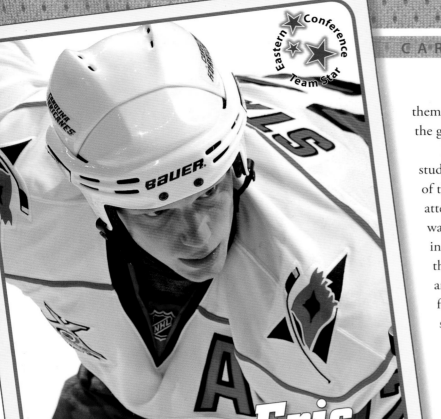

Eric STAAL

CAROLINA HURRICANES – C

them, the Staal brothers were able to relax and learn the game at their own pace.

Eric, the oldest of the four, was certainly a quick study. He was drafted by the Peterborough Petes of the Ontario Hockey League and soon garnered attention from NHL scouts. His final year of junior was Eric's best, as he scored 39 goals and 98 points in 68 games. He was selected second overall by the Carolina Hurricanes at the 2003 entry draft and found himself playing on the big team the following season as an 18-year-old. Staal did not set the world on fire in his rookie year, recording 31 points in 81 games during the 2003–04 season. The lockout wiped out the next year of NHL play, but Staal was able to skate in the American Hockey League and had a banner year with Lowell, netting 26 goals and 77 points in 77 games.

Nobody expected much from the Hurricanes or Staal in the 2005–06 season, but GM Jim Rutherford felt he had made the right moves for the new NHL. Not only did the Hurricanes make the playoffs, they won the Stanley Cup. Much of Carolina's improvement is directly related to the rise of Staal as one of the best players in the league. From the beginning of the season, Staal showed an incredible drive to the net that usually started by undressing a defenseman or two. Using his long legs to great advantage, the 6-foot-3, 200-pound Staal embarrassed more than one defender by simply blowing past him and then going straight to the net. He also demonstrated a strong desire to score and his shot was deadly — nobody else could pick the far side of the net the way Staal did throughout the 2005–06 season. He finished the year seventh in league scoring with 45 goals and an even 100 points. He was 24 points better than the Canes' second-leading scorer, Justin Williams, indicating just how valuable he was to Carolina.

Staal's great performance did not end with the close of the regular season. He scored the overtime winner in the third game of the playoff series against Montreal after

Eric Staal grew up like a typical Canadian kid living in a northern Ontario town. Born and raised in Thunder Bay, he learned to skate and play hockey on the backyard rink built by his father, Henry, on the family farm. The rink was constructed so Eric and his three brothers could enjoy the great game of hockey and have fun. The senior Staal eventually added lights so the boys could continue playing later into the evening after dinner. Henry and Linda Staal did not set out to raise hockey players — they just wanted to see their boys doing what they loved. The Staal parents did not make any suggestions to their sons, nor did Henry make it a point to critique how the boys played and he certainly never got upset with them when it came to results or achievements. With little pressure placed on

12 Eric STAAL

- A second-team NHL All-Star in 2006
- Oldest of the four hockey-playing Staal brothers
- Scored 100 points in his sophomore season (2005–06)
- Has missed only one game in his NHL career
- Had 10 points in nine games for Canada's 2007 gold medal World Championship team

25 Rang up **28** points in playoff games en route to Carolina's first Stanley Cup in 2006 | *By the Numbers*

his team had dropped the first two games at home. That turned out to be a big goal, as the Hurricanes swept the Habs out of the post-season with four consecutive wins.

In the following matchup, as New Jersey was about to tie the series after scoring a late goal in the second game, it was Staal who planted himself in front of the Devils net to score the tying goal with just three seconds remaining. This sent the game into overtime, where the Hurricanes won it. It was difficult to believe Staal, at such a young age, had won a Stanley Cup and led all playoff scorers with 28 points.

While Staal has remained a star, the Hurricanes have not fared so well since the Cup win. Staal's production dropped by 30 points in 2006–07, while Carolina finished three spots back of the final playoff slot. In 2007–08, Carolina narrowly missed the post-season by losing three of its last four games, including a very crucial division matchup with the Washington Capitals, who ousted the Hurricanes from their playoff spot. Stall upped his point total to 82, and proved his leadership qualities when captain Rod Brind'Amour was injured. The Hurricanes need to shore up their blueline and that will get their very talented team back to the playoffs.

Tomas **VOKOUN** 29

FLORIDA PANTHERS – G

the red, white and blue. It was all of 20 minutes, and in that time Tomas Vokoun allowed four goals in his only action for Montreal before being claimed by the Nashville Predators in the 1998 expansion draft.

Going to an expansion club is considered a big break for a goaltender who wants to get his career going. The downside is he is often backstopping a weak team. But Vokoun, who got some further seasoning by playing in the American Hockey League, had the right attitude and the other players liked playing for him. He got off to a good start with the newly minted Predators by winning 12 games in 37 appearances as an NHL rookie. He won only nine games the following year and lost 20, but was back up to double digits in 2000–01 with 13 wins. He won only five contests in 2001–02 and his future appeared to be shaky in Nashville, where Mike Dunham was the regular goalie. The Predators kept adding good players through the draft and eventually the team got better through player development and some good trading. Injuries finally gave Vokoun the opportunity he needed to become the No. 1 goalie.

The 2002–03 season saw Vokoun play 69 games, posting a very respectable 25–31–11 record. The following season was a major breakthrough for the entire organization, when the team

The Montreal Canadiens have always had a good eye for goaltenders. A look through their long and illustrious history shows team management was keenly aware of just how important netminding is to the success of a hockey team. Georges Vezina, George Hainsworth, Bill Durnan, Jacques Plante, Ken Dryden and Patrick Roy were all goalies developed by the organization and they all led the Canadiens to Stanley Cup victories. In 1994, the Canadiens selected two goalies: one of them was future league MVP Jose Theodore, who also helped Montreal pull off a couple of playoff upsets before he was dealt away to the Colorado Avalanche; the other received far less mention than Theodore and only played in one game for

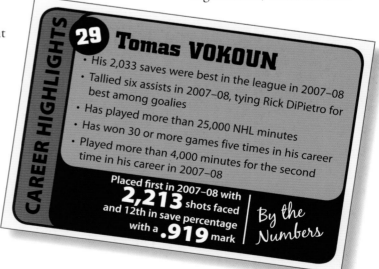

CAREER HIGHLIGHTS

29 **Tomas VOKOUN**

- His 2,033 saves were best in the league in 2007–08
- Tallied six assists in 2007–08, tying Rick DiPietro for best among goalies
- Has played more than 25,000 NHL minutes
- Has won 30 or more games five times in his career
- Played more than 4,000 minutes for the second time in his career in 2007–08

Placed first in 2007–08 with **2,213** shots faced and 12th in save percentage with a **.919** mark

By the Numbers

secured its first playoff spot in franchise history and shook the Detroit Red Wings in the first round of the playoffs before losing in six games. Vokoun also had his first winning year, with a 34–29–10 record. By this point, Vokoun was no longer looking over his shoulder for someone to take his job and he came back from the lockout year to have his best season to date in 2005–06. Vokoun was very steady, playing 61 games and winning 36 contests while losing 18 with four ties. He had a .919 save percentage and added four shutouts. More importantly, the Predators made the playoffs for the second straight year and recorded franchise highs with 49 wins and 106 points.

The 6-foot, 195-pound Vokoun is the type of goalie who puts his size into play by implementing a mostly standup style. He has a good glove hand and is not especially exciting in terms of stopping the puck, but that's because he is so good at being in the right position. Vokoun is very strong, in good condition and his coaches and teammates know he can be relied upon to play a quiet, consistent game. He rebounds well from bad games and goals, and does not take out any misfortune on his teammates.

The 2006 playoffs were a terrible disappointment for both Vokoun and the Predators. A serious bout with blood clots forced Vokoun out of the post-season and backup Chris Mason was not equal to the task of stopping the hot San Jose Sharks in the first round. After a 27–12–4 season in 2006–07, Vokoun got back into playoff action, but the Sharks prevailed once again in five games.

Ownership issues forced the Predators to deal away many players, including Vokoun, who went to the Florida Panthers for a pair of draft choices. While he couldn't quite push the Panthers into the playoffs, Vokoun held his team in many games during 2007–08. He posted a 30–29–8 record while facing more shots than any other goaltender in the league. His strong play helped Florida fans forget about the departed Roberto Luongo and he will be a central figure in any hopes the Cats have of making the post-season for the first time since 2000.

Alex KOVALEV 27
MONTREAL CANADIENS – RW

season. He split that year between New York in the NHL, where he popped 20 goals and 38 points in 65 games, and Binghamton of the AHL, adjusting quickly to a new style of game. He improved to 23 goals and 56 points in 1993–94 and tasted the ultimate success with a Stanley Cup win in the 1994 playoffs as the Rangers won the big prize for the first time since 1940. Kovalev was a major contributor to the title, notching nine goals and 21 points in 23 post-season games. He appeared to be on the verge of a major breakout the next year. But, it just didn't happen.

The lockout-shortened 1994–95 season saw Kovalev produce just 28 points in 48 games. He bounced back with a decent year in 1995–96, with 24 goals and 58 points for the Rangers. It was his last good year in New York as he settled into the 50-point range. With some reluctance, Kovalev was dealt to Pittsburgh in November, 1998. He quickly produced 20 goals and 46 points in 63 games and then improved his point total to 66 in 1999–2000. Once again, it appeared the slick Russian was on the precipice of a breakout. This time, he did not disappoint. In 2000–01, he had his best season with 44 goals and 95 points. It was impeccable timing on Kovalev's part as the outburst came just as his contract expired. The Penguins re-signed him, but traded away Jaromir Jagr in a cost-cutting move.

Kovalev has a dangerous shot and shows a willingness to crash the net to get what he wants. He takes his share of abuse and has let his temper get the best of him in the past, leading to some suspensions. But Kovalev has matured and does a better job of squashing the desire to retaliate. He had 32 goals and 44 assists in 2001–02, but with the Penguins in financial trouble, his future with the team was in jeopardy.

When Kovalev came on the trade market after he had 27 goals and 64 points in the first 54 games of 2002–03, the Rangers picked him up for their playoff push. The Blueshirts ended up missing the post-season again, but Kovalev made an impact with 10 goals in 24 games.

Alex Kovalev is one of those frustrating players who dot many NHL rosters. Enormously gifted physically and blessed with terrific hockey sense, players like Kovalev just don't bring their top game every night. Eventually, people in management get fed up and deal these talented players to new clubs, which often turns out to be a big mistake. All you have to do is ask the New York Rangers about Kovalev. They dealt him away in late 1998, only to re-acquire him in February, 2003.

At 6-foot-2 and 222 pounds, Kovalev has excellent size and that caught the eye of the Ranger scouts in 1991 when they selected him 15th overall at the entry draft. He became the first Russian to be selected in the first round. A skilled puckhandler who is very strong on his skates, Kovalev came over to North America for the 1992–93

The Rangers decided to go in a completely different direction the next season and GM Glen Sather shipped Kovalev to Montreal, which was looking for talented goal-scorers. He helped the Canadiens make the 2004 playoffs and upset the Boston Bruins in Round 1, then re-signed with Montreal after the lockout. In 2005–06, he led the Habs in scoring with 23 goals and 65 points in 69 games, but he had trouble finding the range in the playoffs and the Canadiens were out in the first round. He was awful in 2006–07, recording a mere 47 points. But an off-season chat with Canadiens GM Bob Gainey seemed to be a turning point for Kovalev.

Re-dedicated to playing hockey at a top level, Kovalev led the Canadiens with 35 goals and 84 points in 2007–08. He also took on the role of team leader and was a big help to a couple of young brothers from Belarus, Andrei and Sergei Kostitsyn. Coach Guy

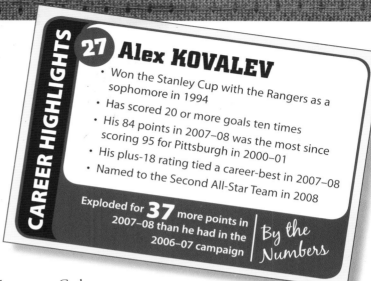

CAREER HIGHLIGHTS

27 Alex KOVALEV

- Won the Stanley Cup with the Rangers as a sophomore in 1994
- Has scored 20 or more goals ten times
- His 84 points in 2007–08 was the most since scoring 95 for Pittsburgh in 2000–01
- His plus-18 rating tied a career-best in 2007–08
- Named to the Second All-Star Team in 2008

Exploded for **37** more points in 2007–08 than he had in the 2006–07 campaign

By the Numbers

Carbonneau showed plenty of faith in his star performer, forgetting any previous comments Kovalev made about his mentoring style. The Habs made the playoffs in 2007–08, but were upset in the second round by Philadelphia. The question now becomes, can Kovalev continue to play at a high level for the Habs?

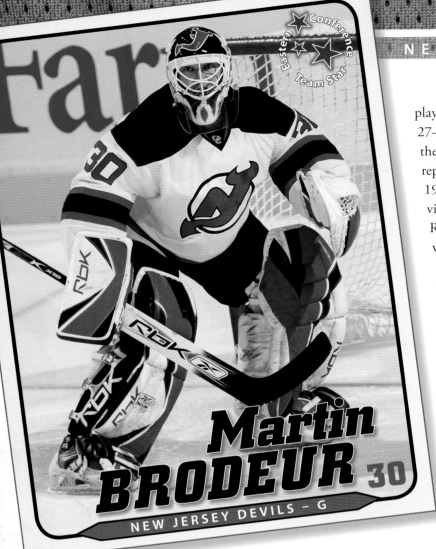

Martin BRODEUR 30

NEW JERSEY DEVILS – G

played in 47 games that year, sporting a very impressive 27–11–8 record and took away the Calder Trophy as the league's best rookie. He cemented a rock-solid reputation by beating Buffalo in the first round of the 1994 playoffs, which featured a Game 7 overtime victory over goalie Dominik Hasek. The New York Rangers eventually derailed the dream, but the best was yet to come for the Devils.

In the lockout-shortened 1994–95 season, Brodeur won 19 of his 40 games, but saved his best for the playoffs when he won 16 of 20 starts as the Devils took the Stanley Cup. Brodeur was spectacular at times and finished with a playoff goals-against average of 1.67, tops in the post-season. At the tender age of 23, Brodeur had won a Cup. The Devils held their parade at the arena parking lot in East Rutherford, New Jersey; not exactly like the celebration in Montreal years earlier, but it would have to do.

Since the 1995 Cup victory, Brodeur has proven to be a solid, consistent goalie. He has been a workhorse for the Devils, often playing more than 70 games in a season. Brodeur makes the most of his 6-foot-1, 205-pound frame and plays a predominantly classic stand-up style, but will drop down when needed. He has a great glove hand and high confidence in his abilities. With the exception of the 2000–01 New Jersey squad that led the league in goals, Brodeur rarely gets much in the way of offensive support. However, the Devils have made strong defensive play a franchise trademark and that has benefited Brodeur tremendously throughout his career. A technically sound goalie, Brodeur is also very tough mentally and bounces back from the few goals he gives up. After a few shocking first round losses following the 1995 Stanley Cup win, Brodeur finally took the Devils all the way back with a fine performance in the 2000 postseason. New Jersey's second championship secured Brodeur's place among the elite in the NHL. The team made the final again in 2001, losing to Patrick Roy and Colorado in seven games. The next year, Brodeur topped his father's 1956

Martin Brodeur was just 14 years old when his hometown Montreal Canadiens won the Stanley Cup in 1986. The teenager skipped school to attend the victory parade held in the streets of the old town. He hoped the day would come when he would hoist the Cup in a parade. His father, Denis, had been a goalie for the bronze medal-winning Canadian team at the 1956 Olympics and young Martin eventually ended up strapping on the pads as well.

After a great career with St-Hyacinthe in the Quebec Major Junior League, Brodeur was selected 20th overall by the New Jersey Devils in the 1990 NHL draft. By the time the 1993–94 season began, the Devils decided to give Brodeur, who had spent a year in Utica in the American Hockey League, a chance at an NHL job. He achievement by backstopping Canada to the 2002 Olympic gold medal.

With Pat Burns behind the bench, New Jersey tied Philadelphia for fewest goals allowed in 2002–03, while Brodeur led the league with nine shutouts and had his lowest goals-against average, 2.02, in five years. He also became the first goalie in NHL history to record his fourth 40-win season. For that, Brodeur won his first Vezina Trophy as the league's best goalie and was named to the NHL's First All-Star Team. In the playoffs, Brodeur won Game 7 against Ottawa in the Eastern Conference final and shut out Anaheim 3–0 in Game 7 of the Stanley Cup final to win his third ring in nine years.

Brodeur has had to face many new challenges the past couple of seasons. The decline and ultimate retirement of Scott Stevens was a blow to the defense, as was the loss of free agent blueliners Scott Niedermayer and Brian Rafalski. Still, he managed to set an NHL record with 48 wins in 2006–07, topping the previous mark of 47 set by former Philadelphia goalie Bernie Parent. However, playoff success has eluded New Jersey since the last championship. The Devils need more offense if they hope to take advantage of having a future Hall of Famer guarding the net for the next few years. Cutting back on the amount of games he plays in the regular season may also help Brodeur be fresher when the playoffs begin.

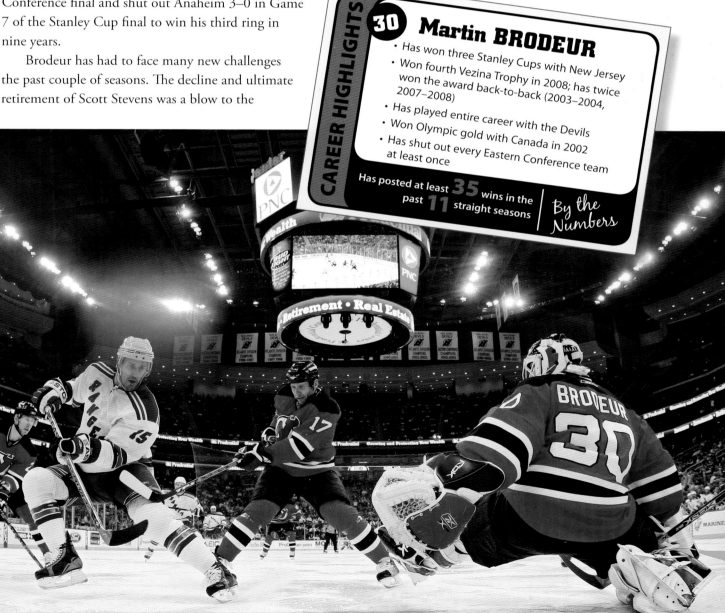

CAREER HIGHLIGHTS

30 Martin BRODEUR

- Has won three Stanley Cups with New Jersey
- Won fourth Vezina Trophy in 2008; has twice won the award back-to-back (2003–2004, 2007–2008)
- Has played entire career with the Devils
- Won Olympic gold with Canada in 2002
- Has shut out every Eastern Conference team at least once

Has posted at least **35** wins in the past **11** straight seasons

By the Numbers

Rick
DiPIETRO
39
NEW YORK ISLANDERS – G

When the New York Islanders signed goaltender Rick DiPietro to a 15-year contract in September of 2006, most people thought only the wacky club from Long Island could do such a thing. The deal called for DiPietro, who was just 25 at the time and had yet to establish himself as a superstar, to make $4.5 million dollars a year for a total value of $67.5 million. Perhaps DiPietro got the longest deal in NHL history because the GM, Garth Snow, was a former goaltender himself? Maybe it was because Isles owner Charles Wang had yet to learn from his previous multi-year, multi-million-dollar bust with Alexi Yashin? In the end, the Islanders were merely heading the wave of the future under a salary-cap system as other clubs have since followed suit by signing franchise players

to long-term contracts. (Examples can be found in Washington where Alex Ovechkin signed for 13 years and in Philadelphia where Mike Richards signed for 12 years).

The fact DiPietro was on Long Island in the first place was a shock. The Isles had the top pick at the 2000 entry draft by virtue of winning the NHL draft lottery and moving up from fifth overall to the top spot. The New York club already had a star goalie in development with Roberto Luongo (drafted fourth overall in 1997), who played in 24 contests for the Islanders in 1999–2000. The Islanders GM at the time was Mike Milbury and 'Mad Mike' certainly confounded the experts by taking DiPietro with the first selection (passing on Dany Heatley and Marian Gaborik in the process). Avoiding any controversy about the Islanders goaltending situation, Luongo was soon dealt to the Florida Panthers, leaving the No. 1 netminding job for DiPietro when he was deemed ready. Milbury certainly believed it would not be long before DiPietro would be in the NHL, mostly based on the fact the young goalie was the best he had seen at handling the puck. He also liked the fact DiPietro had excelled at Boston University in the 1999–2000 season with a 18–5–5 record and took the Terriers to the NCAA tournament before losing to St. Lawrence University in overtime while making 77 saves. Prior to that, DiPietro was named the top goalie at the 2000 World Junior Championship.

The 2000–01 season saw DiPietro start with the lackluster Islanders, going 3–15–1, before being sent down to the Chicago Wolves of the American Hockey League for some more work. The following year, the acrobatic netminder recorded 30 wins while playing for Bridgeport in the AHL and he stayed with the Islanders farm team for most of 2002–03 season as well. Injuries were also holding back his development, but he finally became the Isles' first-string goalie during the 2003–04 campaign, posting a 23–18–5 record. His exciting style of play turned more heads — and earned

him his lucrative deal — when he won 30 games in 2005–06. The next year, he led New York to a playoff berth with 32 victories. The Isles really had no business making the post-season, but DiPietro's strong play throughout the year propelled them there nonetheless. And while the team was ousted in Round 1 by the Buffalo Sabres, the emerging stopper picked up his first career playoff win.

DiPietro has no lack of self confidence. He is a bit of a gambler in goal, but has supreme confidence in his reflexes, which are some of the best in the NHL. Anyone who watches DiPietro ply his trade can see a certain brashness in his approach to stopping the best shooters in the game, but he would not have it any other way. His style is a little too flashy at times and he has to work on his technique to become one of the best, but his tremendous athleticism will allow him to make that transition a little more smoothly. The new rules have curtailed his excellent puck-handling

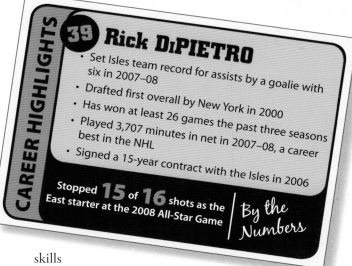

CAREER HIGHLIGHTS

39 Rick DiPIETRO

- Set Isles team record for assists by a goalie with six in 2007–08
- Drafted first overall by New York in 2000
- Has won at least 26 games the past three seasons
- Played 3,707 minutes in net in 2007–08, a career best in the NHL
- Signed a 15-year contract with the Isles in 2006

Stopped **15** of **16** shots as the East starter at the 2008 All-Star Game

By the Numbers

skills to some degree, but he still loves to be a part of the action.

Injuries struck again in 2007–08, cutting his season to 63 games and his win total to just 26. The Islanders must upgrade the entire team if they hope to take advantage of DiPietro's obvious talent in the near or distant future.

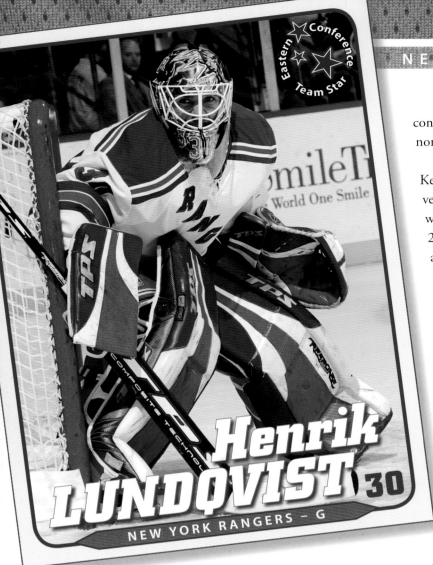

Eastern Conference Team Star

Henrik LUNDQVIST 30

NEW YORK RANGERS – G

contender, all while racking up three Vezina Trophy nominations!

The Rangers had actually signed perennial backup Kevin Weekes in the hopes he might give the team a veteran presence in goal. While Weekes performed well in 32 games, he was still no better than a No. 2 goalie. Lundqvist, on the other hand, quickly adapted to his new environment and grabbed the No. 1 netminding reins and never let go all season long. New York also brought in goaltending coach Benoit Allaire to help out the young man, but the mentor quickly found all he had to do with Lundqvist was assist him with his angles and teach him how to play in the smaller North American rinks.

The 6-foot-1, 192-pound goalie builds his game around positioning — getting square to the shooter consistently and controlling his rebounds effectively. His style of game is somewhere between standup and butterfly, and he moves easily from side to side to get proper positioning. Like all top goalies, Lundqvist is very competitive and hates to lose. He is so driven that he may be a little too intense, especially on game days, for his own good. Lundqvist was so well known in his native Sweden that he actually came to New York to seek a level of anonymity. However, by the third game of his first season, the Madison Square Garden fans were chanting his name. That made the young netminder feel at home and he fed off the energy of the crowd and his new teammates. Early in the year, Lundqvist allowed two goals or fewer in 12 of his starts and his stats were among the best in the league in all goalie categories. Coach Tom Renney was at first reluctant to name Lundqvist as the No. 1 man, but the more he played the more it was obvious who should be the starter. By the time the season was over, the Rangers had secured a playoff spot and Lundqvist posted a record of 30–12–9 in 53 games. He also had a sparkling .922 save percentage and a 2.44 goals-against average.

As if his NHL performance wasn't enough,

Swedish goaltender Henrik Lundqvist was already a decorated player in his homeland when he came to North America. He won the Swedish Elite League championship with Frolunda and was named the most valuable player on that circuit. He had also played in several World Championships for his country. Lundqvist brought all this experience with him when he reported to the New York Rangers as a 23-year-old for the 2005–06 season. The Rangers were essentially starting over with many new players on their roster and were trying to shed their reputation as a high-payroll, low-result team that hadn't made the playoffs for seven consecutive seasons. Not only has Lundqvist, the 205th selection in the 2000 draft, got his team back into the post-season, but he has also made them a consistent

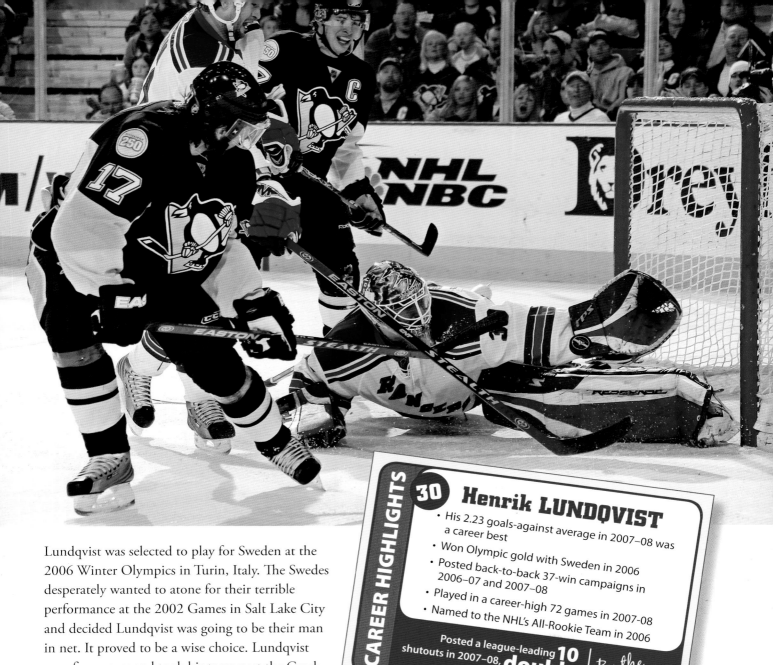

Lundqvist was selected to play for Sweden at the 2006 Winter Olympics in Turin, Italy. The Swedes desperately wanted to atone for their terrible performance at the 2002 Games in Salt Lake City and decided Lundqvist was going to be their man in net. It proved to be a wise choice. Lundqvist won five games and took his team past the Czech Republic in the semifinal and then past ancient rival Finland, 3–2, in the gold medal game. The victory only solidified Lundqvist's position in Sweden as the best goalie since the late Pelle Lindbergh and the country had a great party after the gold was captured.

However, the 2006 NHL playoffs did not go as well for a sick and battered New York team. The New Jersey Devils took advantage and knocked them off in four games. At the time it was a great disappointment to all Ranger fans, but retribution wouldn't be very far away.

The 2007–08 campaign was somewhat difficult for Lundqvist as his father took ill, but the agile goaltender still managed to post a 37-win campaign. He also netted

himself a six-year contract extension worth $41.25 million. The Rangers faced the Devils in a rematch of their 2006 Round-1 series, and Lundqvist's superb play helped eliminate the Devils in five games. Ultimately the upstart Pittsburgh Penguins derailed the Rangers, defeating them in Round 2.

The Blueshirts' future looks bright with the Swedish puckstopper — who has built a pretty good reputation on this side of the ocean, too.

Eastern Conference Team Star

Daniel ALFREDSSON 11

OTTAWA SENATORS – RW

drafted at 133rd overall in 1994. The Sens chose him as a 21-year-old and after another season with Frolunda of the Swedish League, he made an immediate impact in the NHL. The Senators missed the playoffs in his first year, but Alfredsson scored 26 goals and won the 1996 Calder Trophy as the league's top rookie.

Playing a lesser role to the likes of Alexei Yashin, Alfredsson grew steadily as an NHL player and was often more physically aggressive during the playoffs than the regular season, perhaps a response to the "soft" label many had stuck his team with. After scoring 24 goals and increasing his point total to 71 in his sophomore season, Alfredsson's climb toward elite status leveled off for four seasons when he missed a total of 90 games because of injuries. But, in that span, he still potted 73 goals and tallied 207 points.

When Yashin held out for a new contract in 1999–2000, the Sens made Alfredsson their temporary captain. Even when Yashin returned the next season, the 'C' stayed on No. 11's sweater, as Ottawa officially became Alfredsson's team. He really broke into the NHL's upper echelon in 2001–02, scoring 37 goals and 71 points while averaging 20:19 minutes of ice time per game. His goal total dropped to 27 in 2002–03, but his point total rose to 78. He upped that to 32

There is no player who personifies the Ottawa Senators' puzzling, frustrating history of contrasts more than Daniel Alfredsson. The classy right winger is the only Senator who has been involved in each post-season series Ottawa has played during a remarkable 11 straight seasons in the playoffs. And, as the Senators' captain for nearly a decade now, he has been forced to explain how he and his team always seem to come up short in the crunch. He does not like that part of the job, but credit must be given because he shows up after every game, win or lose, to speak for the team.

Alfredsson is one of those classic late-round gems Ottawa's keen scouting staff

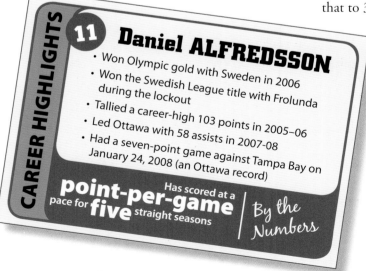

CAREER HIGHLIGHTS

11 Daniel ALFREDSSON
- Won Olympic gold with Sweden in 2006
- Won the Swedish League title with Frolunda during the lockout
- Tallied a career-high 103 points in 2005–06
- Led Ottawa with 58 assists in 2007-08
- Had a seven-point game against Tampa Bay on January 24, 2008 (an Ottawa record)

Has scored at a **point-per-game** pace for **five** straight seasons | By the Numbers

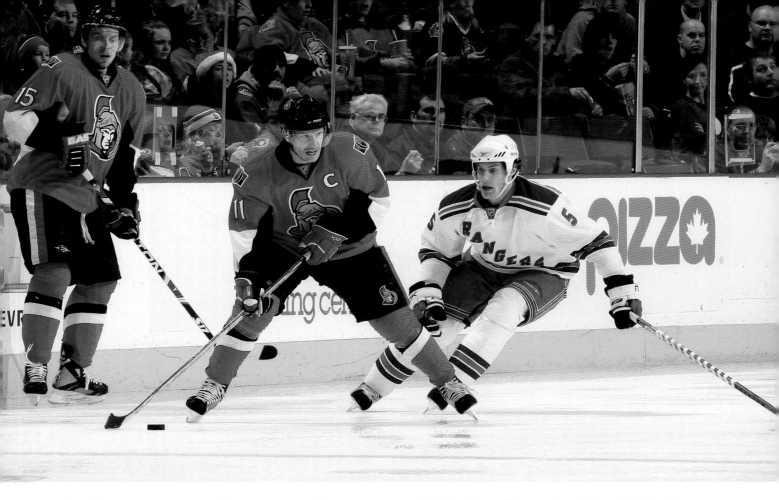

goals and 80 points in 2003–04, signing a new five-year contract near the end of that season.

Alfredsson is the Senators' all-time leader in regular season points, goals and assists. But despite winning four regular season division titles with superior teams, the failure to advance to the Stanley Cup final haunted the Senators and their captain. Yet Alfredsson also exemplified the positives of the Ottawa franchise. With his stickhandling mastery, speed, velvet hands and vision on the ice, he's always a threat to score or set up a highlight-reel goal.

During the lockout of 2004–05, Alfredsson propelled Frolunda to the Swedish League championship, leading all scorers with 12 goals and 18 points in the playoffs. He was also the leading scorer for Team Sweden on its way to the 2006 Olympic gold medal. Alfredsson had a career year in 2005–06, in the new speed-oriented NHL, which seemed to be created specifically for his team. He tied for fourth place in the scoring race recording career highs in goals (43) and points (103), and his plus-29 was more than double his previous best. Unfortunately, his superb regular season is not what

most hockey fans will remember about Alfredsson's year. Unfairly or not, they will always recall Buffalo's Jason Pominville skating around him for the shorthanded overtime goal that eliminated the Senators in Round 2. And they will also remember that a 43-goal shooter managed just one tally against the Sabers during a series in which all five games were decided by a single goal.

Alfredsson had his redemption in the 2006–07 playoffs, as the Senators faced the Sabers again, this time in the Eastern Conference final. The captain and two teammates, Jason Spezza and Dany Heatley, sat tied atop playoff scoring with 22 points, and none was bigger for the Senators than Alfredsson's key overtime winner to knock Buffalo out of the playoffs. The moment, however, was short lived for the Senators as they lost the Cup to Anaheim in five games. Alfredsson recorded 40 goals and 89 points in 2007–08, but the Senators fell apart as the season wore on and were easy prey for Pittsburgh in the playoffs. As valuable as the 35-year-old right winger has been to Ottawa, the team may have to consider trading him at some point as part of a natural rebuilding process.

Daniel
BRIERE 48
PHILADELPHIA FLYERS – C

The summer of 2007 proved how far Daniel Briere had come along in his NHL career. Given up by Phoenix, who drafted him 24th overall in 1996, and shunned by the Buffalo Sabres where he had performed superbly, the smallish center, who is generously listed at 5-foot-10 and 179 pounds, was suddenly a hot property as he became a free agent. The Montreal Canadiens pursued the Quebec native with a vigor they often show French-Canadian stars but he turned the Habs down for the Philadelphia Flyers who landed him with an eight year, $52-million contract. It took awhile for Briere to be comfortable in his new surroundings, but by the end of the 2007–08 campaign he had scored 31 goals and totaled 72 points. Montreal fans will never let Briere forget that he rejected the famed red, white and blue

sweater, as was made evident when the Flyers were back in the post-season and dueling with Montreal in Round 2. Despite the chorus of boos that rained down on Briere at the Bell Centre he and the Flyers eventually knocked the Canadiens out of the playoffs!

Briere was born in Gatineau, Quebec, and his father had him on skates by the age of two. Robert Briere was a junior player in his day and he wanted Daniel to learn the game as soon as possible. The backyard was flooded during the winter, giving Briere a chance to play hockey whenever he could. Briere took to the game very quickly and, while he was almost always the smallest player on his team, he was also the most creative and usually the leading point producer. Eventually, he was noticed by teams in the Quebec Major Junior Hockey League and played three seasons for Drummondville. Briere's first year, 1994–95 saw him named rookie of the year thanks to his 51 goals and 123 points. In his second season, the draft-eligible Briere led the league in every major offensive category with 67 goals, 96 assists and 163 points.

For the next number of years, Briere was shuffled between the minors and the Coyotes. He suffered a concussion one year, which wrecked his game for some time and he lost some confidence as well. But he told his minor league coach that the 2000–01 season was going to be different and he kept his word, with 21 goals and 46 points in just 30 American Hockey League games with the Springfield Falcons. That performance got him back up with the Coyotes and the next season saw him finish with 32 goals and 60 points, earning a new contract in the process. It appeared Briere had won over Phoenix management, but late in 2002–03 he was dealt to Buffalo for 6-foot-4, 220-pound Chris Gratton, a much larger and older player. The Coyotes would love to have that trade back.

Briere was dynamic from the moment he arrived in Buffalo. He worked hard on his game at both ends of the ice and showed he is a talented goal-scorer with a nose for the net. His stature does not stop him from getting in the thick of the action, which combined with his good shot, makes him a dangerous attacker. Briere is a very good skater with a nice burst of speed and he's a deft passer as well. Dedicating himself to getting fitter, he instituted a strongman type of weight-training program that saw him do things like lift large boulders as part of his preparation regimen. His off-ice preparation made him capable of thriving against larger players.

During the final three seasons Briere played in Buffalo, he became a very effective playmaker and goal-scorer for the Sabres. In 2003–04 he scored a career-high 28 goals and 65 points and was on pace to set new marks in 2005–06, but a sports hernia injury held his season to just 48 games. However, he was ready for the playoffs and helped the Sabres get past Philadelphia and Ottawa in the early rounds before losing to Carolina. In 2006–07 he recorded career highs with 63 assists and 95 points and added another 19 points in the playoffs, signaling his arrival among the NHL's elite.

Perhaps the Sabres felt they could not achieve playoff success with Briere and did not make much of an attempt to sign him. He was exceptional in the 2008 playoffs with 16 points in 17 games as the Flyers beat Washington and Montreal before losing to Pittsburgh.

CAREER HIGHLIGHTS

48 Daniel BRIERE

- Played in the past three Eastern Conference finals (twice with Buffalo)
- Posted a career-high 95 points in 2006–07
- Rang up 72 points in 79 games in 2007–08
- Tallied 45 points in 36 games for Bern (Swi.) during the lockout
- Has 53 points in 56 career playoff games

Led the Flyers in 2008 playoff scoring with **16** points in **17** games

By the Numbers

Eastern Conference Team Star

Sidney CROSBY 87

PITTSBURGH PENGUINS – C

1984, the Penguins were fortunate enough to select Mario Lemieux first overall and save their floundering franchise. But times and circumstances had changed. When they chose Lemieux, the Penguins had been assured the first selection simply by finishing last the previous season. The draft lottery system, which doesn't guarantee the first pick simply by virtue of finishing last, was implemented to negate the possibility of teams losing games on purpose. The 2005 draft was complicated by the fact there had been no season the previous winter due to the lockout. Teams' chances of winning were based on a weighting system that took the three seasons leading up to the lockout into account. The smile on Lemieux's face said it all when it was decided Pittsburgh, a team he both partially owned and still played for, would select first overall. To nobody's surprise the Penguins took Crosby with the No. 1 pick. They had a new savior for their team and maybe the entire NHL.

Son of parents Troy and Trina, Crosby was like most other kids as he grew up. He enjoyed playing with Pogs and loved the Teenage Mutant Ninja Turtles. He also enjoyed reading about the Second World War. His love of history eventually led to him visiting Normandy, France, where one of the War's most important battles took place. Of course, young Crosby was also a hockey player, a very good hockey player. The first-ever story about him was published when he was just seven years old. Crosby wanted to be a netminder like his father, who was selected by the Montreal Canadiens during the same '84 draft in which the Pens took Lemieux. But when Troy saw how good a skater Sidney was and how quickly he understood the game, he told his son he needed to give up the idea of being a goalie.

After playing one season with Shattuck–St.Mary's, a private high school in Minnesota, Crosby joined the Quebec Major Junior Hockey League's Rimouski Oceanic for two seasons. In his final year of junior, he scored 66 times and totaled 168 points in 62 games. The

As the Detroit Red Wings were hoisting the 2008 Stanley Cup, Sidney Crosby was in the Pittsburgh dressing room with his emotions out for all to see. The Penguins had romped to the final, easily dispatching the Ottawa Senators, New York Rangers and Philadelphia Flyers, but came up against the well-prepared, veteran-laded Red Wings for the title. Crosby was outstanding in the playoffs with six goals and 27 points in 20 games, but it was clear the young Penguins needed more development time before reaching their ultimate goal. Based on his reaction to the loss, it certainly appears Crosby is going to do everything in his power to one day lift the Cup over his head.

The Pittsburgh Penguins were hoping history would repeat itself with the draft lottery of 2005. Way back in

Oceanic went to the Memorial Cup that year, but were no match for the London Knights of the Ontario League in the final. Crosby led all scorers in the tournament and references to him as "the next one" grew louder.

Crosby joined the NHL as an 18-year-old and managed a point in his first contest by setting up Mark Recchi for the lone goal in a 5–1 loss to New Jersey. The Penguins' home opener was attended by 17,132 fans, who saw Crosby score his first NHL goal against the Boston Bruins, just as Lemieux had done years earlier, although the game ended 7–6 for the visitors. He had five points in his first three games and the Penguins looked poised to be a competitive team.

While Crosby met the incredibly high expectations placed on him by becoming the youngest player ever to record 100 points in one season, the Penguins quickly disintegrated, starting with the retirement of Lemieux. There were changes behind the bench and in the front office. The Penguins started to mature

in Crosby's sophomore year, making the playoffs before being bounced in the first round. Crosby had a league-high 120 points that season and earned his first Art Ross and Hart Trophies, as well as the Lester B. Pearson Award in the process. A high-ankle sprain limited Crosby to just 53 games in 2007–08, though he still notched 72 points. If the Penguins can keep their team together, they have a good chance to win a championship with captain Crosby leading the way.

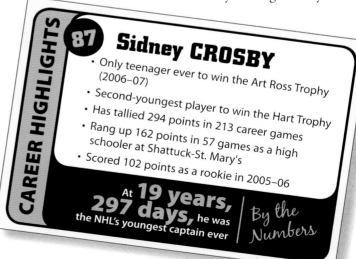

CAREER HIGHLIGHTS

87 Sidney CROSBY

- Only teenager ever to win the Art Ross Trophy (2006–07)
- Second-youngest player to win the Hart Trophy
- Has tallied 294 points in 213 career games
- Rang up 162 points in 57 games as a high schooler at Shattuck-St. Mary's
- Scored 102 points as a rookie in 2005–06

At **19 years, 297 days,** he was the NHL's youngest captain ever

By the Numbers

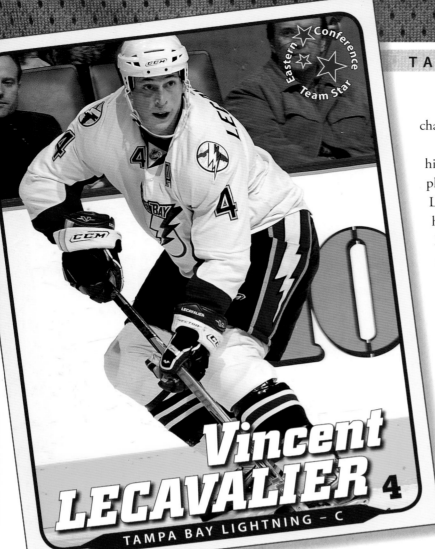

Vincent LECAVALIER 4
TAMPA BAY LIGHTNING – C

champions in 2004.

Lecavalier was groomed to be an NHLer by his father, Yvon, a firefighter and one-time junior player in his native Quebec. Well-learned lessons got Lecavalier playing against nine-year-old boys when he was just four. Lecavalier went to the famed Notre Dame prep school in Wilcox, Saskatchewan, for further development, scoring an astounding 52 goals and 104 points in just 22 games in 1995–96. He then went to Rimouski of the Quebec Major Junior Hockey League for two seasons, scoring 86 times and totaling 217 points in 122 games before becoming the top pick in the '98 draft. No matter where Lecavalier played, he knew he had to be a leader and going to Tampa Bay was no different. So it was no shock when the 19-year-old was made captain of the team.

Lecavalier has shown the skill, talent and maturity that made him worthy of a first overall selection. As a rookie in 1998–99, he scored 13 goals and recorded 28 points in 82 games. It was not a great start, but his second season quickly turned into a top performance with 25 goals and 67 points. His third year was less impressive, with a drop in goals to 23 and points to 51. He was even benched for a time by new coach John Tortorella, but it was all part of the development process for the slick center. Tortorella, who was let go by Tampa at the end of 2007–08, also removed the 'C' from Lecavalier's sweater and demoted him to assistant captain. At one point, Lecavalier was very nearly traded to Toronto, but the deal never quite came to fruition.

Lecavalier is a quiet leader, but his talent speaks volumes. With his outstanding puck-handling skills, Lecavalier makes moves once reserved for the likes of Wayne Gretzky or Mario Lemieux. He shows a good burst of speed and can make his move with the puck very quickly. Lecavalier takes great pride in his play and wants badly to excel. He certainly did that in 2002–03, when the Lightning jumped off to a quick start and won the Southeast Division for the first time. Lecavalier had a

T**alk about being under pressure! Try putting yourself in the shoes of young Vincent Lecavalier on draft day. Your hopes of becoming an NHL player are about to be fulfilled and being selected first overall only adds to one of the greatest days of your life. Then, just before your selection, the owner of the club you'll be joining compares your talent to that of a sporting legend the world over! Such was the case when Art Williams, who had just purchased the Lightning before the 1998 NHL draft, declared the 18-year-old center to be "the Michael Jordan of hockey."

Five years later, Williams was gone from the hockey scene and Lecavalier finally started to establish himself as an elite NHL player. Eventually, the entire Lightning team followed his lead and became Stanley Cup great season with 33 goals and 78 points. The Lightning lost in the second round to New Jersey, but it was apparent Tampa Bay was on its way to playoff glory.

Lecavalier scored 32 goals and 66 points during the 2003–04 campaign and was outstanding in the playoffs. In 23 post-season games, Lecavcalier scored nine goals and totaled 16 points as the Lightning knocked off Philadelphia and Calgary, each in seven games, over the the final two rounds to take home its first Cup. Lecavalier was so determined to succeed that he fought tough Calgary captain Jarome Iginla during the grueling final. It brought a new measure of respect for the Lightning star.

The 2005–06 season was not nearly so kind to Tampa Bay, which was quickly knocked out of the playoffs by a more talented Ottawa Senators squad. The following season saw Lecavalier continue to excite, as he inched closer to the lofty status he was tagged with as an 18-year-old.

The slick center took the NHL by storm, winning the Maurice Richard Trophy for most goals in a season. His 52 tallies were a career high, as were his 108 points. His good play continued in 2007–08 with 40 goals and 92 points, but his great performance wasn't enough to save a faltering Lightning club that finished last in the league.

CAREER HIGHLIGHTS

4 **Vincent LECAVALIER**

- Received the King Clancy Trophy for humanitarian efforts in 2008
- Scored 217 points in two seasons of junior with Rimouski (122 games)
- First Lightning player to ever score 50 goals in a season (2006–07)
- MVP of the 2004 World Cup with Team Canada

Scored or assisted on **44 percent** of Tampa's goals in 2006–07 **(108/243)** | *By the Numbers*

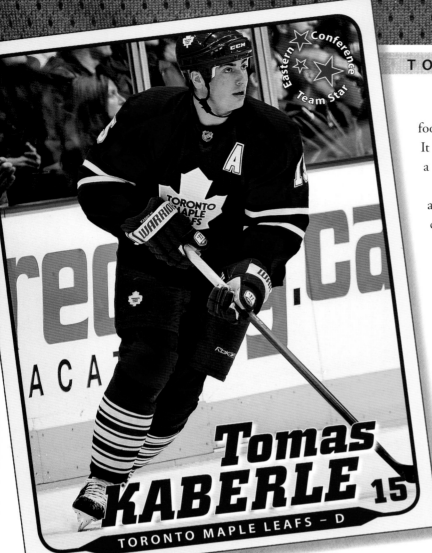

Eastern Conference Team Star

Tomas KABERLE 15

TORONTO MAPLE LEAFS – D

When the Toronto Maple Leafs hired coach Pat Quinn before the start of the 1998–99 season, he knew he had to make some significant changes if one of hockey's most storied franchises was going to get back on the winning track. It appeared the Leafs had little to offer the new coach in terms of young talent, especially on the blueline. But Tomas Kaberle changed all that with a surprising year that launched his NHL career.

Not many expected the defenseman, selected 204th overall in 1996, to make the Leafs starting lineup. But Kaberle's poise with the puck convinced Quinn to add him to his opening night roster. The youngster played 29 minutes and 13 seconds in the contest against Detroit, the most of any player, and the Leafs got off on the right

foot with a 2–1 win over the Stanley Cup champions. It quickly became apparent Quinn had found himself a gem.

Kaberle began playing hockey at the age of five and had a good chance to succeed in the sport, considering his father, Frantisek, was once an elite international player for the Czech Republic. His older brother, Frantisek Jr., was also playing the game and went on to be an NHL player as well with Los Angeles, Atlanta and Carolina. Kaberle's numbers were not overwhelming as he worked up the Czech system averaging roughly 20 points per season. Perhaps that's why he was available to the Leafs with their 13th selection of the '96 draft. The baby-faced blueliner was ticketed for development in St. John's in the American Hockey League, but Kaberle never made it to Canada's east coast. An impressive training camp earned Kaberle a start in Toronto and he has never looked back.

Toronto realized the young defenseman, despite his impressive showing upon landing in North America, still needed work and wisely held him out of some games when he began to struggle as a rookie. He played in 57 games in 1998–99 and contributed four goals and 22 points. He showed flashes of the qualities that got him on the team to begin with, especially his deft puck-handling skills. Kaberle is a strong skater and a very good passer. He reads the play easily and has a knack for knowing when to join the attack.

Kaberle's shot is by no means devastating, but it is somewhat deceiving and tends to be accurate, which he demonstrated when he won the accuracy shooting competition during the Superskills event at the 2008 All-Star Game. Fans often yell at him to shoot more, but he's a passer by nature. As with many skilled players in today's game, Kaberle tends to get into trouble when he overhandles the puck or when the game gets physical. He is listed at 6-foot-2 and 200 pounds, but can have trouble handling big forwards in front of the Leafs net.

During the 2000–01 season, the Maple Leafs had a chance to acquire Eric Lindros from Philadelphia if they would include Kaberle in the deal. The Leafs coveted the former Flyers captain, who was still considered a star at the time, but balked at putting Kaberle into a package to get him. Hanging on to Kaberle has proven to be a wise move by the Leafs. During the 2005–06 season, Kaberle recorded a career-best 67 points, including a team-high 58 assists, and was a vital member of the Leafs' highly ranked power play. Kaberle set up fellow blueliner Bryan McCabe with perfectly placed passes McCabe could blast toward the net. McCabe rightly credited Kaberle for much of his success that year and Toronto management certainly agreed by locking Kaberle up to a long-term deal at a very reasonable $4.2 million a season. The smooth-skating Kaberle is ideally suited to the new NHL, but his evasive maneuvers and puck-possession game can leave him vulnerable to bad turnovers, which have more than once hurt his club. This fact keeps the

15 Tomas KABERLE

ICE CHIPS

Tomas Kaberle's 402 career points as a Maple Leaf rank him fourth all-time for defensemen who have played for Toronto. He trails only Borje Salming (768), Tim Horton (459) and Ian Turnbull (414).

CAREER HIGHLIGHTS

- Has tallied at least 45 assists in the past three seasons
- Scored on two of his three shootout attempts in 2007–08
- Originally drafted 204th overall by the Leafs in 1996
- Recorded a career-high 67 points in 2005–06

tireless Kaberle from becoming one of the truly elite defensemen in the league.

The Leafs have stagnated the last three years with no playoff appearances, but Kaberle has played well enough to produce 58- and 53-point seasons. He may never be a crusher, but any team would love to have the talented puck-moving blueliner on its roster.

Eastern Conference Team Star

Alex OVECHKIN 8

WASHINGTON CAPITALS – LW

W itness an Alex Ovechkin goal and the first thing you'll see is an explosion of pure joy. While whipped goalies slump their shoulders, Ovechkin leaps in to the arms of teammates or jumps into the glass. The gap-toothed Washington Capital loves to celebrate and in 2007–08 he had plenty to rejoice about with a league-leading 65 goals. Young, fast and always dangerous on the attack, Ovechkin is worth the price of admission each and every night he plays. Washington owner Ted Leonsis obviously agrees because he locked up the superstar to a 13-year contract that is set to pay him a whopping $124 million over the duration of the deal. Considering Ovechkin won the '08 Art Ross, Maurice Richard and Hart Trophies, and earned a spot on the league's first all-star squad, the

Capitals have made a wise investment in their future.

The ultra-talented Ovechkin may have inherited his mother Tatiana's athletic genes. She won two gold medals as an Olympic basketball player in 1976 and 1980 for what was then the Soviet Union. But life wasn't always easy for Ovechkin. When he was just 10 years old he lost his older brother, Sergei, in a car accident. The two had a strong bond forged out of the fact it was Sergei who ensured Alex kept playing hockey as a youngster after a period of time when his parents were too busy to get him to practices and games. A young Ovechkin found a way to put the pain behind him and skate on. Ovechkin has another brother, Mikhail, who lived with him when he initially joined the Caps to help with the adjustment to North American.

In Russia, Ovechkin once predicted he would score 50 goals in one season, but the most he ever tallied there in one year was 20. Ovechkin did, however, score 52 in his first year in the best league in the world, potting two in his very first NHL game against Columbus. Perhaps his prediction had been just a little premature!

He scored many great goals as a rookie, but none was more spectacular than his tally against the Phoenix Coyotes on January 16, 2006. As he drove to the Coyotes net with his usual gusto, Ovechkin was taken down and briefly lost control of the puck as he hit the ice. He did not lose sight of it, however, swinging his stick over his head and sweeping the puck into the net as he finished his sprawl on the ice. It became the goal of the year — merely one of many memorable efforts by the young Russian. His highlight-reel tallies helped Ovechkin claim the Calder Trophy as rookie of the year and he also earned a First Team All-Star distinction.

Ovechkin is a right-hand shooting left winger who has blazing speed and an offensive flair rarely seen among players who also posses a strong physical edge. The 6-foot-2, 215-pounder would just as soon go through a defender than around him and does both with great dexterity. He can score on a breakaway, a tip-in near the crease or a rebound — he can beat you with a hard shot, or by picking corners. He is a threat on either the power play or if he is out killing a penalty. Ovechkin plays hard all the time and likes to get every ounce of his talent on display. Most Russian players are rather reserved and tend to shy away from the media, especially in their early years in the league. But Ovechkin happily does interview after interview, usually with a big smile on his face.

The Capitals were not a very good team in 2005–06, winning just 29 games. They were, however, a very hard-working club under coach Glen Hanlon and focused on using young players. His second NHL season saw Ovechkin score 46 goals and 92 points for another berth on the first all-star team, but the Capitals were still not a playoff team.

A major change took place when Hanlon was replaced by offense-minded Bruce Boudreau early in 2007–08 and the Capitals cracked the post-season. No longer left on his own to lead the attack, Ovechkin now has Nicklas Backstrom, Alexander Semin and Mike Green to dish the puck to. But he also took the time to deliver a league-high 446 shots on goal. It's no wonder he is the most flamboyant goal-scorer in the NHL since Bobby Hull roamed the ice for the Chicago Blackhawks.

8 Alex OVECHKIN

ICE CHIPS

Ovechkin recorded two five-point games in 2007–08, both times posting four goals and one assist. The first came against Ottawa on December 29 in an 8–6 victory, the second came against Montreal on January 31 in a grueling 5–4 overtime win that saw Ovechkin get a broken nose and the winner.

CAREER HIGHLIGHTS

- Scored the game winner in his first NHL playoff game
- His 163 goals since the lockout is the most in the NHL
- Won gold with Russia at the 2008 World Championship
- Won his first scoring title in 2007–08 with 112 points

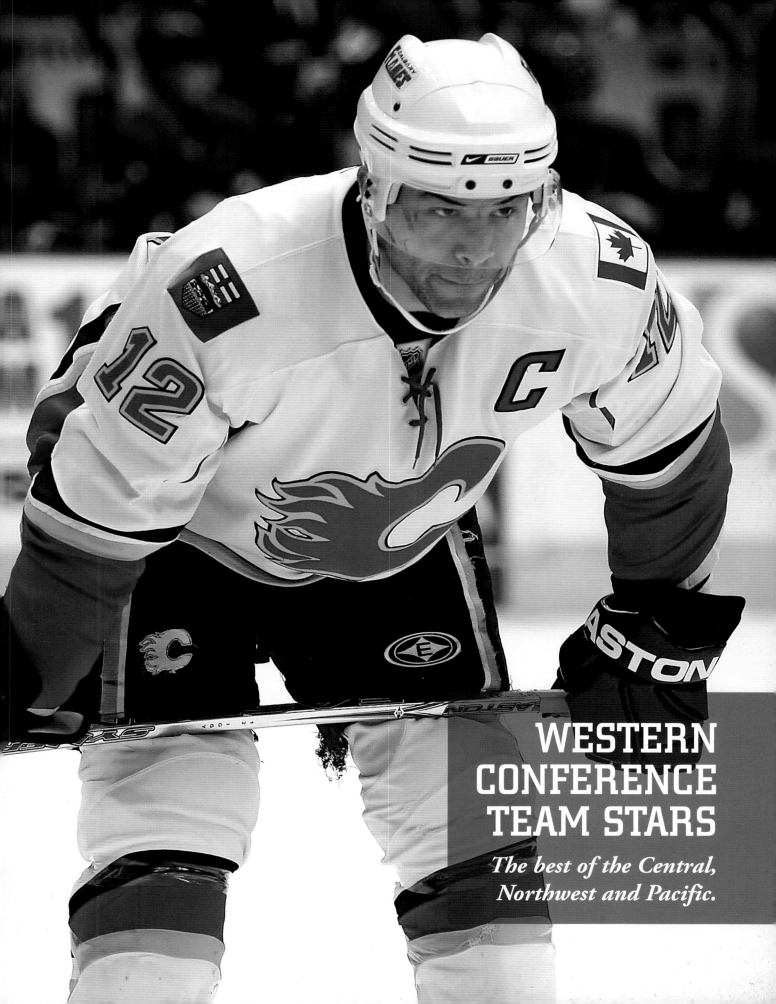

WESTERN CONFERENCE TEAM STARS

The best of the Central, Northwest and Pacific.

Western Conference Team Star

Chris
PRONGER 25

ANAHEIM DUCKS – D

scouts was Pronger's 6-foot-6, 207-pound frame and his incredible reach. Throw in some toughness and leadership potential, and Pronger looked like a can't-miss prospect. But his youth and immaturity quickly surfaced in Hartford and he developed a reputation off the ice that displeased Whalers management. Pronger's conditioning was also nowhere near where it needed to be. Soon, the trade rumors began.

He played just two years in Hartford and scored a total of 10 goals and 44 points.

By this time, Mike Keenan was coach-GM of the St. Louis Blues. When he heard Pronger might be available, he moved in fast. Keenan paid a high price for Pronger, dealing the very popular and talented Brendan Shanahan, but the coach felt it was worth it. However, Keenan was furious after seeing firsthand Pronger's poor conditioning and told his new player in no uncertain terms this was not acceptable. It was a turning point for the young blueliner, who got the message to get serious about his career loud and clear. His first season as a Blue, 1995–96, was rough, with only seven goals, 25 points and a minus–18 rating. But he started to bloom in the playoffs and Pronger has never looked back.

Joel Quenneville, a former NHL defenseman, eventually replaced Keenan as coach of the Blues. This change helped Pronger enormously; he now had a mentor to teach him how to play on the blueline properly. In 1996–97, he scored 11 goals and 35 points and posted a plus-15 mark. Now his name was being mentioned among the NHL's best rearguards as he developed a strong two-way game. He could contribute on the power play or dish out a terrific bodycheck. In 1999–2000, Pronger became the first defenseman since Bobby Orr to win the Hart and Norris Trophies in the same year, when he had 14 goals and 62 points, helping the Blues to the best record in the NHL.

He had an injury-filled 2000–01 season, but still managed 47 points in 51 games. In the 2002 playoffs

As GM of the Hartford Whalers, Brian Burke felt defenseman Chris Pronger could be just what his floundering club needed. Burke also knew if he was to have any chance at selecting Pronger at the 1993 draft, he would have to move up from his sixth position. He waited nervously while the Ottawa Senators selected first. They accommodated Burke nicely by taking Alexandre Daigle. Burke had his opening and quickly struck a deal with San Jose that included a flip of first round choices and Burke, now picking second, grabbed Pronger's rights.

Pronger played junior with the Peterborough Petes and recorded 62 and 77 points in his last two seasons there. He was by far the best defenseman in the Canadian Hockey League. What attracted all the he had eight points in nine games, but suffered a serious knee injury. That injury and three operations to his wrist kept him out of all but five games in 2002–03. The Blues had learned to play without him, but were ecstatic to have their captain back the following year.

Pronger had a good season in St. Louis during 2003–04 with 54 points, but the Blues' fortunes were taking a downturn. The rebuilding squad could not see paying Pronger a big contract after the lockout and dealt him to Edmonton for a package of younger players, including defenseman Eric Brewer. He had a difficult time adjusting to the new game at first, but he came on strong at the end, finishing with 12 goals and 56 points, as the Oilers made the playoffs. He was their best player in the post-season as Edmonton defeated Detroit, San Jose and Anaheim before dropping a seven-game final against the Carolina Hurricanes.

Despite the springtime success, Pronger's family

couldn't adjust to life in Edmonton and he requested a trade. It caused a major controversy for Oiler fans, but the same GM who'd traded up to get him in the draft came calling again. This time, as GM of the Anaheim Ducks, Burke landed what he hoped was the final piece of a Stanley Cup puzzle. As it turns out, he was right. Pronger teamed with all-world defenseman Scott Niedermayer to help lead the Ducks to their first-ever Cup in 2007.

25 Chris PRONGER

ICE CHIPS

Chris Pronger plays a nasty brand of hockey, which led him to his eighth career suspension in 2007–08. He claims he is a target and that he only dishes out what he receives. However, it could be argued that Pronger's aggressions against Pat Peake and Dean McAmmond were completely unwarranted.

CAREER HIGHLIGHTS

- Has won Olympic gold, a Stanley Cup and world junior gold
- Took home Hart and Norris Trophies in 2000
- Three-time NHL All-Star
- Has tallied 92 points in 134 playoff games
- Is a career plus-153

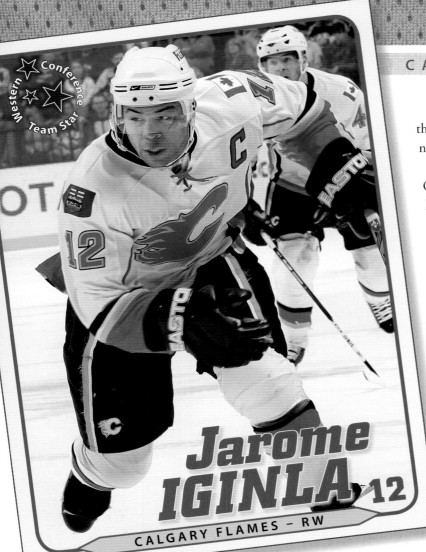

Jarome IGINLA 12
CALGARY FLAMES – RW

that Gretzky and coach Pat Quinn couldn't help but notice the player they hadn't even originally invited.

When Iginla used the confidence gained from the Olympic camp to jump into the NHL goal-scoring lead and stay there, Team Canada's management knew it had to put him on the roster for the Olympics. By the gold medal game in Salt Lake City, Iginla had graduated to Canada's top line beside Joe Sakic and, ironically, Gagne. The trio dominated the final showdown with the United States. Iginla became a household name when he scored twice in the final, once on a deflection to break a 1–1 tie and then on a hard shot to give Canada an insurmountable 4–2 lead.

Canada's first Olympic men's hockey gold in 50 years gave him further confidence and he returned to the Flames to become the NHL's only 50-goal scorer in 2001–02.

The career year was a huge leap from 2000–01, when Iginla scored 31 goals, the first time he'd reached 30 in his five NHL seasons. But he'd been steadily improving his play since he joined the Flames for the 1996–97 season.

As a junior player, Iginla led the Western Hockey League's Kamloops Blazers to back-to-back Memorial Cups in 1994 and '95, and was named most outstanding forward of the World Junior Championship when Canada won the

Hockey history can be changed gradually or in an instant. For Jarome Iginla and the Canadian Olympic team, it was both. Wayne Gretzky, point man on the crew that was putting Team Canada together for the 2002 Winter Games, phoned the 24-year-old, hard-shooting Calgary Flames right winger in the middle of the night in early September, 2001 and asked if he had a couple of days to spare. Simon Gagne had suffered a shoulder injury and Team Canada's orientation camp in Calgary was in need of another player so the club could scrimmage properly. Iginla figured the call came only because he was already in Alberta, but he jumped at the chance and was on the ice the next morning. He played so well

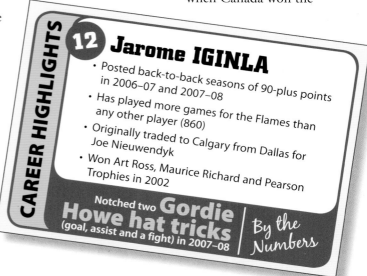

CAREER HIGHLIGHTS

12 Jarome IGINLA
- Posted back-to-back seasons of 90-plus points in 2006–07 and 2007–08
- Has played more games for the Flames than any other player (860)
- Originally traded to Calgary from Dallas for Joe Nieuwendyk
- Won Art Ross, Maurice Richard and Pearson Trophies in 2002

Notched two **Gordie Howe hat tricks** (goal, assist and a fight) in 2007–08 | *By the Numbers*

tournament in 1996. Just two weeks prior to that event Iginla was traded by the Dallas Stars, the team that drafted him 11th overall in 1995, to Calgary for Joe Nieuwendyk.

As an NHL rookie in 1996–97, he had 21 goals and 50 points, then helped Canada to the World Championship title at the end of the season. He dipped to just 13 goals as a sophomore, but gradually increased his output to 28, 29 and 31 over the next three years.

In Calgary's first 52 games of the 2002–03 season, Iginla posted a disappointing 15 goals, but he confidently told everyone he would finish strongly in the final 30 games. He was true to his word, scoring 19 goals in the next 20 games and ended up with 35. Darryl Sutter took over as Flames coach during that season and he had his club ready to go for the 2003–04 campaign. Sutter named Iginla team captain and he responded to the challenge by tying for the league lead with 41 goals, winning a share of his second Maurice Richard Trophy.

Iginla was outstanding in the 2004 playoffs, scoring 13 goals and 22 points in 26 games as the Flames

returned to the Stanley Cup final for the first time since 1989. In the playoffs Iginla showed he could score, set up plays, hit and fight if necessary. His tussle with Tampa Bay star Vincent Lecavalier in the final is the stuff of legend. However, Iginla and his teammates fell just short of the big, shiny prize, losing in seven tough games to the Lightning.

Great expectations were placed on Iginla's shoulders for the 2005–06 season, but he had trouble getting started after not playing any hockey during the lockout. He recovered nicely to score 35 times and lead the team with 67 points, but it was clear he missed not having at top-flight center to play alongside. The Flames had a terrific season with 103 points, but were dispatched by Anaheim in the first round of the playoffs.

The Flames have not been able to duplicate their playoff success from 2004 despite the fact Iginla continues to shine. He scored 39 goals in 2006–07 and then 50 in 2007–08, helping him land a First Team All-Star selection, but Calgary has remained an inconsistent team that hasn't realized its full potential.

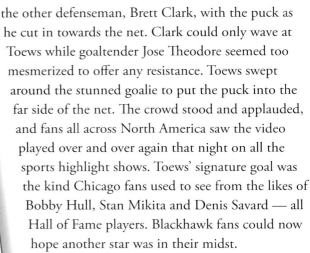

Jonathan TOEWS 19

CHICAGO BLACKHAWKS – C

Western Conference Team Star

the other defenseman, Brett Clark, with the puck as he cut in towards the net. Clark could only wave at Toews while goaltender Jose Theodore seemed too mesmerized to offer any resistance. Toews swept around the stunned goalie to put the puck into the far side of the net. The crowd stood and applauded, and fans all across North America saw the video played over and over again that night on all the sports highlight shows. Toews' signature goal was the kind Chicago fans used to see from the likes of Bobby Hull, Stan Mikita and Denis Savard — all Hall of Fame players. Blackhawk fans could now hope another star was in their midst.

Toews highlight reel goal was not the only time he produced memorable footage. During the 2007 World Junior Championship, Toews scored three goals, including the game-winner, during a semifinal shootout against the United States. Toews showed a soft touch and remarkable coolness in putting all three chances past American netminder Jeff Frazee. The win allowed Canada to advance to the final, where it took the gold medal. The sturdy 6-foot-1 203-pound center has always been able to produce goals. Although he is a native of Winnipeg, Manitoba, Toews stayed out of the Canadian junior system and played one year of high school hockey in Minnesota. He attended the same institution, Shattuck-St. Mary's, that's produced NHL players like Sidney Crosby and Zach Parise. He scored 48 goals to go along with 62 assists in 64 games during the 2003–04 high school season. He then enrolled at the University of North Dakota for the next two seasons, scoring a total of 40 goals and 85 points in 76 games played. The Blackhawks, who were failing miserably for a number of years, had another high draft position in 2006 and GM Dale Tallon was bent on selecting Toews (only Erik Johnson and Jordan Stall were selected ahead of him). There is no doubt Tallon is more than pleased with his choice because Toews may prove to be the best player selected that year.

When the Chicago Blackhawks decided to keep youngsters Jonathan Toews, the third overall pick in 2006, and Patrick Kane, drafted first overall in 2007, with the team for the start of the 2007–08 season, they were not sure exactly what to expected from the highly touted pair. If there was any doubt about Toews it was quickly erased on the night of October 19th when Chicago hosted Colorado at the United Center. With the game scoreless, Toews started deep in his own end and took a pass from Kane as he crossed the red line. Gathering speed as he outraced Milan Hejduk of the Avalanche along the boards, he crossed the opposition blueline on his own while facing two defenders. Toews deftly cut across the ice to beat defenseman Scott Hannan rather easily and then teased

Toews had a bit of a rough start to the 2007–08 season thanks to a visit from the injury bug. He broke a finger during training camp and then suffered a knee injury on New Year's Day. Later, after he had returned from his injury, he took an ugly hit to the head that opened a nasty gash. But through all the pain and discomfort, Toews has shown he is a leader, speaking up when the rest of his teammates needed to hear that they did not hate losing enough. Even though he was just 19 years of age during his rookie season, that didn't dissuade Blackhawk management from handing him the leadership of the team in July 2008 — making him the third-youngest captain in league history. Once Toews recovered from his broken finger, he hit the ice running by recording a point in each of his first ten games. He displays a strong skating ability and can really put something behind a terrific wrist shot. Despite the fact he will be counted on to score and set up plays, Toews knows he must contribute to the defensive side of the game as well. He ended his first season with 24 goals and 54 points in 64 games.

Chicago now has an assortment of young forwards and defensemen to build around, as well as a quality goaltender in Christobal Huet. You can bet the new and improved Blackhawks will be led by a young superstar named Jonathan Toews.

Western Conference Team Star

Paul STASTNY 26

COLORADO AVALANCHE – C

ponds and took every opportunity possible to play hockey. It became obvious the youngster had great hockey sense — something that cannot really be taught. He began playing organized hockey in New Jersey after his father was traded to the Devils and continued his development around St. Louis when Peter finished up his illustrious career with the Blues. Although he lacked the foot speed that attracts the eye of scouts, it was clear his on-ice smarts were going to give him a chance to play professional hockey.

Stastny played Jr. A hockey with the River City Lancers of the United States Hockey League and scored 30 goals and a league-leading 47 assists in 56 games in 2003–04. His skills and ability to anticipate the play were noticed by the University of Denver, which recruited him for the 2004–05 season and he responded with a 45-point campaign in 42 games. He was drafted 44th overall in 2005 by the Colorado Avalanche, but returned to school for one more year, posting 53 points in 39 games. Stastny didn't waste any time making a good first impression upon entering the big show in 2006–07. He scored 28 goals in his rookie season and his 78 points represented the fourth-highest total for a freshman in franchise history. Stastny found a nice niche playing as the second center behind Avs legend Joe Sakic. He also developed some chemistry with fellow rookie Wojtek Wolski, a left winger who produced 22 goals and 50 points. Stastny made the NHL's all-rookie team and was edged out for the Calder Trophy by Pittsburgh's Evgeni Malkin. Although the Avalanche recorded 95 points, it missed the playoffs, but vowed to make the post-season in 2007–08.

Watching Stastny play in the NHL as a rookie, it was easy to see he had great playmaking abilities and a knack for scooping up loose pucks. Former Avs coach Joel Quenneville did not hesitate to play him in any and all situations, and liked his game away from the puck as well — a compliment not often paid to young players. Stastny has built his game around being at the right place

Most NHL players would kill for Paul Stastny's pedigree. His father, Peter, is a member of the Hockey Hall of Fame by way of a great career with the Quebec Nordiques, the same franchise Paul now plays for. His uncles, Marian and Anton, were also top performers for many years with the Nordiques. All three brothers defected from the former Czechoslovakia in the early 1980s, a time when Europeans still weren't exactly welcomed with open arms by North American NHLers. Despite his family's huge hockey heritage, Paul was never pushed to play the game by those closest to him. His father stressed having fun with hockey and playing other sports, but it was clear from an early age that Paul was a gifted athlete who excelled on the ice. Born in Quebec City, Paul began skating on frozen and his competitive nature makes him a natural out on the ice. The 2007–08 season was not as easy for Stastny as a major injury kept Sakic out of the lineup for most of the season. Not only did that mean Stastny was now the first-line center by default, it also meant his mentor was not there to help him out. Stastny started the year in terrific fashion with a hat trick in the opening game against the Dallas Stars. He also recorded his 100th career point in just 99 games played. It looked like Stastny was going to improve on his fine rookie totals, but he missed 15 games after having his appendix removed. He was able to return and picked up right where he left off, ending the season as the Avalanche leader in points with 71. Colorado also made good on its promise to make the playoffs.

If there is a one reason why Stastny is as successful as he has been to date, it may have something to do with embracing his family history. He was extremely grateful to teammate John-Michael Liles for giving up sweater No. 26 so he could wear his father's former digits. Many might want to distance themselves from such a legacy to keep the pressure off, but instead Stastny seems to thrive on it. You can bet the Avs are glad they invested a second-rounder to select Stastny, a player who, in many ways, helps them connect with their past.

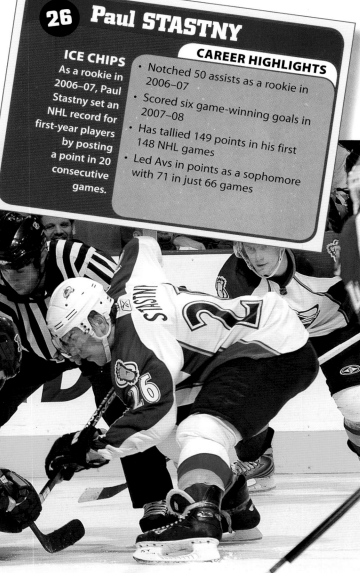

26 Paul STASTNY

ICE CHIPS
As a rookie in 2006–07, Paul Stastny set an NHL record for first-year players by posting a point in 20 consecutive games.

CAREER HIGHLIGHTS
- Notched 50 assists as a rookie in 2006–07
- Scored six game-winning goals in 2007–08
- Has tallied 149 points in his first 148 NHL games
- Led Avs in points as a sophomore with 71 in just 66 games

Rick NASH 61
COLUMBUS BLUE JACKETS – LW

Western Conference Team Star

second, was poised to take goaltender Kari Lehtonen. MacLean, holding the third pick, was able to secure the No. 1 spot by promising the Panthers a swap of future first-rounders at Florida's discretion. It was the best move the Blue Jackets have made in their brief history.

A native of Brampton, Ontario, Nash had thought about being a goaltender, since he played that position in lacrosse. His dad suggested he make a choice when he was about 10 years old and Nash decided to stay out of the hockey nets and play forward instead. Nash first came to prominence when he scored 61 goals in the 1999–2000 season as a bantam for the Toronto Marlboros of the Greater Toronto Hockey League. He then jumped to major junior hockey with the London Knights of the Ontario Hockey League, where he was named to the All-Rookie Team by scoring 31 goals in 59 games. A 32-goal season in 2001–02 wasn't extraordinarily high, but the Blue Jackets had done their homework and knew what they wanted. Nash stayed on with the big team after his first training camp and experienced the thrill of scoring in his first NHL game, against Chicago on October 10, 2002. He went on to score 17 times and add 22 assists to earn a spot on the NHL's All-Rookie Team.

The next season saw the youngster tie Jarome Iginla and Ilya Kovalchuk for the league lead in goals with 41. That performance got noticed all over the NHL as the 6-foot-4, 215-pound left winger started to emerge as a top power forward.

Nash is very intense and has a great nose for the net. He is especially deadly around the crease and his quick release is difficult for goalies to handle. Nash is not afraid to battle for the puck and his large frame, a huge load for any defenseman to handle, helps him gain favorable positioning. Even when it appears he is tied up, Nash is able to keep his stick free and get off his rocket shot.

After spending the lockout year in Switzerland, Nash returned to Columbus for the 2005–06 season expecting the Blue Jackets to make a jump in the standings. But

Former Columbus GM Doug MacLean did not have an easy time trying to build the expansion Blue Jackets into a contending team. They began NHL play in 2000–01 and have never competed in a single post-season game, while watching their expansion cousins, the Minnesota Wild, qualify for the playoffs three times. Additionally, the Blue Jackets have struggled to lure top-notch free agents to Ohio. MacLean has been replaced by Scott Howson and the team is now coached by Ken Hitchcock, a Stanley Cup winner with Dallas in 1999. However, the one move made by MacLean that nobody can question was his maneuvering to select forward Rick Nash first overall at the 2002 entry draft. The Florida Panthers held the first pick and knew they wanted defenseman Jay Bouwmeester, while Atlanta, picking things got off to a terrible start before the year even began as he sprained his ankle badly in the summer. He came back only to suffer a knee injury and played in a total of just 54 games — still managing 54 points. The rest of the team was not nearly as effective without him as Columbus finished 2005–06 with 223 goals for — fourth lowest in the league. Only David Vyborny and Nikolai Zherdev seemed to excel for coach Gerard Gallant and even Russian legend Sergei Fedorov struggled after he was acquired in a deal with Anaheim. There's hope Gallant's replacement, Hitchcock, will extract the most out of players like Jason Chimera, Kristian Huselius, Raffi Torres and Derick Brassard. Goalie Pascal Leclaire took a huge step forward in 2007–08 and the belief is Columbus has finally found a stopper capable of getting them to the playoffs.

Nash, armed with a five-year, $27-million deal, is the cornerstone of the Columbus franchise. He has scored 27 and 38 goals over the last two seasons and has become a more varied goal-scorer who is confident in making moves and beating defenders 1-on-1 to score a picture-perfect goal — as he did on Jan 17, 2008, when he dangled around both Derek Morris and Keith Ballard of Phoenix before dekeing goaltender Mikael Tellqvist and popping the puck into the open net for the game-winning goal, and one of the best markers of the year.

61 Rick NASH

ICE CHIPS

In 2007–08 Rick Nash won the 'Three Stars Award' for the Columbus Blue Jackets for the fourth straight season. Nash was named the first star of the game nine times, the second star five times and the third star four times.

CAREER HIGHLIGHTS

- Won gold with Canada's 2007 World Championship squad
- Youngest player ever to lead NHL in goals with 41 in 2003-04 (tied with Iginla and Kovalchuk)
- Put up 46 points in 44 games for Davos (Swi.) during the lockout
- Ranked sixth in the league with 329 shots in 2007–08

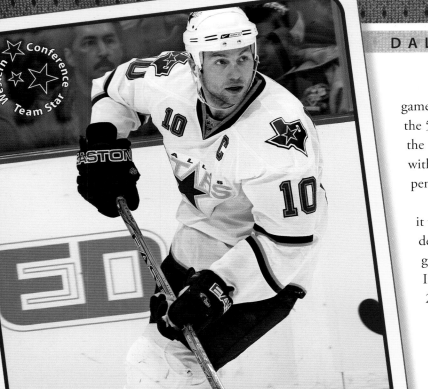

Western Conference Team Star

Brenden MORROW
DALLAS STARS – LW
10

game caught the eye of the Dallas Stars, who selected the 5-foot-11, 210-pounder 25th overall during the 1997 NHL draft. He played one more season with Portland, scoring 41 times and racking up 248 penalty minutes.

As with most young players with rough edges, it was anticipated Morrow would spend sometime developing in the minors. He spent all of nine games playing for Michigan of the now-defunct International Hockey League during the 1999–2000 campaign, scoring twice. An injury to Jere Lehtinen provided an opening for Morrow in the Stars lineup and he has not looked back. It was not easy for the youngster who joined a Stanley Cup-winning roster, but he acquitted himself very well by scoring 14 goals and recording 33 points and 81 penalty minutes in 64 games played. The Stars were back in the final in 2000, but were defeated by the New Jersey Devils in six games. In the four seasons that followed, Morrow was consistent, if unspectacular, in his play. Good for 20 to 25 goals a season and roughly 40 points, and usually well over 100 penalty minutes, Morrow seemed to settle into the role of dependable two-way player. However, something seemed to change after the lockout. He came back determined to do more and was ready to adapt to the new style of game.

Backed by his strong work ethic and superb skating skills, Morrow posted 23 goals and 65 points in 2005–06 and established himself as star player on Dallas. He creates space for himself on the ice by dishing out strong hits and keeps coming at the opposition all over the ice. Morrow is especially strong in front of the crease, where he is willing to take the hits to get goals. He drives defensemen crazy by gaining position on them, often winning races to capture the loose puck. Morrow had great success playing alongside center Jason Arnott, but also showed he could play without his familiar pivot after Arnott left the Stars as a free agent. Just as he was gaining confidence in his offensive play in his new

By his own admission, left winger Brenden Morrow takes his time to develop. It started when the native of Carlyle, Saskatchewan, began his major junior career with the Western Hockey League's Portland Winter Hawks in 1995–96. Moving away from home at 15 and living with a billet family forced him to mature quickly, although it took time before that showed in his play. Even though he scored 117 goals in 60 major bantam games for Estevan in Saskatchewan, he tallied just 13 times in his first year in Portland. But he scored 39 times the following year and then 34 the following season, a year that saw the Hawks win the Memorial Cup. Morrow contributed 18 points in 16 post-season games en route to the big victory. His constantly improving play and aggressive approach to the

role as team captain, Morrow suffered a serious wrist injury that required surgery and kept his 2006–07 season to just 40 games. Even in that stretch, Morrow managed 16 goals and 31 points while playing alongside a new center, Mike Ribeiro. The two developed great chemistry and opponents were forced to focus a lot of time and energy on diffusing the pair.

Morrow bounced back during the 2007–08 season to record 32 goals and 74 points, both career highs. Armed with a new six-year contract, Morrow has now played over 500 career games and his leadership skills and toughness make him one of the most complete players in the entire league. Former Stars player Brett Hull is now co-GM in Dallas and he is encouraging Morrow to evolve beyond playing the role of crease-

CAREER HIGHLIGHTS

10 Brenden MORROW

- Scored the game winning playoff-elimination goal in the fourth overtime against San Jose in Round 2 of the 2008 playoffs
- His team-leading 74 points in 2007–08 were a career high
- Also led the team in, goals (32) and game-winning goals (seven)

By the Numbers

Has rang up at least **49** points and **100** penalty minutes in **four** of the past **five** seasons

crasher. Morrow is beginning to understand the value of lurking a little deeper in the slot and utilizing the extra space to release his high-velocity shot.

Morrow was a strong force in the 2008 playoffs and led his team to upsets of Anaheim and San Jose, finishing with nine goals and 15 points in 18 games. Of his nine tallies, none was bigger than his quadruple-overtime elimination goal in Game 6 against San Jose, as he pushed the puck past a sprawling Evgeni Nabokov in the eighth longest game in NHL history. It may not have been as dramatic as Hull's overtime cup-winner for Dallas in 1999, but it was still very important and exciting for the underdog Stars.

Western Conference Team Star

Nicklas LIDSTROM 5

DETROIT RED WINGS – D

the first time in 16 seasons. It was a classy move by the Red Wings' leader.

Since his arrival in the NHL, Lidstrom has played a quiet, steady game on the blueline. He is not at all flashy, but rarely loses any 1-on-1 battles. He is a superb skater and executes a highly intelligent game by stressing positional play in his own end. He has good size at 6-foot-2 and 190 pounds, but is hardly the physical type. Lidstrom will not shy away from the heavy going, but he likes to move the puck up quickly to Detroit's very capable forwards. With two-way skills similar to his boyhood idol, Hall of Famer Borje Salming, Lidstrom is in on virtually every important situation for the Red Wings.

Lidstrom began his NHL career in 1991–92, when he scored 11 goals and 60 points. His numbers slipped slightly the next season, but he quickly recovered in 1993–94 to post 56 points. In 1994–95, the rebuilt Red Wings got their first taste of success by making it to the Cup final — where they lost to New Jersey — and Lidstrom led the way with 16 points in 18 playoff games. He followed up with a great regular season of 17 goals and 67 points in 1995–96, but the Wings lost in the playoffs to the Colorado Avalanche. Detroit, tired of playoff disappointments, was ready for the 1996–97 season. Lidstrom contributed 57 points and then another eight points in the playoffs, as the Red Wings won the Cup final in four straight games over Philadelphia. In the sweep, Lidstrom and partner Larry Murphy effectively shut down Eric Lindros and his Flyer teammates to clinch the Wings' first championship in over 40 years.

The stellar defenseman was outstanding in 2000–01, when he finally won the Norris Trophy after three straight years as the runner-up. He won it again the next two seasons, becoming the first three-peat winner since Bobby Orr. When the Red Wings won the Cup again in 2002, he won the Conn Smythe Trophy as playoff MVP. In 2002–03 he led the league in ice time per game at 29:20, the highest of his career. He was also named a First

Some people actually believed a European captain would never lead his team to a Stanley Cup. But on the night of June 4, 2008, Swede Nicklas Lidstrom accepted the Stanley Cup from commissioner Gary Bettman and the doubts were forever erased. It took a few years for the talent-laden Detroit Red Wings to reach the top of the mountain, but they finally broke through. Some began to doubt if the super-smooth Lidstrom had enough fire in him to take a team all the way. There should have been no questioning the abilities of one the greatest defensemen in NHL history, but it's a safe bet Lidstrom relished being the first European captain to lift the trophy high over his head. Lidstrom then gave the Cup to teammate Dallas Drake, a longtime NHL veteran who made it to the final for

Team All-Star, joining Orr and Doug Harvey as the only defensemen to be selected for six consecutive seasons.

Lidstrom recorded just 38 points in 2003–04, his lowest full-season total since he joined the Red Wings. However, after taking the lockout year off completely, he came back strong in 2005–06. Urged to shoot more by new Detroit coach Mike Babcock, the consistent Lidstrom heeded the advice and worked his power play magic to score nine goals and 50 points with the extra man — more than half of the career-high 80 points he posted. The Red Wings won the Presidents' Trophy for racking up the most regular season points, but were upset by the Edmonton Oilers in the first round of the 2006 playoffs. However, the highlight of that season for Lidstrom was scoring the goal that gave Sweden the gold medal in a 3-2 win over their historic Finnish rivals at the 2006 Winter Games in Turin, Italy.

Detroit faced the agony of another playoff exit when Anaheim knocked off the Red Wings in the Western Conference final in 2007, but in 2007–08, Lidstrom scored 70 points to help lead his team to the best record in the NHL. He then cemented his reputation in Detroit and around the hockey world forever by leading the Wings to their fourth Cup in 11 seasons.

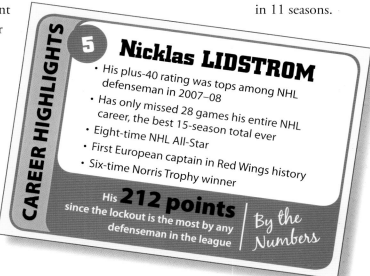

CAREER HIGHLIGHTS

5

Nicklas LIDSTROM

- His plus-40 rating was tops among NHL defenseman in 2007–08
- Has only missed 28 games his entire NHL career, the best 15-season total ever
- Eight-time NHL All-Star
- First European captain in Red Wings history
- Six-time Norris Trophy winner

His **212 points** since the lockout is the most by any defenseman in the league

By the Numbers

Dustin
PENNER 27
EDMONTON OILERS – RW

Western Conference
Team Star

other than it was a chance to play hockey, Penner drove two hours to get registered at the school before an important deadline passed. He was in school the next day. The team at Minot State-Bottineau played exhibition games only and Penner was rarely used. He then suffered a season-ending injury, but came back the following year to score 20 times in 23 games and won the Most Determined Player award. The second event that affected Penner's life was attending an evaluation camp in Saskatoon. It was there that an assistant coach from the University of Maine spotted Penner and offered him a scholarship. Although he had to sit out a year because of the transfer, he then helped the Black Bears get to the championship game of the 2004 NCAA tournament. He scored the game-winning goal in the semifinal against Boston College, but lost the title game 1–0 to Denver University.

Just as he was leaving after the final game against Denver, he experienced another life-changing moment when Anaheim Ducks pro scout and assistant GM David McNab approached him. McNab told Penner he had a chance to play professional hockey. McNab loved what he saw of Penner and thought he had played some great hockey during the tournament. Penner's confidence soared when he talked to McNab, as he finally got the sense he had accomplished something significant. Since he had played so little at the highest levels, the Ducks were able to sign him as a free agent and assigned the 6-foot-4, 245-pound left winger to their farm team in Cincinnati for the 2004–05 season. Penner scored ten times and added 18 assists in 77 games while compiling 82 penalty minutes. The following season saw the Ducks farm team move to Portland, Maine and Penner had a great year with 39 goals and 84 points in just 57 games. He also spent 19 games with the Ducks, scoring four goals and then getting called back up for 13 playoff games. Penner had finally arrived.

The bruising winger took a huge step forward the next season, which was officially his rookie year. He

Dustin Penner always believed he could be a hockey player, but he was rejected so often it was hard to maintain the faith at times. He began playing at the age of four and strived to compete at the highest level possible, but virtually every team he tried out for cut him. Penner did not get to play junior hockey or triple-A hockey for that matter. He had to settle for high school hockey in his hometown of Winkler, Manitoba. When that was over, Penner contemplated leaving hockey altogether and going to work at a plant. But a series of events would change his life and eventually get him into the NHL.

The first was a phone call from a cousin who asked Penner if he had any interest in attending junior college in nearby North Dakota. Not knowing anything else

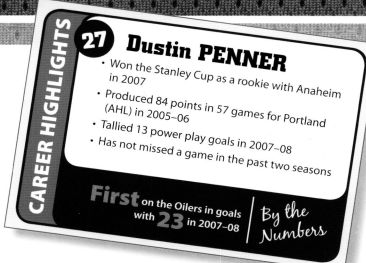

CAREER HIGHLIGHTS

27 Dustin PENNER

- Won the Stanley Cup as a rookie with Anaheim in 2007
- Produced 84 points in 57 games for Portland (AHL) in 2005–06
- Tallied 13 power play goals in 2007–08
- Has not missed a game in the past two seasons

First on the Oilers in goals with **23** in 2007–08 | *By the Numbers*

scored 29 times in the regular season before adding three goals — two of which were game-winners — and eight points in the playoffs, as the Ducks claimed their first Stanley Cup. His impressive performance in the post-season, especially when he basically ran over the Ottawa Senators in the final, drew rave reviews and a monster contract offer from the Edmonton Oilers in the summer. The Ducks were furious that Kevin Lowe, the GM of the Oilers, gave such a rich contract ($21.25 million over five years) to a player they felt was not yet a proven commodity. It made Lowe and Ducks GM Brian Burke bitter enemies.

It's easy to see what the Oilers liked in the young power forward. Penner is large, but has the touch of a much smaller man. He has a good, accurate shot and he knows he needs to hang around the front of the net to be most effective. His skating has improved steadily and his toughness is not to be questioned. He got off to a difficult start with Edmonton, but finished first on the team with 23 goals in 2007–08. Penner is a large part of the Oilers' future and along with Edmonton's other young forwards — Sam Gagner, Andrew Cogliano, Ales Hemsky, among others — he will help provide the team with a varied, dangerous attack for years to come.

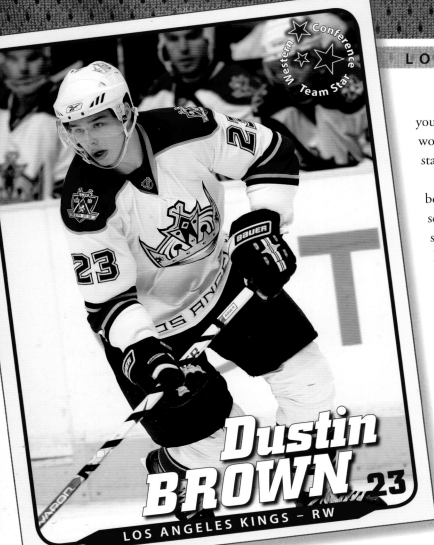

Dustin BROWN 23
LOS ANGELES KINGS – RW

youthful talent the Kings have in their system and hard-working right winger Dustin Brown, who was 22 at the start of 2007–08, only adds to the impressive mix.

Although the 6-foot, 200-pound Brown was born in Ithaca, New York (where he played two seasons of high school hockey), he developed his skills playing for the Guelph Storm of the Ontario Hockey League for three seasons. In 2001–02, he scored 41 goals and totaled 73 points, while the following season saw him record 76 points. Team management in Guelph liked Brown's scoring touch and his very competitive nature. His good play caught the eye of the Kings, who selected him 13th overall in the 2003 NHL draft. Brown became the fifth-youngest player in Kings history when he cracked L.A.'s lineup in 2003–04, but most of his season was washed out with an ankle injury he suffered late in November. He did mange to get into 31 contests and score his first goal (against Colorado) and record five points. During the lockout year of 2004–05, Brown was assigned to Manchester and had an excellent campaign with 29 goals and 74 points in 79 games to go along with 96 penalty minutes. Brown was now ready to re-join the big league team in time for the 2005–06 season.

Brown began to contribute modestly to the Kings attack, scoring 14 times that year and chipping in 17 the next season (13 came on the power play) to go along with 46 points in 81 contests. It was also becoming very evident Brown was going to contribute in more ways than one to the Los Angeles attack when he registered 258 bodychecks, second most in the NHL. He then scored a career-high 33 goals and added 27 assists as the Kings continued to build their team slowly in the 2007–08 campaign. Brown has quickly become known as a two-way player who will take on an opponent physically at every opportunity. Difficult to play against, he does not hesitate to use his stocky frame to initiate contact all over the ice. Brown threw 311 hits in 2007–08, more than any other NHLer. But he also has the finesse skills

When the 2007–08 season began, the Los Angeles Kings roster was sprinkled with a talented variety of players 25 years of age or under. Forwards Anze Kopitar (20 years old), Alexander Frolov (25), Mike Cammalleri (25), Patrick O'Sullivan (22) plus defenseman Jack Johnson (20) and goaltender Jonathan Bernier (19) all began the year with the NHL squad. Cammalleri, who was ultimately traded to Calgary, missed time with injury and Bernier was eventually sent back to junior, but the young nucleus was in place. Waiting in the wings to join the green group are Teddy Purcell (20) and Brian Boyle (22), both centers who earned playing time with Kings during the season based on their fine play with Manchester of the American Hockey League. Few NHL clubs can boast the kind of to be a consistent 25-plus goal-scorer. He is still learning how to use his good shot by getting into the right spots, but that should come with maturity and experience. Brown needs to be more consistent and avoid taking bad penalties, but that too will improve with time. At this point,

Brown is the kind of player every team in the NHL would love to have.

The Kings certainly recognized his value by signing him for the next six seasons on a deal that will pay him in excess of $19 million over the course of the contract. Los Angeles GM Dean Lombardi did not want to face the possibility of losing this rising talent as a restricted free agent, so a deal was worked out with Brown that was quite to the player's liking. Brown could have certainly waited longer to sign his new deal, but he recognized the Kings, despite a run of missing the playoffs in recent seasons, are in good position to build a great team in the coming years and he did not wish to miss out on such an opportunity. Time will tell if he and the club made the right choice.

23 Dustin BROWN

CAREER HIGHLIGHTS

- Recorded a career-high 60 points in 2007–08
- Also posted six multi-goal games
- Nearly doubled his career best for goals with 33 in 2007–08
- Despite his 2007–08 hit total, tallied just 55 penalty minutes
- Has been a member of Team USA at the World Championship three times

Was **first** in the NHL in hits with **311** in 2007–08 | *By the Numbers*

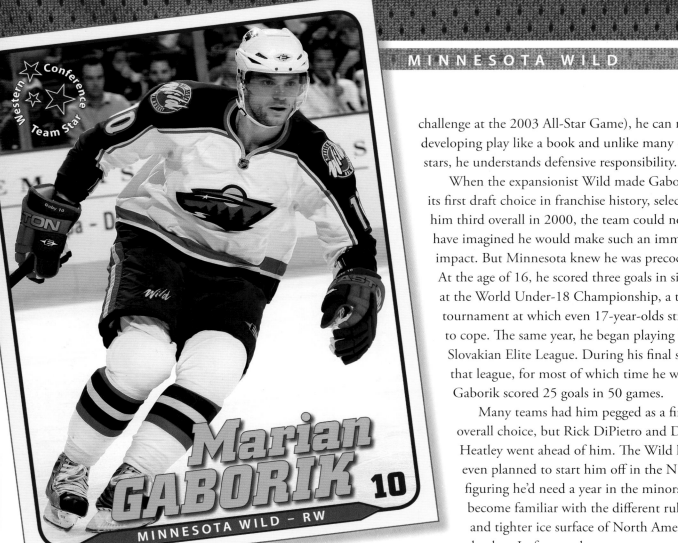

Western Conference Team Star

Marian GABORIK 10

MINNESOTA WILD – RW

challenge at the 2003 All-Star Game), he can read a developing play like a book and unlike many offensive stars, he understands defensive responsibility.

When the expansionist Wild made Gaborik its first draft choice in franchise history, selecting him third overall in 2000, the team could not have imagined he would make such an immediate impact. But Minnesota knew he was precocious. At the age of 16, he scored three goals in six games at the World Under-18 Championship, a tough tournament at which even 17-year-olds struggle to cope. The same year, he began playing in the Slovakian Elite League. During his final season in that league, for most of which time he was 17, Gaborik scored 25 goals in 50 games.

Many teams had him pegged as a first overall choice, but Rick DiPietro and Dany Heatley went ahead of him. The Wild hadn't even planned to start him off in the NHL, figuring he'd need a year in the minors to become familiar with the different rules and tighter ice surface of North American hockey. In fact, at the prospects camp his first summer, Gaborik was so accustomed to having no center red line he went offside on nearly every play. The Wild also felt Gaborik would need to work on defense. But what the team, and everybody else, had not understood was that Gaborik was a quick study. By the end of his first training camp, he had adjusted to the new rules and rink dimensions, had overcome his distaste for North American food and had bought into coach Jacques Lemaire's stifling trap game. He was never sent to the minor leagues.

From the first whistle, Gaborik began creating history. He scored the Wild's first pre-season goal. He scored its first regular season goal in the team's first game and was chosen the third star of the contest. He also scored the first game-winning goal in franchise history. Gaborik bagged his first two-goal game just three games into his NHL career. He took a whopping 19 shots in his first five NHL contests. On a young team that thought

Whatever they're putting in the water in Trencin, they should export it to the rest of the hockey world. The Slovakian city has produced some of the finest players ever to come out of Europe: Ziggy Palffy, Pavol Demitra, Miroslav Satan, Zdeno Chara, the Hossa brothers, Marian and Marcel — all of them were raised in Trencin.

So was Marian Gaborik, who has turned his hockey hotbed roots into quite a reputation in the NHL. It was no less an authority than Mario Lemieux, who in 2002–03 said of Gaborik, who was just shy of his 21st birthday at the time, that he was already among the top five players in the NHL. The 6-foot-1 Minnesota right winger shoots hard and often and is an incredibly fast skater (he won the fastest skater competition in the skills

about defense long before offense, he finished with 18 goals and 36 points in his rookie season. Lemaire and GM Doug Risebrough kept a careful watch on their franchise player and repeatedly deflected attention away from him. As a result, for more than a year, Gaborik was one of the best-kept secrets in the NHL.

But the anonymity couldn't last, not the way Gaborik was playing. He nearly doubled his offensive output in his sophomore season, scoring 30 goals and notching 67 points to again lead the Wild, which moved up to 73 points. When the NHL decided to crack down on neutral-zone interference for the 2002–03 season, many observers felt the Wild would suffer the most. But Lemaire's trap was built on speed and discipline, not illegal moves, so Minnesota thrived under the new system and improved dramatically in its third season. By mid-December, the Wild was in first place and Gaborik led the NHL with 19 goals.

The expected slide came after Christmas, but Minnesota did make the playoffs,

advancing all the way to the Western Conference final.

He scored only 18 times in 2003–04, but bounced back nicely in 2005–06 to lead the team with 38 goals and record 66 points. A 30–goal season in 2006–07 was followed by a career-high 42 tallies in 2007–08, making Gaborik one of the most consistent scorers in the NHL. He had the night of his life during a game against the New York Rangers that year, becoming the first player since Sergei Fedorov in 1996 to record five goals in one game.

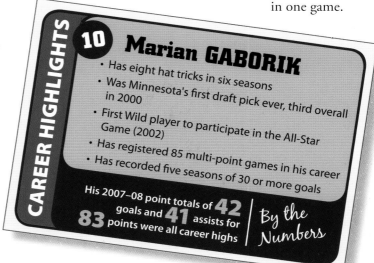

CAREER HIGHLIGHTS

10 Marian GABORIK

- Has eight hat tricks in six seasons
- Was Minnesota's first draft pick ever, third overall in 2000
- First Wild player to participate in the All-Star Game (2002)
- Has registered 85 multi-point games in his career
- Has recorded five seasons of 30 or more goals

His 2007–08 point totals of **42** goals and **41** assists for **83** points were all career highs | *By the Numbers*

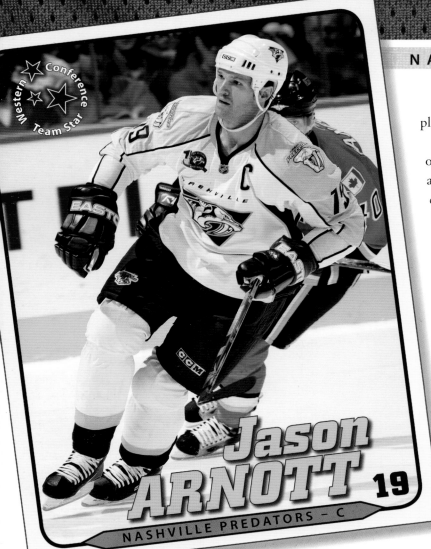

Western Conference Team Star

Jason ARNOTT 19
NASHVILLE PREDATORS – C

Every youngster who plays hockey dreams of scoring the goal that wins the Stanley Cup, especially in overtime. On June 10, 2000, Jason Arnott lived the dream. His New Jersey Devils team was locked in a fierce battle with the Dallas Stars in the sixth game of the final. The Devils held a 3–2 advantage in the series and a victory by the Stars would force a seventh and deciding game back in New Jersey. Suddenly, at the 8:20 mark of the second overtime period, Arnott found himself open in front of the Stars net. He was spotted by teammate Patrik Elias and a quick pass from the wing to a waiting Arnott ended up in the Dallas goal past a sprawling Ed Belfour. Arnott leaped for joy and the excited Devils mobbed him in celebration of a dream come true. Ironically, within two years, Arnott would be playing for the team he had just beaten.

The goal actually marked a return for Arnott as one of the game's elite. A classic power forward at 6-foot-4 and 220 pounds, Arnott had not been meeting the expectations that developed after his first season. The big, strong center first came to prominence when he broke into the NHL in 1993–94 with the Edmonton Oilers. As the seventh overall pick in the 1993 draft, Arnott made a huge splash with 33 goals as a rookie, finishing second in the Calder Trophy race to goalie Martin Brodeur of New Jersey. The Oilers' drafting record had not been worth talking about since their glory days, but they finally hit on a winner with the selection of Arnott. It also looked like he would be a future leader and a likely replacement for Mark Messier. However, it all quickly unraveled in Edmonton and soon Arnott found himself incurring the wrath of Oiler fans and facing some off-ice issues.

Oilers GM Glen Sather quickly solved the situation by dealing Arnott to New Jersey for Bill Guerin, who was holding out in a contract dispute, in January, 1998. With the Devils, the power forward rediscovered his game, in part because he was shifted from wing back to his natural position at center. Teamed with Elias and Petr Sykora, the trio formed one of the top lines in the entire NHL. After winning the Cup in 2000, the Devils made the final again in 2001, but Arnott missed a couple of key playoff games with injuries. He had held out at the start of that season, but signed on to play 54 games and record 55 points. At the 2002 trade deadline in March, Devils GM Lou Lamoriello dealt Arnott and tough guy Randy McKay to Dallas in a monster deal for Joe Nieuwendyk and Jamie Langenbrunner. It was a good deal for both teams. Although McKay opted for free agency, Arnott's 23 goals and 47 points helped Dallas finish first in the Western Conference in 2002–03, after it had missed the playoffs in 2002. The Devils, paced by Langenbrunner and Nieuwendyk, won another Stanley Cup in 2003.

Arnott uses his body to great effectiveness. He

combines skill with a heavy shot that he can one-time as well as anyone in the league. A solid passer, Arnott is able to keep up with speedy wingers and most of all, he gives them the room they need to operate. Arnott has come to understand he must keep his intensity up at all times to be effective.

After a mediocre season in 2003–04 saw Arnott score just 21 goals, he came back in the 2005–06 season to record a career-best 76 points and was second on his team with 32 goals. Arnott played with a leaner, more sculpted body and proved he could keep up in the new style of NHL play. The Stars won 53 games in 2005–06, but did not appear to be ready for the playoffs and were quickly disposed of by Colorado.

Dallas decided against re-signing the 32-year-old Arnott in the summer of 2006, but the Nashville Predators stepped up and gave him a five-year contract.

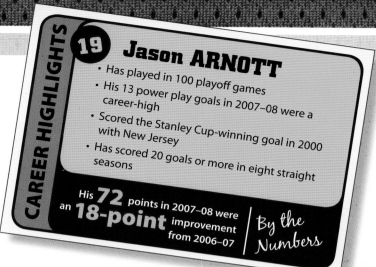

CAREER HIGHLIGHTS

19 Jason ARNOTT

- Has played in 100 playoff games
- His 13 power play goals in 2007–08 were a career-high
- Scored the Stanley Cup-winning goal in 2000 with New Jersey
- Has scored 20 goals or more in eight straight seasons

His **72** points in 2007–08 were an **18-point** improvement from 2006–07

By the Numbers

He has been one of the Predators best players since his arrival in Nashville, scoring 27 goals in 2006–07 and 28 in 2007–08. More importantly, he made it clear he wants to remain in Nashville and was rewarded with the team captaincy in 2007–08. Arnott should remain an effective player for the remainder of his deal with the Predators.

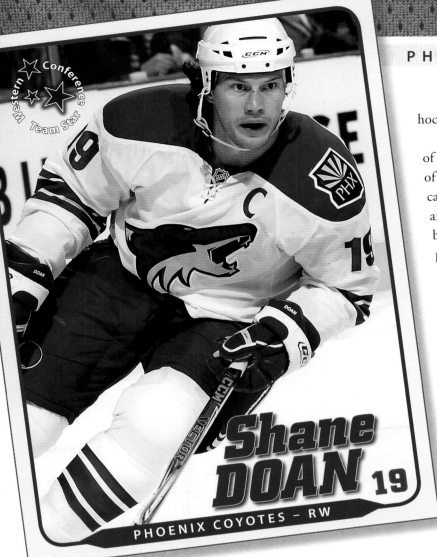

Western Conference Team Star

Shane DOAN 19

PHOENIX COYOTES – RW

hockey and he learned his lessons well.

Doan was a junior star with the Kamloops Blazers of the Western Hockey League. He was named MVP of the 1995 Memorial Cup, won by Kamloops, capping a great season that saw him score 37 goals and 94 points. Doan was drafted seventh overall by the Winnipeg Jets that same year and posted 17 points while playing for the club in its last season in Manitoba, as the franchise moved to Phoenix for the 1996–97 season. His play over the next few seasons was not especially distinguished, but he was learning the pro game at the NHL level. His lack of production got him sent to Springfield in the American Hockey League for half of the 1997–98 season, but he quickly proved he did not belong there by scoring 21 goals and posting 42 points in just 39 games. The following year saw him get just six goals and sixteen assists for the Phoenix Coyotes in 79 games and many wondered if Doan would ever hit his stride in the big league.

The 1999–2000 campaign proved to be a turning point for Doan, who broke through with a 26-goal, 51-point season. He followed that with four consecutive years in which he eclipsed the 20-goal barrier, establishing himself as a consistent two-way performer. Doan's strength is his ability to be fast and physical, especially as he bears down on opposing defensemen. His sculpted 6-foot-2, 216-pound body allows him to be a hard hitter and gives him the confidence to play with an edge. Doan keeps his mean streak under control, but it can be roused in certain circumstances and he is very willing to stand up for a teammate. He forechecks efficiently and knows what to do when he pries the puck loose. Much more than just a checker, Doan utilizes a strong shot to make himself a threat around the net. The Coyotes acknowledged Doan's development by making him team captain before the 2003–04 season. The rest of the NHL took notice when Doan went out and popped 27 goals and 68 points that year, booking his place in the All-Star Game. His

When one considers Shane Doan's family history, it's little wonder the bruising right winger is involved in professional sports. His sister, Leighann, did well in track and field and went on to play pro basketball in Europe, while many of the men in Doan's family excelled in rodeo. Doan's cousin is married to speed skater Catriona LeMay-Doan, who won gold medals while skating for Canada in the 1998 and 2002 Olympics. Shane's father, Bernie, was drafted 80th overall by the St. Louis Blues in 1971. He didn't end up seeing any NHL action, but he played minor pro hockey for a while before deciding to raise a family. Shane was born in Halkirk, Alberta, and grew up on a ranch where he learned to ride horses and help move cattle. In addition, young Shane found lots of time for

performance also earned him an invitation to join Team Canada for the 2004 World Cup of Hockey, where the Canadian squad won the title.

Doan turned in another good season during the 2005–06 campaign, when he scored a career-high 30 goals and totaled 66 points, tying him for the team lead with Mike Comrie. Doan also led the team with 123 penalty minutes, but the Coyotes missed the playoffs again. In 2006–07, Doan's point total slipped to 55, although he only played in 73 contests. Despite his dip in production, Doan earned the distinction of being named captain for Team Canada's entry at the 2007 World Championship, where he led the Canadian squad to the gold medal.

Doan bounced back for 2007–08 recording 28 goals and 78 points in 80 games. Coach Wayne Gretzky was pleased with his captain's play, believing Doan was taking the Coyotes upon his shoulders. He now leads a young group of talented players that includes Peter Mueller, Martin Hanzal, Daniel Winnick, Daniel Carcillo and

Kyle Turris. The Coyotes nearly made the playoffs in 2008 and are finally poised to make people excited about hockey in the desert. Doan has limited playoff experience thus far and that must change for him to be truly considered among the game's elite.

CAREER HIGHLIGHTS

19 Shane DOAN

- Only member of the Coyotes left who also suited up for the Winnipeg Jets
- Captained Canada's 2007 gold medal-winning World Championship team
- Led the Coyotes in points (78) and assists (50) in 2007–08
- Has scored 20 or more goals for eight consecutive seasons

By the Numbers

Hit **50 assists** for the first time in his career in 2007–08

Joe
THORNTON 19
SAN JOSE SHARKS – C

once-proud Original Six team held the first overall pick in the draft and wanted to select a player the team could rebuild its future around. Boston, which also held the eighth pick overall, could not afford to mess up what was a golden opportunity for the organization. There were some tantalizing choices available to the Bruins, including Patrick Marleau, Olli Jokinen, Roberto Luongo and Eric Brewer. But as far as Boston was concerned, a 6-foot-4 center named Thornton stood out from all the rest.

Joe Thornton had put together an excellent major junior career with the Ontario Hockey League's Sault Ste. Marie Greyhounds. In his two years with the Hounds, Thornton scored a combined 71 goals and 198 points. Big things were expected from him right away, though Bruins coach Pat Burns wasn't about to immediately make his rookie a regular. Thornton got into 55 games during his first year and struggled for the most part, with three goals and seven points.

Immaturity was holding Thornton back. He needed to understand dedication was required to be a full-time NHL player. Thornton's second season was a little better. He scored 16 goals and 41 points in 81 games as the Bruins crawled back into the playoffs. Thornton improved further in 1999–2000, leading the team with 23 goals, 60 points and 82 penalty minutes. The biggest improvement to his game was a more intense approach. Thornton is the type of player who needs to get involved physically. His big, strong body is imposing and when he is in the mood, Thornton can make life very difficult for any defenseman who tries to check him. He does have good vision on the ice, which makes him a strong playmaker, but he is most effective when he goes to the net and causes havoc.

When Mike Keenan was brought in to take over the team he challenged Thornton even more. The young man responded with his best year to that point in 2000–01, scoring 37 times and recording 71 points. He had 68 points in six fewer games the next year. But

When you put up great numbers the way Joe Thornton has year after year, people come to expect those performances to lead to a Stanley Cup. Since joining the San Jose Sharks, Thornton has recorded point totals of 92, 114 and 96, but has never advanced past the second round of the playoffs. Until he takes his team further into the postseason, Thornton's detractors will be forced to look upon the center as only a regular season performer, especially with a team as potent and ripe with talent as the Sharks. Despite this, not even his detractors can question how gifted Thornton is, as evidenced by his ascendance to the NHL's elite.

The Boston Bruins were in an unusual position in the summer of 1997. After finishing last overall, the

Thornton really broke out in 2002–03, his first year as captain. He finished third in NHL scoring with 36 goals and 101 points, the first Bruin to surpass 100 points in nine seasons.

Despite his development, Thornton wore out his welcome in Boston with poor playoff performances, prompting former GM Mike O'Connell to send him to San Jose in a blockbuster deal that landed Boston

Marco Sturm, Brad Stuart and Wayne Primeau. Many in the hockey world scratched their heads at the deal; to nobody's surprise, O'Connell was relieved of his GM duties later that season. Thornton thrived in San Jose, scoring 92 points in the 58 games he played wearing teal in 2005–06. He led the league in scoring that season with 125 points, and he took home the Hart Trophy as league MVP as well. His first post-season in San Jose ended in a second round defeat at the hands of the Edmonton Oilers.

Thornton's fine play continued in 2006–07 as the Sharks finished second in the Pacific division, but were again unable to get past the second round of the playoffs. It was more of the same in 2007–08. This time San Jose was a Cup favorite and Thornton piloted the Sharks to the second best record in the NHL. Again San Jose faltered in Round 2, losing to the Dallas Stars. Over the 2007 and '08 post-seasons, Thornton has recorded 21 points in 24 games, but has scored only three goals. Until he leads a team to the Stanley Cup final there will always be questions about Thornton's true value.

19 Joe THORNTON

CAREER HIGHLIGHTS

ICE CHIPS
Thornton led the NHL in assists with 67 helpers during the 2007–08 campaign. He also led the league with 96 assists in 2005–06 and with 92 in 2006–07.

- San Jose's all-time leader in post-season assists with 25
- Only player ever to win the Hart Trophy in a season in which he was traded (2006)
- Has recorded at least 20 goals in eight consecutive seasons
- Orginally drafted first overall by Boston in 1997

Brad
BOYES 22
ST. LOUIS BLUES – C/RW

Stuart) for Nolan. At the time of the deal, Boyes was playing for the Leafs' farm team in St. John's where he produced 51 points in 65 games and had to switch to the San Jose feeder team in Cleveland, notching 13 points in 15 games. It appeared Boyes had taken the swap in stride and was now ready to contribute to a rebuilding Sharks squad.

Boyes played a grand total of one game with San Jose in 2003–04 and another 61 in Cleveland, where he recorded 60 points, before he found himself a member of the Boston Bruins. It seems the Sharks were enamored with defenseman Jeff Jillson and were willing to part with Boyes to complete a deal in March of 2004. Boyes dusted himself off once again and made the move to Providence, scoring six goals in 12 games to finish the season. He played the entire 2004–05 campaign with Providence, scoring 33 goals and 75 points. When NHL play resumed after the lockout ended, Boyes found regular work with the Bruins and proved his good play in the AHL was no fluke by scoring 26 times and recording 69 points in 82 games played.

His performance gained him a spot on the NHL's All-Rookie Team and it looked like Boyes' perseverance would pay off with a long career as a Bruin.

Listed at 6-foot-1 and 197 pounds, Boyes makes up for a relative lack of brawn by playing a smart game. He has very soft hands and a deceptively quick shot that tends to hit the goal. Boyes moves efficiently on the ice and reads the play well, allowing him many opportunities to demonstrate his quick release — which he often scores goals with by taking shots right along the ice. He will drive the net for loose pucks and scores most of his goals in tight. You can bet if the disk comes to him, it will be a difficult stop for the netminder. His skating is more centered around quickness than pure speed, but Boyes has worked diligently to get off the mark as fast as possible and most of all, to always keep his feet moving. Well liked by his teammates, Boyes also works hard at learning to play in the heavy traffic areas,

Given the number of times he's been traded during what is still a very young NHL career, you could forgive Brad Boyes for wondering what he should have done differently. The native of Mississauga, Ontario was a first round draft pick (24th overall in 2000) of the Toronto Maple Leafs and he looked forward to joining the team closest to his hometown. However, the Leafs had other ideas for the former Erie Otter of the Ontario Hockey League and traded his rights to San Jose in a 2003 deal that netted Toronto robust winger Owen Nolan. The high-scoring center recorded 90 points for the Otters in 2000–01 and was supposed to be one of a stable of young players the Leafs were forging their future around, but Boyes was traded away along with Alyn McCauley and a first round draft choice (Mark

but it is unlikely he will ever be a physical force.

The 2006–07 season saw the Bruins miss the playoffs and Boston management wanted to improve its blueline brigade. As a result, Boyes was dealt yet again — this time to the St. Louis Blues for defenseman Dennis Wideman. After scoring only 13 goals and 34 points to go along with an unimpressive rating of minus-17 while with Boston for 62 games that season, he put up 12 points in 19 games after he joined the Blues and got his plus/minus rating to an even zero. The Blues were thrilled to land Boyes, believing his soft hands were just the tonic to ignite their attack. It was a good thought since he started the 2007–08 season by scoring 20 goals in his first 31 games — the only Blue ever to reach 20 goals faster in a season was Brett Hull!

Boyes went on to score 43 goals in 2007–08 while recording 65 points in 82 games. He also scored 11 power play goals and his

shooting percentage was 20.7. Playing right wing on the Blues' top line with Paul Kariya and newcomer Andy McDonald, Boyes transformed himself into one of the most dangerous snipers in the NHL. And in the process, perhaps finally found himself a permanent home.

22 Brad BOYES

ICE CHIPS
Brad Boyes' junior team, the Erie Otters, retired his No.16 jersey on January 26, 2007. He is the first Otters player to be so honored. In four seasons with Erie, Boyes recorded 309 points in 223 games played.

CAREER HIGHLIGHTS
- His 20.2 shooting percentage was second in the NHL in 2007–08
- Also led the Blues in goals with 43 and tied Paul Kariya for first in points with 65
- His 43 goals shattered his previous career-best of 26
- Produced 16 multi-point games in 2007–08

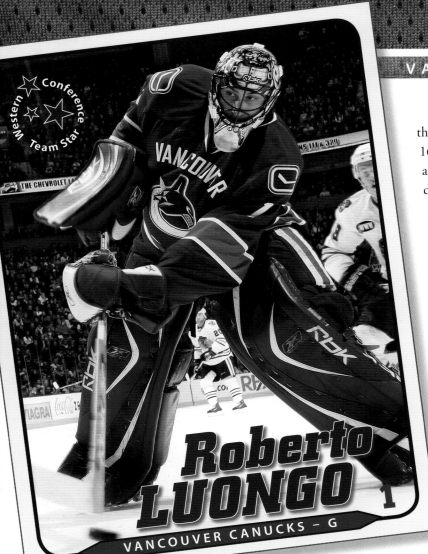

Western Conference Team Star

Roberto LUONGO
VANCOUVER CANUCKS – G

the Quebec Major Junior Hockey League at the age of 16. At 18, he led the Foreurs to a league championship and all the way to the 1998 Memorial Cup final, despite having to face as many as 60 shots per game.

Although the New York Islanders selected Luongo fourth overall in 1997, he stayed in junior as the Isles already had two starting goaltenders in Tommy Salo and Felix Potvin. His junior rights were traded to Acadie-Bathurst during the season and Luongo once again made it back to the Memorial Cup, only to fall short of the big prize for a second time. Luongo, after a brilliant training camp in 1999, suited up for Lowell of the American Hockey League where he played in 26 games. When backup Wade Flaherty was injured, Luongo was called back to Long Island and played 24 contests. His first NHL game was a 2–1 victory at Boston. Behind a terrible defense, he finished the season with a 3.35 goals-against average and .904 save percentage. He had a lucrative bonus clause in his contract that kicked in after 25 games and the Islanders refused to play him in the 25th game. That hurt Luongo and he wasn't terribly upset when the Islanders traded him to Florida on draft day, 2000.

The Panthers immediately tabbed Luongo as the goalie of their future, which arrived in a hurry. He started 2000–01 behind veteran Trevor Kidd, but by the all-star break he had become the No. 1 goalie. His 2.44 goals-against average in 47 games was nearly a goal per game better than Kidd's and his .920 save percentage ranked seventh in the league. His five shutouts also broke a Panthers record. In 2001–02, Luongo was firmly established as the starter and a key to Florida's rebuilding plans. Mike Keenan, who has a history of yanking goalies, became the Cats coach early in the season and it took a little while for Luongo to adjust to him. But Luongo's mental toughness and calm demeanor helped him handle Keenan's antics: he dealt with them like he dealt with bad goals — he forgot them quickly.

The Panthers were not able to make the playoffs

A butterfly goalie with super reflexes and a darting glove hand, Roberto Luongo is one of many Quebec-born goalies who grew up idolizing netminders Patrick Roy and Martin Brodeur. While he tries, with far less success, to handle the puck like Brodeur, his style is much more like Roy's because of his size. At 6-foot-3, Luongo is even an inch taller than the Hall of Famer. Before changes were made to reduce the size of goaltending equipment, shooters complained knee flaps at the top of goalie pads helped plug the five-hole. Luongo, however, realized the opposition would say anything to unnerve a goalie. Luckily for him and his team, the big stopper is not easily disturbed. He's always been a confident, mature athlete and was targeted for the NHL from the time he joined the Val-d'Or Foreurs of despite the impressive performance of Luongo, who posted a 2.77 goals-against average in 58 games. Keenan turned over the coaching reins in Florida to Jacques Martin for the 2005–06 season, however, he was still the team's GM. Keenan's ultimate goal was to get his star netminder signed to a new contract, and taking Luongo to salary arbitration in the summer of 2005 may have turned out to be a strategic error by the hard-nosed GM. Despite the contractual drama, the big goaltender posted his first-ever winning season in 2005–06, and when Keenan could not get Luongo to sign an extension to his deal, he was quickly dealt to Vancouver for a package of players that included Todd Bertuzzi and goalie Alex Auld. Luongo then signed a four-year deal with the Canucks.

Since Luongo's arrival in Vancouver the Canucks have built their team around his superb netminding. In 2006–07, he played in 76 games and won 47 contests as the Canucks set a club record with 105 points. He also guided Vancouver to the second round of the playoffs, finally getting his first taste of post-season action along the way. The Canucks and Luongo were not nearly as good in 2007–08, with the team missing the playoffs despite Luongo playing 73 games and registering 35 victories with six shutouts and a .917 save percentage. Vancouver needs to add scoring to truly take advantage of Luongo's prodigious talent.

1 Roberto LUONGO

ICE CHIPS

Luongo set a Canuck record in November, 2007 by going 195 minutes and 34 seconds without allowing a goal. The sequence included three straight shutouts: 2–0 over Chicago on the 25th, 4–0 over Anaheim on the 27th and 2–0 over Columbus on the 29th.

CAREER HIGHLIGHTS

- Has logged more than 4,000 minutes of playing time in four consecutive seasons
- NHL All-Star in 2004
- Has won at least 35 games in three straight seasons
- Backstopped Team Canada to the 2004 World Cup
- Owner of 38 career shutouts

Henrik
ZETTERBERG 40
DETROIT RED WINGS – LW/C

Miikka
KIPRUSOFF

IMPACT PLAYERS

Players who elevate their game with everything on the line.

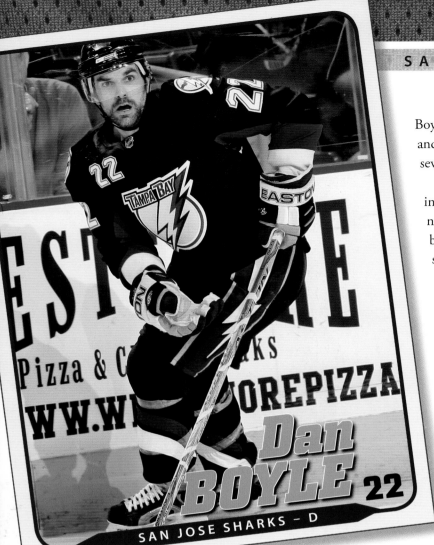

Dan
BOYLE 22
SAN JOSE SHARKS – D

Boyle recovered from the shocking events of that night and so did the Lightning, which eventually won the seventh game on home ice to capture the Stanley Cup.

Boyle was certainly never a lock to be playing in the NHL, let alone the Stanley Cup final. The native of Ottawa, Ontario, played Jr. A hockey before Ohio-based Miami University offered him a scholarship. He put up good numbers while playing four years in the NCAA with the RedHawks and his final two seasons saw him record 54 and 40 points, respectively. However, no NHL team was willing to spend a draft pick on the 5-foot-11, 190-pound defenseman. But in March of 1998, the Florida Panthers signed Boyle as a free agent and he played 22 games for them the next season, recording eight points. He spent the rest of the year with Kentucky of the American Hockey League, where he had a very respectable 42 points in 53 games. By the 2000–01 season, Boyle was more or less a regular with the Panthers and got into 69 contests, notching 22 points. About a quarter of the way through the next season, the Panthers suddenly traded him to the Lightning for a measly fifth round draft choice. It was a move the Panthers would regret.

Boyle's game is more about finesse than anything else. Not a large defender by any means, he has found a way to keep his offensive numbers reasonably high without sacrificing his defensive play. At first, Boyle was seen as a rather questionable defender, but he worked very hard to improve in his own zone because he knew that would ensure him NHL employment. Competent at both ends of the ice, Boyle's name now often comes up when the best defenders in the NHL are discussed; he was even named to the 2006 Canadian Olympic team, although he did not see any action. He is not the dominating defenseman every team craves, but he will quarterback a power play with a good low shot that can be tipped by forwards in front of the net. Boyle is not a speedster, but is smart enough to know when to jump in and when to stay back. He often faces the opposition's best line.

The Tampa Bay Lightning was thrilled to be starting its first-ever Stanley Cup final at home against the Calgary Flames the night of May 25, 2004. The Flames, however, were not good guests and took the contest by a 4–1 score. Naturally, Tampa Bay defenseman Dan Boyle was upset to lose the opener, but that was just the start of what was to be a terrible night. When the game was over, Boyle was told his house in the Tampa area had suffered extensive damage from an apparent electrical fire. At first, Boyle thought it was a joke, but a loss estimated at somewhere around $300,000 was nothing to laugh at, even for a well-paid hockey player. A good portion of the home was destroyed, as were his clothes and many other personal items. Luckily, many of his hockey mementos survived.

During the 2002–03 season, Boyle recorded 13 goals and 53 points, and in the Lightning's Cup year he had a 39-point season followed by 10 points in 23 playoff contests. Tampa Bay struggled mightily during the 2005–06 season, but Boyle matched his career best with 53 points which included notching 15 goals — another career mark. The Lightning were knocked out in the first round of the 2006 playoffs by Ottawa in just five games, but during one contest Boyle beat former Senators goalie Ray Emery with one of the best goals of the post-season, spinning with the puck and firing in a shot on the glove side.

The 2006–07 season was the best of Boyle's career with a 20-goal, 63-point effort. A freak injury that occurred when Boyle's skate fell from his locker and onto his wrist, severing a tendon, kept Boyle out for most of the 2007–08 campaign. Upon his return he was in great form,

collecting 25 points in just 37 games, as well as a hefty, $40-million contract. With a new ownership group taking over the Lightning in the summer of 2008, management decided to cut ties with Boyle's large contract. Despite his no-trade clause, the Lightning got Boyle to consent to a deal with the San Jose Sharks. Boyle will now be the go-to offensive blueliner for the Sharks, who lost defenseman Brian Campbell to free agency in the summer of 2008.

22 Dan BOYLE

ICE CHIPS

On February 29, 2008 Boyle scored in overtime against the Toronto Maple Leafs to become Tampa Bay's all-time leader for goals by a defenseman with 66. Boyle's goal surpassed Pavel Kubina, who was a Leaf at the time.

CAREER HIGHLIGHTS

- Posted at least 30 assists from 2002–03 to 2006–07
- Played for Djurgardens (Swe.) during the lockout
- Tallied 10 post-season points in the 2003–04 Cup run
- Led the Lightning with a 27:24 ice time average in 2007–08
- Traded to San Jose for Matt Carle and Ty Wishart

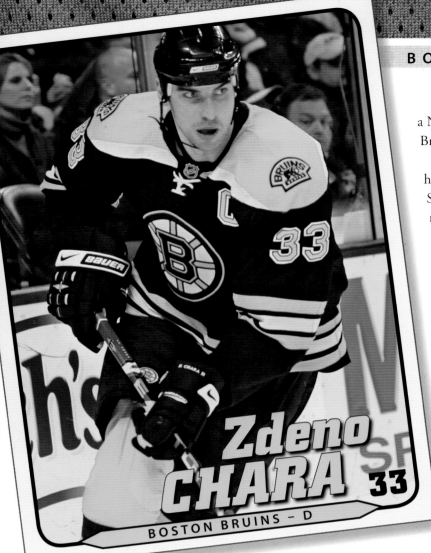

Zdeno
CHARA 33
BOSTON BRUINS – D

a Norris Trophy finalist and helping the beleaguered Bruins back to the post-season.

When the 6-foot-9 Chara arrived in Ottawa, he was more a curiosity item than an answer to the Senators' well-known lack of physicality. But that was nothing new to him. When Chara started playing hockey in the Slovakian town of Trencin, everyone told him he was too big for the game. Chara's muscles and coordination could not keep up to his surging height. He was awkward and easy to get around. In fact, Chara nearly quit playing hockey at age 16. However, he opted to stick with it and became determined to prove his critics wrong.

The Islanders selected Chara 56th overall in the 1996 draft. He came to Canada for one year of major junior play with the Western Hockey League's Prince George Cougars, then spent the next two seasons alternating between the Islanders and the American Hockey League. He found regular NHL employment beginning in 1999–2000, but took a lot of penalties, scored few goals and had horrible plus-minus.

The Islanders considered him highly expendable, but all Chara needed was to stop growing, fill out a bit and find a comfortable environment. He got all of that in Ottawa. His 10 goals in 2001–02 were four more than he totaled in his entire four years in New York and his plus-minus zoomed to plus-30. He brought a certain edge to an Ottawa team that had always survived on speed and finesse. In fact, when the Senators lost Games 6 and 7 to the undermanned Toronto Maple Leafs in the second round of the 2002 playoffs, the defeat was widely attributed to Chara's absence from the lineup with a knee injury. His physical presence had been an important factor in the Sens getting past Philadelphia in Round 1 and gaining a series advantage on Toronto.

In 2002–03, Chara continued to improve. He set career marks with 30 assists and 39 points. Ottawa coach Jacques Martin often used him as a forward on the power play, where the large defenseman could pose

On June 23, 2001, after toiling for four seasons on Long Island, defenseman Zdeno Chara was traded along with the Islanders' first round draft choice to the Ottawa Senators for disgruntled superstar, Alexei Yashin, in what was thought to be a lopsided trade favoring the Islanders. Two years later, it looked to be the Senators who got the steal of a deal as Yashin's play deteriorated badly, the Senators used the draft choice to take Jason Spezza and Chara became a frontline NHL defenseman. For all the fortune the Senators received with the Islanders deal, they were left with nothing but cap space when they let the hulking defenseman sign with the Boston Bruins as an unrestricted free agent in the summer of 2006. Since that time Chara has continued to excel, earning his second selection as a formidable screen. After four years of early playoff exits, Chara helped the Sens advance to Game 7 of the Eastern Conference final where they were felled by New Jersey. Chara continued his rise with a great 2003–04, besting his previous point total by two — he repeated the feat the following year recording 43 points, his best total with Ottawa.

Chara's strength and long reach make it difficult for forwards to squeeze past him. He can move the league's biggest players from the front of the net with ease and is feisty enough that he has taken 100 penalty minutes or more for six straight seasons. He also has a soft touch on the attack, as evidenced by his four consecutive seasons with 40 or more points.

Ottawa's decision to let Chara go as a free agent has proved a boon for the Bruins, who locked down the big defender to a five-year deal in the summer of 2006. His inaugural year in Boston was his first as an NHL captain, and although he tied his previous best point output of 43,

the season was not great as Boston missed the playoffs and the captain posted a porous minus-21 rating. The 2007–08 campaign saw Chara regain his high caliber of play with 17 goals and 51 points — both career highs — while posting a very responsible plus-14 rating. The Bruins made it back to the post-season for the first time since the 2003–04 season and took the first-place Canadiens to seven games before being ousted by the favored club.

33 Zdeno CHARA

ICE CHIPS
Chara defended his 'Hardest Shot' title at the NHL All-Star Game skills competition held in Atlanta on January 26, 2008, with a drive measured at 103.1 miles per hour.

CAREER HIGHLIGHTS
- Ranked third in the NHL with 26:50 average ice time in 2007–08
- Plus-14 rating was a 35-point improvement from 2006–07
- His 17 goals tied for second among NHL blueliners in 2007–08
- Has represented Slovakia eight times internationally
- Is the 18th captain of the Bruins
- Second Team All-Star in 2008

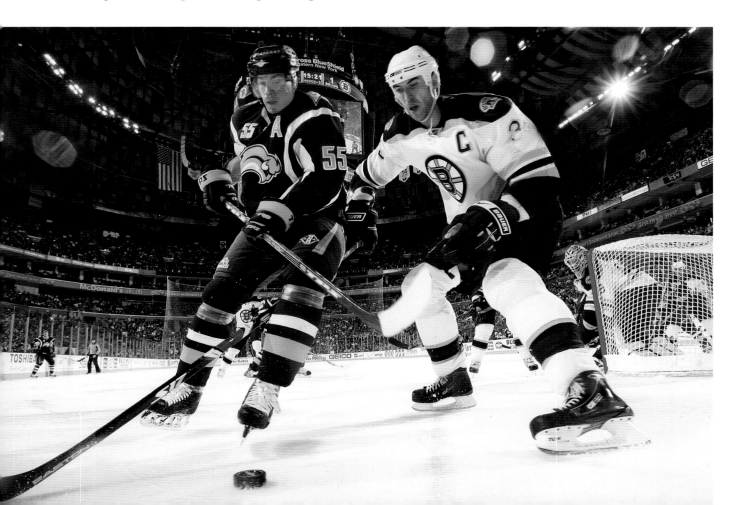

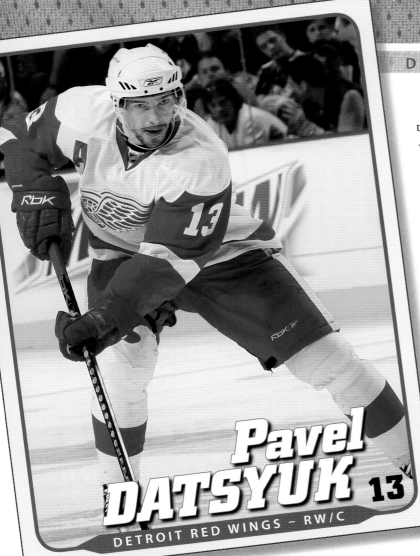

Pavel DATSYUK 13

DETROIT RED WINGS – RW/C

teams have passed on the opportunity to take someone with your talent level. Such was the case for Russian-born Datsyuk, who was finally selected by the Red Wings in 1998. Considered too slight at 5-foot-11 and 180 pounds to compete at the NHL level, the gifted center had something to prove when he came over to play in North America. His timing was good, however, as the Red Wings were going to lose Sergei Fedorov and Igor Larionov, two longtime centers, to free agency in the near future. They needed some youthful legs to step in and take over and Datsyuk did not disappoint.

He began his NHL career starting in the 2001–02 season, when he played in 70 games, scoring 11 goals and recording 35 points. Detroit then went on to win the Stanley Cup and Datsyuk contributed three goals and six points in 21 playoff games. He also played for the Russian team at the 2002 Winter Olympics to complete a dream season for the youngster. The 2002–03 campaign saw Datsyuk up his point total to 51 on the strength of 39 assists, but he also suffered a knee injury and this time the Red Wings were quickly dispatched in the playoffs. The following season saw Datsyuk score a career-high 30 goals and total 68 points in 75 games, as he got the increased ice time that goes

Since entering the NHL in 2001, Pavel Datsyuk has been one of the most consistent players in the game. He has steadily increased his point totals and racked up a very impressive 31 goals and 97 points to lead all Red Wing players in the 2007–08 season. The only drawback to Datsyuk's game was his rather anemic playoff performances. But those troubles were forever put to rest during the 2008 playoffs, when he scored 10 times and totaled 23 points in 22 games as the Detroit Red Wings regained their grip on the Stanley Cup. Datsyuk also won the Lady Byng and Selke Trophies at the '08 NHL awards, entrenching his spot as one of the premier two-way forwards in hockey.

When you get drafted 171st overall, plenty of NHL

13 Pavel DATSYUK

ICE CHIPS

Datsyuk won the Lady Byng Trophy three years in a row from 2006–2008. He became the first player since the New York Rangers' Frank Boucher, in 1935, to three-peat. Boucher won the Byng a record seven times.

CAREER HIGHLIGHTS

- Led the high-powered Wings in scoring with 97 points in 2007–08
- Set a career high in goals with 34 in 2007–08
- Also led the NHL in plus/minus with a plus-41 rating
- Originally drafted 171st overall by Detroit in 1998

with being a regular center. He also shook the reputation of being a player who always looked to pass first and shoot later. Datsyuk was now an established NHL player.

Much of Datsyuk's game is built around his outstanding skating ability. His exceptional lateral movement makes him a very dangerous 1-on-1 player and his moves with the puck can befuddle defensemen and dazzle crowds at Joe Louis Arena. A slick player at both center and wing, Datsyuk is very patient and his top playmaking skills are due to his good vision. He is not very physical, but that does not stop him from excelling as an offensive player.

Datsyuk spent the lockout year back in Russia playing in 47 games for Moscow Dynamo and recording 32 points during the regular season. He added nine points in the playoffs for Dynamo, including six goals. His performance in Russia had him poised and ready for the 2005–06 season, which proved to be an interesting one for both Datsyuk and the Red Wings. He led the team in points with 87 and showed his past

performances were no fluke. He enjoyed showing off his great stickhandling skills during the shootouts that were instituted to settle tied games — Datsyuk's deft and highly creative moves reduced more than one NHL netminder to the role of helpless pee wee goalie. Detroit captured the Presidents' Trophy for having the most points in the league and many expected the Red Wings to romp through the playoffs and recapture the Stanley Cup.

However, the Edmonton Oilers stomped on those dreams by knocking out the Red Wings in six games and Datsyuk's performance was sub par, with no goals to show for the series. In fact, that ran his playoff goalless streak to a dubious 27 games.

Detroit maintained its faith in the dynamic Datsyuk and he's rewarded the franchise the last two springs. He posted eight goals and 16 points and five multi-pont games during a run to the conference final in 2007, before becoming one of the key cogs on the Wings' Stanley Cup-winning team in 2008, where he assisted on the Cup-winning goal.

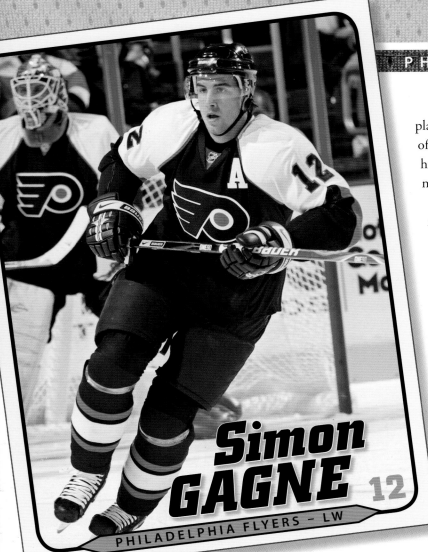

Simon GAGNE 12

PHILADELPHIA FLYERS – LW

play hockey at every turn. He was on skates at the age of two and was playing organized hockey by the time he was four. People marveled at his skating ability, much of it learned on the family's backyard rink.

His father, Pierre, mentored Gagne through minor hockey. The senior Gagne was a good minor pro player in Quebec, as was his father, Roger, a terrific player in the American Hockey League during the 1940s. As a third-generation hockey player in his family, Simon had both the background and the desire to play pro hockey. He played in the prestigious Quebec pee wee tournament on two occasions and eventually plied his craft with Beaufort of the Quebec Major Junior Hockey League.

His last two years of junior saw Gagne play for the Quebec Remparts, where he had a 30-goal, 69-point season in 1997–98. On the recommendation of former Flyer Simon Nolet, who was very familiar with the Gagne family, Philadelphia selected Gagne in the first round of the 1998 entry draft. Gagne went back for one more year of junior and notched 50 goals and 120 points to lead the league in scoring. He made the jump to the Flyers for the 1999–2000 season and cracked the All-Rookie Team with 20 goals and 46 points. He followed that up with 27 markers the next year and then in 2001–02, was outstanding with 33 goals and 66 points. He was also thrilled to be selected for the Canadian squad that won gold at the 2002 Olympics in Salt Lake City. Gagne had four points in six games during the tournament and everyone remembers the front-page photo of him and Martin Brodeur celebrating the end of the gold medal game. Gagne was actually surprised to be selected for the team, but Team Canada GM Wayne Gretzky wanted him there.

At 6-foot and 190 pounds, Gagne is not a huge player, nor is he overly aggressive. He relies on a high skill level to get by. The puck always seems to follow him around and he is deadly when in close. He can get a blast off quickly and is blessed with a tremendously accurate

For the two NHL seasons prior to the 2005–06 campaign, Simon Gagne had not produced to the level expected of him. In 2002–03, he had only nine goals and 27 points in an injury-shortened 46-game season. He played 80 games in 2003–04, but scored only 24 times and totaled 45 points — good numbers for most players, but not for the multi-talented Gagne. He took the lockout year off completely and returned to find the new NHL very much to his liking. He scored 47 goals and 79 points that first year back, leading the Flyers in both categories while setting career bests with both marks as well. The swift left winger was now exceeding expectations and he had the good fortune to do it in a year when his contract was up for renewal.

Growing up in Ste-Foy, Quebec, allowed Gagne to

wrist shot. Gagne is especially good on the power play. The extra room to maneuver helped him score 12 man-advantage goals in 2005–06 and 13 more the following year. Gagne's incredible skating allows him to simply pull away from defenders and few can pivot and turn like he does. He can control the puck, move at full speed and is a very willing passer.

Gagne's unselfish style of play had the Flyers contemplating giving him the team captaincy, but he felt a more senior player on the team deserved the honor, so he passed on it. He continued to fill the net in 2006–07, netting 41 goals. The Flyers had visions of Gagne bagging another 40-goal campaign, but a bad concussion reduced his 2007–08 season to just 25 games.

Gagne needs to avoid the injury bug and improve a little on his playoff performances before he reaches his

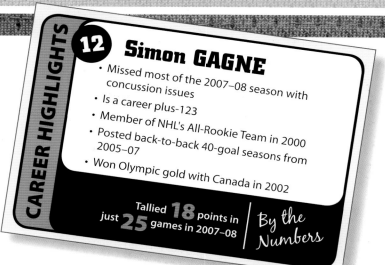

CAREER HIGHLIGHTS

12 Simon GAGNE

- Missed most of the 2007–08 season with concussion issues
- Is a career plus-123
- Member of NHL's All-Rookie Team in 2000
- Posted back-to-back 40-goal seasons from 2005–07
- Won Olympic gold with Canada in 2002

By the Numbers

Tallied **18** points in just **25** games in 2007–08

maximum potential. However, he now has plenty of help on the team with the likes of Mike Richards, Jeff Carter and Daniel Briere giving the Flyers a great set of forwards on the attack. They will need to upgrade their blueline to be considered true contenders.

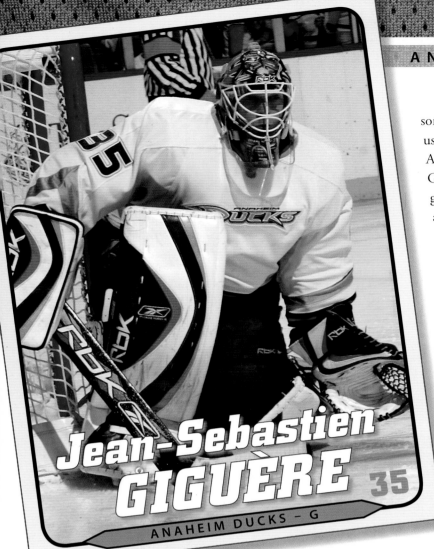

Jean-Sebastien **GIGUÈRE** 35

ANAHEIM DUCKS – G

son. The Ducks supported their netminder fully, using Ilya Bryzgalov in net for the first four games in Anaheim's Round 1 match up with Minnesota, and Giguère responded with a 13–4 record and a 1.96 goals-against average. There were no more doubters about Giguère's netminding abilities.

The Hartford Whalers drafted Giguère 13th overall in 1995, making him the first goalie taken in that draft. During his final junior season in 1996–97, he played eight games for the Whalers, with a 3.65 goals-against average. But that summer, the Whalers moved to Carolina and shipped Giguère to the Flames along with Andrew Cassels for Gary Roberts and goalie Trevor Kidd. Giguère spent the entire 1997–98 season sharing goaltending duties with Tyler Moss in Saint John as the Baby Flames allowed the fewest goals in the American Hockey League. Flames GM Al Coates viewed the big goalie as the heir apparent in Calgary and Giguère played 15 games for the Flames in 1998–99. He looked to join Calgary for good the next year, but the club signed Grant Fuhr and 'Jiggy' was bumped.

Coates had planned to keep Giguère in the expansion draft of 2000, but he was fired and replaced by Craig Button, who wanted to protect only one goalie, Fred Brathwaite. So Giguère was traded to Anaheim for a draft choice that was dealt away to Washington. Once he joined the Ducks, Giguère's career took off. He spent 34 games with Cincinnati of the AHL in 2000–01, but was called up to start a franchise-record 23 straight games for Anaheim. The next year he became the No. 1 goalie as the Ducks floundered, losing 21 games by a score of 3–2 or 2–1. With off-season improvements, the Ducks began winning those close games in 2002–03. But nobody expected them to have the kind of playoff run they posted that spring.

Giguère captured the imagination of the hockey world with an astonishing playoff run in 2003 and the seventh-seeded Ducks rode him all the way into the Stanley Cup final. Despite the fact Anaheim was edged

W hen the NHL lockout ended in 2005, many in hockey were concerned that Jean-Sebastien Giguère's effectiveness might decrease with the size of his goalie equipment reduced. Dubbed the 'Michelin Man' after a bloated advertising character, it was thought Giguère might not be the same netminder who surged onto the scene to win the Conn Smythe Trophy in 2003 when Anaheim lost the final in seven games to New Jersey. But he proved many wrong by posting a 30–15–11 mark during the 2005–06 regular season. He was even better in 2006–07 winning 36 games and then taking his team all the way to the final where the Ducks beat Ottawa decisively in five games. Giguère was able to stay focused during the 2007 post-season despite a severe eye problem with his newborn out by Martin Brodeur and the New Jersey Devils, Giguère was the story of the post-season. It was no surprise he won the Conn Smythe Trophy, becoming just the fifth player to win playoff MVP honors without being on the Cup-winning squad. In the opening round, the Ducks met the defending Stanley Cup-champion Detroit Red Wings, the highest-scoring team in the NHL. Giguère immediately gave a hint of what was to come when he faced 63 shots in the first game, the most ever for a goalie making his playoff debut, and Anaheim won 2–1 in triple overtime. The Ducks went on to an improbable sweep of one of the most powerful teams in hockey history, as the 6-foot-1, 200-pound butterfly-style netminder stopped 165 of 171 shots in the series. Giguère then took the Ducks past Dallas and Minnesota to reach the final round.

It took awhile for Giguère to recapture his good play, posting a poor 17–31–6 record and missing the playoffs

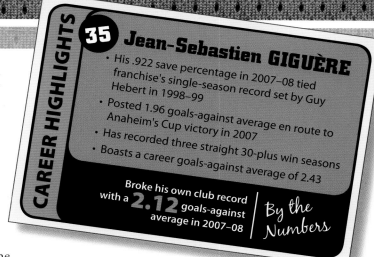

CAREER HIGHLIGHTS

35 **Jean-Sebastien GIGUÈRE**

• His .922 save percentage in 2007–08 tied franchise's single-season record set by Guy Hebert in 1998–99
• Posted 1.96 goals-against average en route to Anaheim's Cup victory in 2007
• Has recorded three straight 30-plus win seasons
• Boasts a career goals-against average of 2.43

Broke his own club record with a **2.12** goals-against average in 2007–08 | *By the Numbers*

in 2003–04. He rebounded well in 2005–06 and by the start of the 2006–07 season, the Ducks were a powerful team, winning 48 times while producing a club-record 110 points. Giguère thrived with all-star defensemen like Scott Neidermayer and Chris Pronger in front of him, as Anaheim won its first championship in 2007. The Ducks could not repeat as champions after the 2007–08 season, but no team has done that since Detroit in 1997 and 1998.

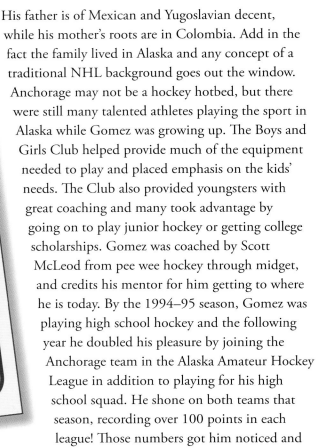

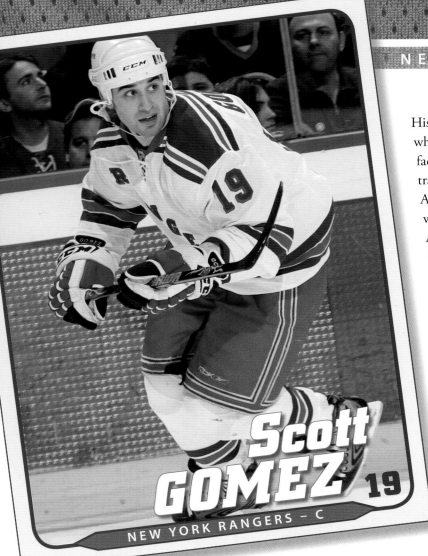

Scott GOMEZ 19

NEW YORK RANGERS – C

His father is of Mexican and Yugoslavian decent, while his mother's roots are in Colombia. Add in the fact the family lived in Alaska and any concept of a traditional NHL background goes out the window. Anchorage may not be a hockey hotbed, but there were still many talented athletes playing the sport in Alaska while Gomez was growing up. The Boys and Girls Club helped provide much of the equipment needed to play and placed emphasis on the kids' needs. The Club also provided youngsters with great coaching and many took advantage by going on to play junior hockey or getting college scholarships. Gomez was coached by Scott McLeod from pee wee hockey through midget, and credits his mentor for him getting to where he is today. By the 1994–95 season, Gomez was playing high school hockey and the following year he doubled his pleasure by joining the Anchorage team in the Alaska Amateur Hockey League in addition to playing for his high school squad. He shone on both teams that season, recording over 100 points in each league! Those numbers got him noticed and he landed in British Columbia for the 1996–97 Jr. A season, where he recorded 124 points in 56 games for South Surrey in the B.C. Junior League.

Gomez then played two years of major junior hockey with Tri-City in the Western Hockey League and recorded 157 points in 103 total games. The Devils selected Gomez 27th overall in the 1998 entry draft and quickly inserted him into their lineup for the 1999–2000 season. Without playing a single game in the minors, Gomez made the New Jersey squad and scored 19 goals and totaled 70 points in 82 games. He was named the NHL's rookie of the year and the Devils won the Stanley Cup. Gomez had 10 points in 20 playoff games. The smiling, happy-go-lucky kid seemed to come out of nowhere to give the Devils a shot in the arm offensively. Gomez then produced fairly modest seasons of 63, 48 and 55 points, while helping the Devils take the Cup once again in 2003. In 2003–04, Gomez increased his

When Scott Gomez was growing up in Anchorage, Alaska, he dreamed of one day making it to New York City. When the opportunity to play on the world's biggest stage came up in the summer of 2007, there was no way he was going to pass on it. The New York Rangers offered an incredible seven-year contract worth $51 million dollars, ensuring Gomez a whooping $10 million in the first season alone. It was certainly a lot of money for a guy who scored all of 13 goals in 2006–07 while skating for the only NHL team he'd ever suited up for to that point, the New Jersey Devils. It was also certainly a long way from his days of playing minor hockey with the Boys and Girls Club in Anchorage.

Gomez' ethnic background is an interesting mix.

offensive output and led the NHL in assists with 56. But it was with the post-lockout rule changes that Gomez really blossomed as he posted his best numbers to date with 33 goals and 84 points in 2005–06.

An arbitration hearing in 2006–07 saw Gomez land the $5-million contract he had been pushing for with Devils GM Lou Lamoriello. Any dispute with the penny-pinching GM, especially one involving salary, typically does not bode well for future negations. Sensing opportunity, Broadway leapt at the chance to sign an unrestricted free agent the caliber of Gomez.

Under Rangers coach Tom Renney, the freedom the swift-skating, offense-minded Gomez was hoping for was granted. Few are better at sensing a scoring chance than the 5-foot-11, 200-pound center, and with the Rangers he gets a lot of shots and gets his nose dirty around the net.

Gomez had trouble living up to expectations in the Big Apple, but he overcome a slow start and notched 70

CAREER HIGHLIGHTS

19 Scott GOMEZ
- Two-time Stanley Cup winner while playing for New Jersey
- Recorded 11 points in 10 playoff games in 2007–08
- Has posted at least 40 assists in five straight seasons
- Played for his hometown Alaska Aces (ECHL) during the lockout

By the Numbers
Has notched **75** points in **106** career playoff games

regular season points. Gomez' first trip to the post-season as a Blueshirt was against his old mates in New Jersey, where he posted seven points in five games, including three helpers in Game 1 in New Jersey, to help the Rangers advance to Round 2. Sydney Crosby and the upstart Penguins bested the Rangers in five games, but for Gomez, it was all part of finding his grove in the Big City.

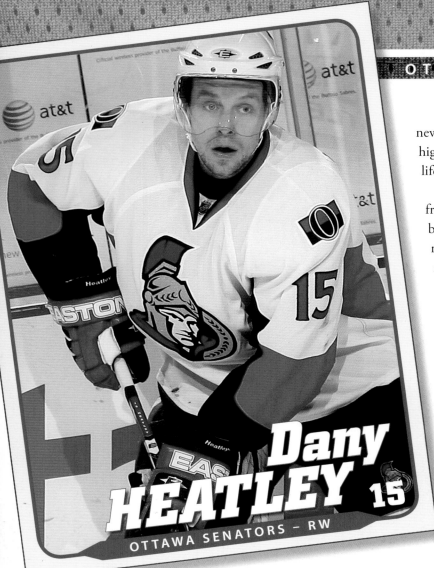

Dany HEATLEY 15

OTTAWA SENATORS – RW

new six-year contract that will see him earn a league-high $10 million in 2008–09 and $45 million over the life of the deal.

Heatley had an immediate impact on the NHL from the moment he was selected second overall by the Atlanta Thrashers in 2000. He has been a remarkably consistent scorer since his first year of midget hockey in Calgary, when he rang up 91 points in just 25 games and was named MVP of the national championship tournament, currently named the Telus Cup. Two years later, he led the Alberta Junior Hockey League with 70 goals and 126 points for the Calgary Canucks. As a freshman with the University of Wisconsin, Heatley had 56 points in 38 games. He followed that up with a 57-point sophomore season and jumped directly from college hockey onto the Thrashers' top line. At 6-foot-3 and 210 pounds, he's big, yet still has a deft touch. But what really impressed observers about Heatley's game was his uncommon poise and patience for a player so young.

Heatley scored 26 goals and 67 points in his rookie year of 2001–02. He won the Calder Trophy as the NHL's top rookie over his teammate Ilya Kovalchuk, but insisted either of them could have been chosen. Coach Bob Hartley noticed Heatley's all-around worth as soon as he took over the struggling Thrashers in January, 2003. Within a few games, he promoted Heatley to the role of assistant captain. After his brilliant NHL debut, Heatley not only avoided the classic sophomore slump, but advanced into the league's elite. In 2002–03, he posted the NHL's sixth-highest goal total with 41 and finished ninth in league scoring with 89 points. He also scored 19 power play goals, third most in the league, even though the Thrashers were thin on talent. Atlanta was not able to surround its two young stars with enough supporting skill to come close to making the playoffs. However, it did make a modest improvement in 2002–03, moving to 74 points from 54 points the previous season.

In early 2003, NHL coaches were asked in a secret poll to name the player they would most like to build a team around. The winner was a 22-year-old right winger named Dany Heatley. If the same question were asked right now there would be more names to consider, but Heatley's would still be near the top of the list. When the Ottawa Senator was injured in February of 2008, the team lost all direction without him. The Senators were 29–10–4 at the time of the injury, but a long slide in the standings saw them barely make the playoffs. Ottawa was quickly dispatched by Pittsburgh in the post-season and while Heatley still managed 41 goals and 82 points in 71 games, he and the Senators never got it going again. It was an unhappy ending to a season that started with Heatley signing a

Heatley was the driver in a horrific car accident prior to the start of the 2003–04 season that killed teammate Dan Snyder and nearly ended his own career. He recovered and returned to the Thrashers lineup for 31 games and recorded 29 points, but his days in Atlanta were numbered. He wisely asked for a trade prior to the start of the 2005–06 season and Thrashers management, recognizing the young man needed a change of scenery to get his life back together, accommodated his request and dealt him to Ottawa for Marian Hossa.

Heatley had a great debut in Ottawa. Playing on a line with Jason Spezza, he racked up 50 goals and 103 points. He was not nearly as sharp in the playoffs, however, and Buffalo eliminated Ottawa in the second round.

A 50-goal, 105-point regular season in 2006–07 was the best of Heatley's career to date and was enhanced by a playoff performance that saw him record seven goals and 22 points. The Senators finally made it to the Stanley Cup final, but were resoundingly defeated by Anaheim. The Senators made it as far as they did largely based on a No. 1 line of Heatley, Spezza and captain Daniel Alfredsson. If Ottawa is to advance to the final again it needs to find some help for its big line and Heatley will have to be a true leader in the post-season. You can be sure that given the size of his new contract, Heatley will be under great pressure to perform better when it counts most.

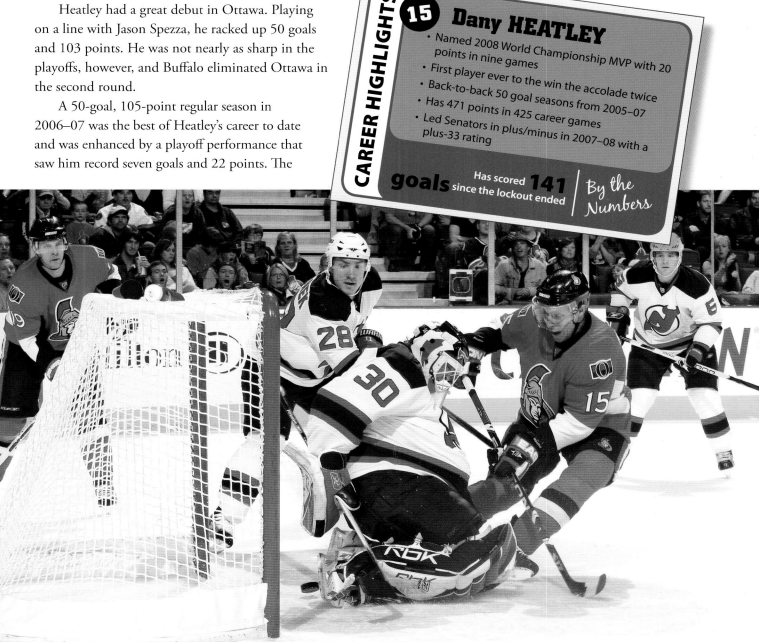

CAREER HIGHLIGHTS

15 **Dany HEATLEY**

- Named 2008 World Championship MVP with 20 points in nine games
- First player ever to the win the accolade twice
- Back-to-back 50 goal seasons from 2005–07
- Has 471 points in 425 career games
- Led Senators in plus/minus in 2007–08 with a plus-33 rating

goals Has scored **141** since the lockout ended | *By the Numbers*

Milan **HEJDUK** 23
COLORADO AVALANCHE – RW

club. In the 2001 playoffs, he finished tied for second among all scorers with 23 points, putting him among the elite in the NHL.

He confirmed that status with a brilliant 2002–03 season, storming back from a disappointing 2001–02 campaign where he missed 20 games with an abdominal injury and only posted 44 points. In his 2002–03 resurgence, Hejduk scored 50 times and won the Rocket Richard Trophy as the league's top goal-scorer. He finished fourth in NHL scoring with 98 points, was fourth in power play goals with eight and tied with linemate Peter Forsberg for the NHL's best plus-minus rating at a phenomenal plus-52. Hejduk had been showing this potential for years. He came to North America from his native Czech Republic, where he had scored 53 goals in 99 games during his last two years while playing for HC Pardubice in the Czech League. He had a good background in sports, since both his parents were athletes: Hejduk's father played hockey and his mother was a tennis player.

He quickly showed a poise and maturity not seen in many young NHL players. Hejduk works very hard and one of his strengths is paying attention to detail, making him a defensively responsible player.

Not big at 5-foot-11 and 185 pounds, Hejduk's strengths are his quick hands and his ability to finish plays. Hejduk shows a willingness to go to the net and is determined to score in spite of his smallish size. His terrific speed and hockey sense take him to all the right places on the ice. Hejduk joined the Avalanche in 1998–99 and made a splash in his first NHL game by scoring a goal and an assist. He ended up with 14 goals and 48 points as a rookie. He was a finalist for the Calder Trophy, but that award went to teammate Chris Drury. Hejduk showed he could handle pressure that first season, recording 12 points in 16 playoff games. He also showed a flair for the dramatic, netting three game-winning goals in the post-season, two of which came in overtime!

By his third season, Hejduk was clearly feeling

The Stanley Cups won by the Colorado Avalanche were an outgrowth of the losing that happened before the team moved to Denver. As the Quebec Nordiques, the franchise made many great draft choices that led to Cups in 1996 and 2001. A good drafting record builds a foundation of talent and affords a team the depth required to make good trades. Some of the best players the Colorado franchise drafted while the team was in Quebec include Joe Sakic, Adam Foote and Milan Hejduk, all of whom played on the 2001 championship team.

The case of Hejduk is a particularly good example of how well the Colorado franchise does its homework. Selected 87th overall in 1994, the right winger has proven to be one of the best choices ever made by the comfortable, scoring 41 times and totaling 79 points in 80 games during the 2000–01 campaign. He was outstanding in the playoffs and scored a signature goal against Los Angeles when he quickly converted a 2–on–1 with Forsberg into a shot past goalie Felix Potvin. The Kings had been pressing, but Hejduk's goal quickly put an end to that.

Hejduk had another fine season in 2003–04 when he had 35 goals and 75 points in 82 games, but he did not enjoy his best year when the NHL returned from the lockout in 2005–06, missing eight games with an injury and posting just 58 points. Hejduk never really got on track, although the Avalanche did make the playoffs and knocked off the Dallas Stars.

He bounced back strongly in 2006–07, when he scored 35 times and totaled 70 points in 80 games. Despite his strong numbers, the inconsistent Avalanche missed the playoffs. Buoyed by the return to form of Jose

Theodore, a key free agent signing in Ryan Smyth and the continued development of the club's young talent, the Avalanche returned to the playoffs in 2007–08. Hejduk had six points in 10 playoff games, but that was hardly typical of the season he had had, where his point total dropped to 54. Hejduk is signed until 2010, which could make him prime trading material as the Avalanche bring in younger players.

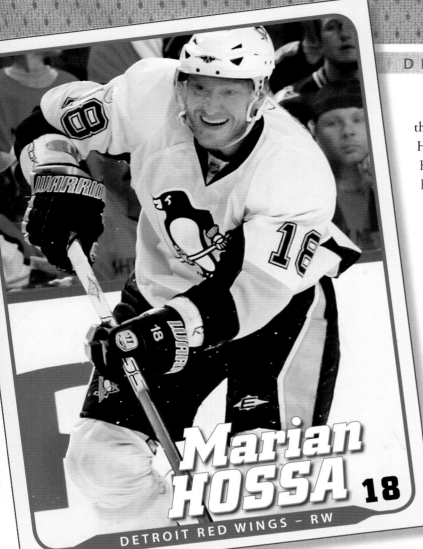

Marian HOSSA 18

DETROIT RED WINGS – RW

their use of the 12th overall choice in 1997 to select Hossa from Dukla Trencin of the Slovakian League. Hossa, who turned 18 only at the end of the season, had 25 goals in 46 games for Dukla, after recording a phenomenal 91 points in 53 games the previous season for Dukla's junior squad. When the Senators opened 1997–98 with the 18-year-old Hossa in the lineup, he was the second-youngest player ever to suit up for Ottawa. Two weeks later, the Senators sent him back to major junior hockey with the Western Hockey League's Portland Winter Hawks and he recorded nine points in his first 10 games. He had 40 goals and 85 points in 53 games for Portland and another 13 goals in 16 post-season games. He contributed nine points in four games as Portland went on to win the Memorial Cup with an overtime victory over Guelph. But in the dying moments of regulation time in the final, he tore ligaments in his left knee and was forced to have off-season surgery.

His knee operation and rehab kept him out of Ottawa's lineup until early December in 1998. But in the remaining 60 games, Hossa served notice he would be a force to be reckoned with. He scored 15 goals and 30 points, and, despite missing a quarter of the season, was named runner-up to Colorado's Chris

A s the 2008 NHL trade deadline approached, a slew of teams were very interested in acquiring winger Marian Hossa from the Atlanta Thrashers. Pittsburgh pulled off the deal by giving up a package of players and a No. 1 draft choice. Sensing they had a chance to go deep into the spring, the Penguins paid the price and then watched as Hossa finally broke through in the playoffs with 12 goals and 26 points in 20 post-season games. Pittsburgh made it to the Stanley Cup final for the first time since their last championship in 1992, proving GM Ray Shero's gamble was indeed worth the risk.

Hossa, a solid right winger, was born to put the puck in the net. The Ottawa Senators collected the dividends of some very good draft positions, including

CAREER HIGHLIGHTS

18 Marian HOSSA

- Signed by Detroit as an unrestricted free agent in the summer of 2008
- Posted back-to-back seasons of 340 shots or more from 2005–07
- Tallied 100 points for Atlanta in 2006–07
- Notched 10 points in 12 regular season games for the Pens in 2007–08
- Has 648 points in 701 career games

Has recorded **seven hat tricks** in his career

By the Numbers

Drury for the Calder Trophy.

Well-balanced, he is hard to knock off the puck. He has great hands and an excellent shot, and in his sophomore season he nearly doubled his goal total to 29, which tied for the Ottawa team lead. But in a game against Toronto late in the season, Hossa fired a shot at the net and on the follow through his stick caught Leaf Bryan Berard in the eye, virtually blinding the talented defenseman. The incident rattled Hossa and it stayed with him well after the season was over.

In 2000–01, Hossa jumped from being a good player into the NHL's upper ranks. Still only 21, he opened the season with a club-record nine-game point streak in which he rang up 13 points. He also had five assists in a game, set another club mark with two shorthanded goals in one game against Florida and was selected for the All-Star Game for the first time. He set career highs with 32 goals and 43 assists as the young Senators won their division and finished second overall in the Eastern Conference. But that excellent season was all but forgotten when the Senators were swept in the opening playoff round by Toronto. There was much said about the Senators' lack of mental toughness in the post-season. It was noted that, as the Senators lost three straight years in the opening round, Hossa had managed only one goal in 14 games.

Hossa continued to excel with Ottawa, consistently putting up 30-plus goal seasons, reaching a career high of 45 tallies in 2002–03. However, when the opportunity to acquire Dany Heatley came up, the Senators shipped Hossa to Atlanta. He played well in Atlanta for two-and-a-half seasons, recording 192 points in his first two years there. But his refusal to sign a new deal led to the trade to Pittsburgh, where he and the young club came up just short, taking the Detroit Red Wings to six games in the Cup final. Hossa then stunned everyone in the summer of 2008 by spurning more lucrative offers and singing a one-year, $7.4 million contract with the Detroit Red Wings.

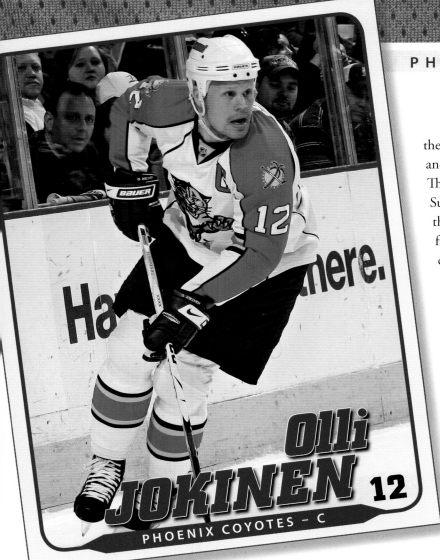

Olli JOKINEN 12

PHOENIX COYOTES – C

By his own admission, he was playing himself off the team. He had even considered leaving the Panthers and returning to Finland to find his self-confidence. Then, on December 3, 2001, Keenan replaced Duane Sutter behind the bench and immediately announced that hockey scouts are rarely wrong and there was far more to Jokinen than the NHL had seen. He challenged and prodded Jokinen the same way he had done to an underachieving Joe Thornton in Boston. Eventually, he got the same results.

Sutter had Jokinen on the fourth line, but Keenan promoted him to the first line, giving him the ice time that would either make him or break him. It made him. After recording just 35 goals and 87 points in 314 games over his first five NHL seasons, Jokinen scored 36 goals and notched 95 points in the 2002–03 season. He was named to the All-Star Game, which was held at Florida's home rink, and for much of the year he combined with Viktor Kozlov and Marcus Nilson to form one of the NHL's most dangerous forward lines.

This was the kind of season expected from Jokinen from the time he began playing in the Finnish Junior League at the age of 14. Less than a year after the Kings drafted him, he was in the NHL, playing in eight games at the end of the 1997–98 season. He registered nine goals the following season, a reasonable output for a 20-year-old making the adjustment to the North American pro game. However, the Kings were desperate for more scoring and included him in a multi-player trade to the Islanders for Ziggy Palffy and Bryan Smolinski. He spent just one year on Long Island, scoring 11 goals, but a large part of his job description with the Islanders was penalty killing.

Although he had great skating and stick skills, his scoring touch remained concealed. Islanders GM Mike Milbury, who wanted to draft goalie Rick DiPietro, traded Jokinen and stopper Roberto Luongo to Florida for Oleg Kvasha and Mark Parrish. In doing so, Milbury dealt the Cats a franchise goalie and premier pivot.

S ome coaches bring out the best in a hockey player and some bring out the worst. At various times to different players in his long NHL career, Mike Keenan has done both. But there is no mistaking the positive influence the demanding coach had on Florida Panthers center Olli Jokinen.

Predicted for NHL stardom since the Los Angeles Kings chose him third overall in the 1997 draft, Jokinen had become a major NHL disappointment by late 2001 and was constantly criticized in the media. Rushed to the big leagues too soon and traded twice before he was 21, he could not find his confidence, or the net. His self-esteem had reached an all-time low early in the 2001–02 season, when he had just one point in the first 25 games for Florida.

However, they didn't realize they had their No. 1 center until Keenan arrived.

In his first year in Florida, Jokinen scored only six goals and his confidence continued to dive. Every time he'd have a bad game, it would affect him for the next five or six. Although he can play a physical game with his 6-foot-3, 205-pound body, Jokinen concedes he wasn't mentally tough until he had to deal with Keenan every day. He responded well to Keenan's demands and after playing well for Finland at the 2002 World Championship, he spent the off-season on a rigorous training program. He returned to Florida much stronger, particularly in the lower body, and previewed what was to come by scoring six goals in five pre-season games.

Keenan, who was also GM in Florida, signed Jokinen to a new contract during a 2005–06 campaign that saw the Panthers captain score 38 goals and 89 points. He followed that up with a 39-goal, 91-point year in 2006–07, but Keenan was eventually replaced by Jacques Martin as coach. Although Jokinen did not especially like the new Panthers bench boss, he did score 34 goals and 71 points in 2007–08, which marked the center's last season in Florida. Jokinen was traded to the Phoenix Coyotes for defensemen Keith Ballard and Nick Boynton and the 49th overall pick in the 2008 draft. The big Finn has played 723 NHL regular season games without tasting post-season action — he hopes to end that drought in the Arizona desert.

12 Olli JOKINEN

ICE CHIPS
In 2007–08 Jokinen set the Florida Panthers franchise record for most career goals, with 188, and most career points, with 419, surpassing the marks previously set by Scott Mellanby.

CAREER HIGHLIGHTS
- Has posted three consecutive 30-goal seasons
- Played for Finland at nine World Championships and two Olympics
- Took at least 340 shots in each of the past three seasons
- Did not miss a game in four straight campaigns (2003–08)

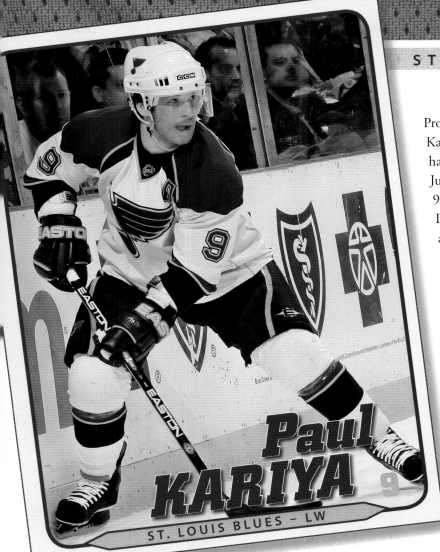

Paul KARIYA

ST. LOUIS BLUES – LW

Pronger second overall before the Ducks selected Kariya with the fourth choice. The Vancouver native had made his reputation in the British Columbia Junior Hockey League, racking up 244 points in just 94 games, before attending the University of Maine. In his first year with the Black Bears, Kariya posted an impressive 25 goals and 75 assists in 39 games. Based on that performance he became the first freshman to win the coveted Hobey Baker Award as the best NCAA player. After helping Canada's Olympic team to a silver medal in 1994, Kariya was ready for the NHL.

When he entered the league in 1994–95, Kariya displayed all the talents necessary for a great career. A superb skater with a terrific anticipation, Kariya also demonstrated a great shot that goalies had to respect. Kariya is always near the top of the list for shots on goal and in 1998–99 he led all players with 429. But the slick winger can do more than shoot and he has the assists to prove it. In 1995–96, Kariya scored 50 goals and added 58 assists in his first full NHL season. He came back with 44 goals and 99 points the next year to show he was for real. The following season was one to forget for young Kariya. First, he had a long contract dispute with the Ducks, then Suter's cross-check to the head kept him out of the 1998 Olympic Games.

The 1998–99 season was much better for Kariya, who played in all 82 contests and recorded 39 goals and 101 points. Kariya has won two Lady Byng Trophies, proving players can excel while still paying attention to sportsmanship. He is also dedicated to the game and is willing to spend the necessary time needed for conditioning.

In 2001–02, the Ducks missed the playoffs for the fourth time in five years and although he scored 32 goals, Kariya's assists slipped to 25, his lowest total for a full season. But although the Ducks were for sale, they brought in some help for their franchise player in 2002–03. Peter Sykora, Adam Oates, Sandis Ozolinsh

Paul Kariya has taken a remarkable number of hard knocks over his 13 NHL seasons. Some have been devastating hits on the ice, like the ugly cross-check delivered by Gary Suter and a senseless elbow from Mathieu Schneider. Some have come from the management of teams he has played on like the Anaheim Ducks and Nashville Predators, as neither club was interested in paying their top player what he was worth. Relatively slight for the modern NHL at 5-foot-11 and 180 pounds, Kariya has learned to survive.

It's hard to believe now, but Kariya was not the first player selected in his draft-eligible year of 1993. The Ottawa Senators had the top selection and wasted it on Alexandre Daigle. A better choice was made by Hartford, which scooped up huge defenseman Chris

and Rob Niedermayer helped the Ducks increase their point total from 69 to 95. Kariya had only 25 goals, but his 56 assists ranked eighth in the NHL. Kariya also became Anaheim's all-time leader in assists with 369 and points with 669.

The Ducks, named after a Disney movie, wrote a script of their own by reaching the 2003 Stanley Cup final, beating powerful teams like Detroit Red Wings and Dallas Stars along the way. Kariya finally had that long NHL spring he had hoped for. The Ducks took New Jersey all the way to the seventh game in the final before losing 3–0.

In a shocking move, Anaheim let Kariya become an unrestricted free agent. He signed with the powerful Colorado Avalanche for one season, but scored only 11 goals and 36 points in 51 games.

Kariya returned after the lockout to play for the upstart Nashville Predators in 2005–06, signing a two-year deal for $9 million. The Predators posted 49 wins and 106 points, but were steamrolled by San Jose in five games during the playoffs. The next season was much the same, with the team improving to 51 wins and 110 points, only to again be ousted in five games by the Sharks. 2007–08 saw Kariya sign as a free agent with the St. Louis Blues, and although he led the team in assists with 49, his goal total dropped to 16 in 82 games — the second worst output of his career. His is 65 points were, however, good enough for a share in the team scoring lead.

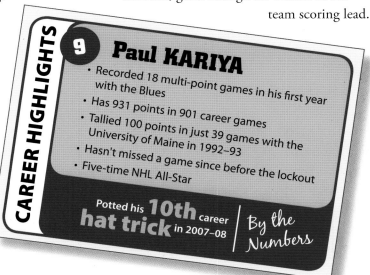

CAREER HIGHLIGHTS

9 Paul KARIYA
- Recorded 18 multi-point games in his first year with the Blues
- Has 931 points in 901 career games
- Tallied 100 points in just 39 games with the University of Maine in 1992–93
- Hasn't missed a game since before the lockout
- Five-time NHL All-Star

Potted his **10th** career **hat trick** in 2007–08 | *By the Numbers*

Miikka KIPRUSOFF 34
CALGARY FLAMES – G

time in seven years and carrying them all the way to the seventh game of the Stanley Cup final.

Kiprusoff had always displayed streaks of brilliance, but lacked consistency. It turned out all he really needed was a legitimate shot to prove himself. Part of a new generation of spectacular Finnish goalies to emerge in the last ten years, Kiprusoff was drafted by San Jose, 116th overall, in 1995. After being named the Finnish Elite League's best goalie in 1999 and most valuable player of the playoffs that same season, the Sharks brought Kiprusoff to North America to replace Evgeni Nabokov on their American Hockey League affiliate in Kentucky. His goals-against average of 2.48 in 1999–20000 was fourth best in the AHL and helped Kentucky win its first division championship.

The next season, he not only ranked third in the AHL in goals-against average and save percentage, but also got into five NHL games, providing a glimpse of what was to come. Kiprusoff won two of three decisions and also won a playoff game against St. Louis as he and Nabokov became the first goaltending duo in six years to capture their first post-season victories in the same series.

The Sharks traded goalie Steve Shields because they thought Kiprusoff was ready for the NHL. They gave him 20 appearances in 2001–02, while Nabokov handled the bulk of the work. In one stretch, Kiprusoff won three straight starts, including his first NHL shutout. But the following season he played only 22 games and had a poor 5–14 record. By the start of 2003–04, he had fallen behind both Nabokov and fellow Finn Vesa Toskala on the depth chart. So Kiprusoff was shipped off in the deal that changed the future of the Calgary Flames.

Using positioning and his 6-foot-1, 186-pound frame to play large in net, Kiprusoff ended the year by establishing a new NHL record with a 1.69 goals-against average. He tied for the league lead with a .933 save

F ans of the Calgary Flames thought they were getting the short-term solution to Roman Turek's injury problems. But GM Darryl Sutter was taking the longer view. Sutter completed a trade in November, 2003, acquiring goalie Miikka Kiprusoff from San Jose for a second round draft choice. Despite the paltry price, Sutter believed he was getting a No. 1 netminder.

Two days after his trade to Calgary, Kiprusoff started his first game for the Flames, won it and never looked back. By early March, he was running neck-and-neck with Martin Brodeur as the best goaltender in the NHL and he had turned the Flames into self-believers. Kiprusoff had very quickly established himself as one of the best goalies in the league, and he further proved the point by getting the Flames into the playoffs for the first percentage and finished runner-up to Martin Brodeur for the Vezina Trophy as the NHL's best goalie. He was a clutch playoff performer, making 26 saves in a seventh-game overtime victory over Vancouver in Round 1, shutting out Detroit in Games 5 and 6 of the next round and exacting revenge on the Sharks by winning four of six games in the conference final. The incredible run did not stop until he was beaten 2–1 in the seventh game of the Stanley Cup final by Tampa Bay.

In September of 2004, Kiprusoff backstopped the underdog Finns to the World Cup final, where they lost to Canada. He then played in Sweden during the lockout before picking up where he had left off in the NHL. Although his scoring-challenged Flames were upset by Anaheim in the opening round of the 2006 playoffs, Kiprusoff was their most valuable player all season, leading the NHL with a 2.07 goals-against average and 10 shutouts and finishing second in wins with 42. He also played more minutes than any netminder in the league. For that stellar performance he took home the

Vezina as the league's top goalie and he was named a finalist for the Hart Trophy as league MVP. Clearly, he was more than a stop-gap solution in Calgary's crease.

The Flames have been an inconsistent bunch the last three years, underachieving while playing for three different coaches. Their fortunes are directly tied to Kiprusoff's performance and he seems to have no trouble shouldering that pressure. However, a return trip to the final is dependant upon Calgary injecting more talent into its lineup and finally settling on a true team identity.

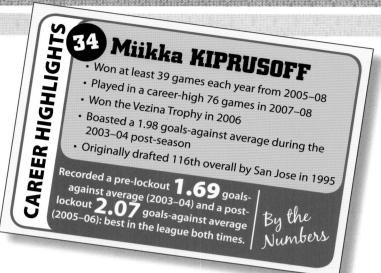

CAREER HIGHLIGHTS

34 Miikka KIPRUSOFF

- Won at least 39 games each year from 2005–08
- Played in a career-high 76 games in 2007–08
- Won the Vezina Trophy in 2006
- Boasted a 1.98 goals-against average during the 2003–04 post-season
- Originally drafted 116th overall by San Jose in 1995

Recorded a pre-lockout **1.69** goals-against average (2003–04) and a post-lockout **2.07** goals-against average (2005–06): best in the league both times.

By the Numbers

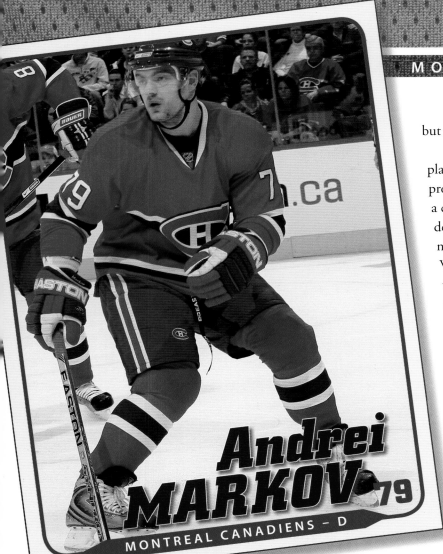

Andrei
MARKOV 79
MONTREAL CANADIENS – D

but that perseverance does pay off.

Markov started skating at the age of five and was playing hockey by the time he was eight. He showed promise while playing hockey close to home and a coach suggested he might be suited to playing defense. It was good advice and Markov first got noticed outside Russia when he played in the 1998 World Junior Championship. His performance in that prestigious tournament caught the attention of the Canadiens, who selected him with their sixth choice in the '98 entry draft. The Habs were hoping to get him to Montreal quickly, but Markov decided to stay home for two more years. He played for Moscow Dynamo, helping that club win one regular season championship. In 1998–99, he scored 17 goals in 50 games and the following season he had 23 points in 29 games for Dynamo. He had established himself as the best Russian player not in the NHL and while he did not wish to leave his family behind, Markov knew it was time to take the plane ride over the Atlantic.

The 2000–01 season saw Markov play 63 games for Montreal, scoring six goals and adding 17 assists. But the Canadiens felt he could use some time in the minors and sent him to their farm club, the Quebec Citadelles of the American Hockey League, for 14 games. He did much the same thing the following season, when he had 24 points in 56 games for Montreal and 10 points in 12 games for the Citadelles. It was difficult for Markov to accept his time in the minors and he very nearly went home. However, he did not want to give up his goal of playing in the NHL. He learned to play better defensively and his minor league days were over by the 2002–03 season, when he firmly established himself as a regular on the Canadiens blueline. In 79 games, Markov scored 13 goals and added 24 assists, and although his numbers dropped somewhat the following year to 29 points, he was still considered a star in the making.

The 6-foot, 203-pounder has broad shoulders and

H ockey players who are not born in North America often want to test themselves by coming across the ocean and playing in the world's best league. They know they can dominate a game in Europe, but can never be sure if they are indeed elite players until they try the National Hockey League. Such was the case for Montreal Canadiens defenseman Andrei Markov. Born in Voskresensk, Russia, the sturdy blueliner took his time before coming to Montreal. When he arrived, Markov suffered the growing pains all defensemen do when they play in the NHL for the first time. He also had to adapt to a language and cultural change he was not quite ready for, but he was determined to make it. By 2008 he was selected as a starter for the NHL All-Star Game, proving not only that he had achieved his goal,

is quite comfortable moving the puck up ice. He is very mobile and likes to join the attack in the offensive zone. Markov is a smooth skater and good passer, but plays his best hockey when he has a bit of an edge to his game. He competes hard and boasts a terrific shot from the point, which helped him post six man-advantage markers in 2005–06. He took only 88 shots on goal that year and scored 10 times, indicating he should fire the puck more. By comparison, former Montreal defenseman Sheldon Souray took 202 shots that same season. Markov is now better equipped to handle the NHL's bigger forwards and his penalty minutes hit a career-high 74 in 2005–06, indicating he is getting more involved in the physical action. He has become the Canadiens' best and most reliable defenseman, improving his point total to 49 in 2006–07 and then a career-best 58 in 2007–08 when he stayed healthy and played all 82 games.

The Canadiens finished first overall in the Eastern Conference last season with 104 points and won one round in the playoffs. Markov needs to be more assertive in the post-season if the Canadiens are to advance any further. The talented blueliner is of all-star caliber and the Habs need him to play that way when it matters most.

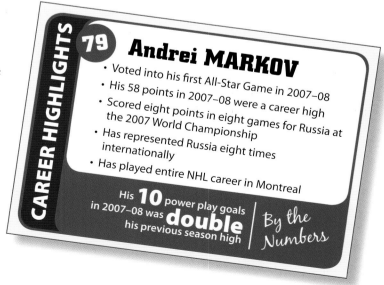

CAREER HIGHLIGHTS

79 Andrei MARKOV

- Voted into his first All-Star Game in 2007–08
- His 58 points in 2007–08 were a career high
- Scored eight points in eight games for Russia at the 2007 World Championship
- Has represented Russia eight times internationally
- Has played entire NHL career in Montreal

His **10** power play goals in 2007–08 was **double** his previous season high | *By the Numbers*

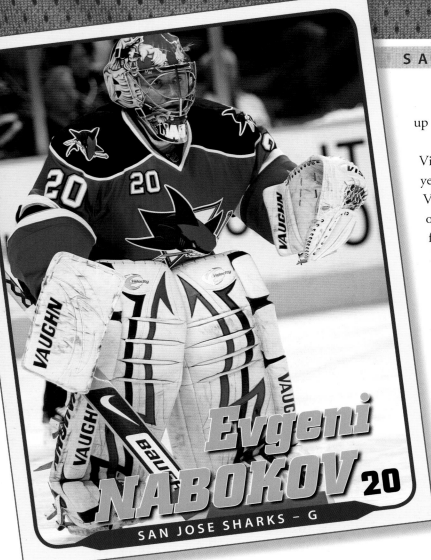

Evgeni
NABOKOV 20
SAN JOSE SHARKS – G

up the Sharks crease for years to come.

Nabokov came to goaltending through his father, Viktor, who played in Russian leagues for many years, and like most Russian hockey fans, admired Vladislav Tretiak — an admiration that was passed on to his son. After hanging up his pads, Nabokov's father assisted in his son's development, ultimately helping him land in the Russian Super League. The Sharks knew Nabokov had to adjust to the North American game and had former goaltender Warren Strelow ready to advise the new arrival. At first, Nabokov could speak no English and Strelow had no understanding of Russian. But, they made it work. The goaltending specialist reminded his protégé to stay focused, work on his fundamentals and always remember to have fun. He only won 10 of 33 AHL games in 1997–98, but the second season saw Nabokov record a 26–14–1 record. He was in the minors for most of the next season, but got into 11 contests with the Sharks and won two games. By the start of the 2000–01 season, Nabokov's minor league days were over.

By posting a 32–21–7 record in 66 games during the 2000–01 campaign, Nabokov won the Calder Trophy as NHL rookie of the year. He quickly got used to the idea of playing a high number of games and only injuries seemed capable of slowing him down. Nabokov followed his great rookie year with a 37-win season in 2001–02, but collapsed somewhat in 2002–03 with only 19 wins and 28 losses. Another problem for Nabokov and the San Jose club was their consistently poor playoff showings. The Sharks kept adding depth to their goaltending roster and at one point had Vesa Toskala and Miikka Kiprusoff in the fold. Eventually both were traded away and that left the net solely in the hands of Nabokov by the time the 2007–08 season began. Under extreme pressure to succeed with a talented team, Nabokov responded with a career year that saw him play 77 games and lead the entire league with 46 wins! His old mentor Strelow, who passed away in April of

When a goaltender gets drafted in the ninth round, 219th overall, it is pretty easy to forget about him. Add in the fact Evgeni Nabokov was playing for Ust-Kamenogorsk in Kazakhstan and it becomes even easier to pay little attention to a puckstopper who's not facing the best shooters in the world. In fact, the Sharks had never even seen him play or watched any film of the very athletic Nabokov before selecting him in 1994. San Jose was looking to add goaltending depth to the organization in 1997, and the Sharks scouts liked what they saw of Nabokov while playing for the Moscow Dynamo that year. Believing he was worth the risk, they sent him to their farm team in Kentucky of the American Hockey League for two seasons. Little did they know the move would help shore

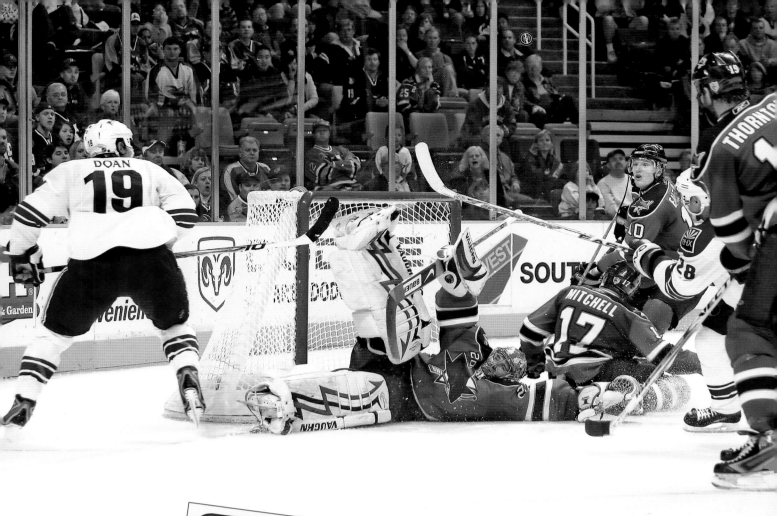

2007, would have been very proud. Nabokov was especially good in the early going of 2007, when he won many close games and posted a 2.14 goals-against average. The 2008 playoffs were a little up and down for Nabokov, who looked ordinary at times and spectacular at others. He got the Sharks past Calgary in the first round, but a loss to Dallas in the next series ended the San Jose hopes once again. Even though he was disappointed with the Sharks elimination, Nabokov agreed to play in the World Championship and backstopped the Russian team to a gold medal with

20 Evgeni NABOKOV

ICE CHIPS
On March 10, 2002, Evgeni Nabokov became the seventh goalie in NHL history to score a goal. He was the first European-born netminder to do it and also the first goalie to score a power play goal.

CAREER HIGHLIGHTS
- Backstopped Russia to a gold medal at the 2008 World Championship
- His 2.14 goals-against average was third best in the NHL in 2007–2008
- Named First Team All-Star in 2008
- Has won 30 or more games four times in his NHL career

a 5–4 overtime win over the host Canadian team.

At 6-foot and 200 pounds, Nabokov is not the biggest goalie in the league, but he is very aggressive in the crease. Like many goalies in the NHL today, he is very difficult to beat down low and he also relies on his lightning-quick reflexes to survive. Nabokov never gives up on a shot and is quick to uses his legs to kick drives out. He rarely gives the shooter a good angle, but must be more aware of his positioning at all times to be truly effective. Nabokov also seems to posses the ideal temperament and personality to be an NHL goaltender. He has now established himself as one of the best in hockey — not bad for a goalie nobody saw before he was drafted!

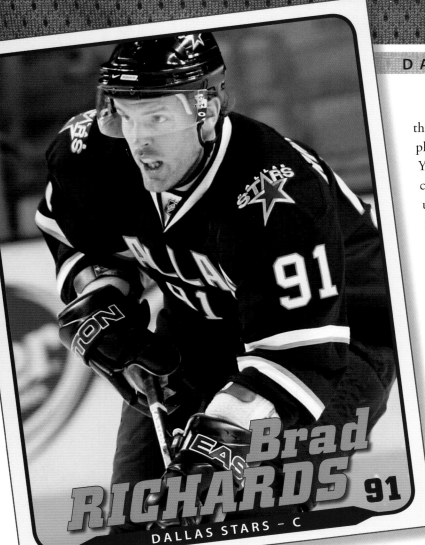

Brad RICHARDS 91

DALLAS STARS – C

the Lightning made Richards the second-highest paid player in the NHL, behind Jaromir Jagr of the New York Rangers, with a $39-million, five-year deal. The contract meant the Lightning would be spending just under $20 million on the dynamic trio through to the 2008–09 season.

Come the 2007–08 trade deadline, the Lightning sat with a 25–30–7 record. It was obvious the team was not going to make the playoffs for the first time since 2001–02, and with holes to fill and not much cap space to do it with, Richards became the expendable member of the Lightning's big three. Along with Goaltender Johan Holmqvist, Richards was traded to the Dallas Stars for Jussi Jokinen, Jeff Halpern, Mike Smith and a 2009 fourth round pick.

Richards is the kind of player who can carry a team and Dallas was happy to land the slick center. He has a fine all-around game and is one of the best playmakers in the NHL. He is not afraid to let fly at the net either, logging over 250 shots a season. He can block shots, quarterback a power play and generate spectacular set-ups off the rush.

Richards' father, Glen, is a third-generation lobster fisherman, but his son was never attracted to the profession. Instead, Richards ended up in the land locked Canadian province of Saskatchewan, playing for the Hounds of Notre Dame College. When he was 14, he met another young Hound player of the same age — Vincent Lecavalier — and the two became roommates. When Lecavalier headed to play major junior for the Rimouski Oceanic, Richards stayed at Notre Dame for a season of Jr. A and was named rookie of the year. Richards joined the Oceanic a year later in 1997, and following that season the Lightning drafted him 64th overall after taking Lecavalier with the first pick in the 1998 draft.

Richards spent two more years with Rimouski. His final season of major junior, 1999–2000, was one for the ages. Richards led the league in scoring with 72 goals and 115 points. He was the Quebec Major Junior Hockey

W hen Brad Richards was three years old, he learned to skate on a pond behind his grandfather's house on Prince Edward Island. Twenty years later, Brad Richards carried the Stanley Cup to that very same house so his grandfather could have his picture taken with the trophy and the grandson who had just won it. Not only did Richards' Tampa Bay Lightning win the 2004 Stanley Cup, the creative center was named the winner of the Conn Smythe Trophy as playoff MVP. He also claimed the Lady Byng Trophy for sportsmanlike and effective play for the 2003–04 season.

That season was the height of good times for a Lightning squad that boasted three of the best play-making forwards in the league in Richards, Vincent Lecavalier and Martin St-Louis. In the spring of 2006,

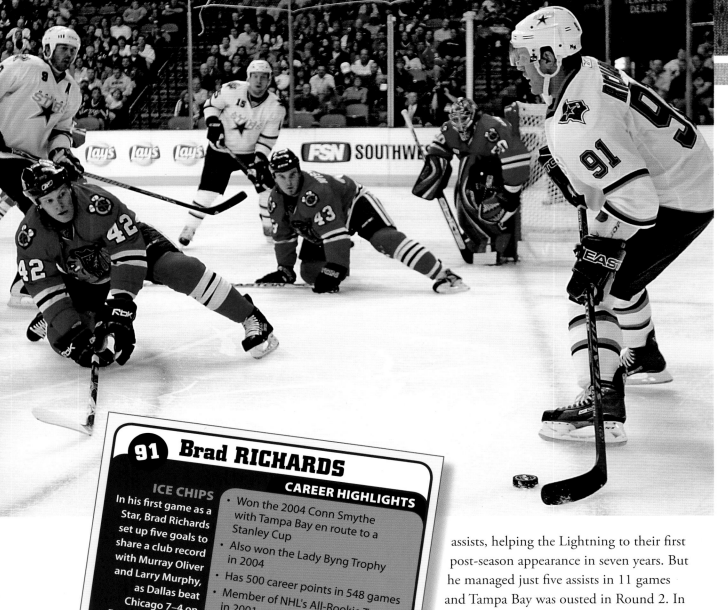

91 Brad RICHARDS

ICE CHIPS
In his first game as a Star, Brad Richards set up five goals to share a club record with Murray Oliver and Larry Murphy, as Dallas beat Chicago 7–4 on February 28, 2008.

CAREER HIGHLIGHTS
- Won the 2004 Conn Smythe with Tampa Bay en route to a Stanley Cup
- Also won the Lady Byng Trophy in 2004
- Has 500 career points in 548 games
- Member of NHL's All-Rookie Team in 2001
- Set an NHL record with seven game-winning goals in the 2004 playoffs

League's regular season and playoff MVP. Richards then led the Oceanic to a Memorial Cup triumph, the icing on the cake coming when he was named the Canadian Hockey League's player of the year. He then joined the Lightning for the 2000–01 season and didn't miss a beat. Richards' 21 goals, 41 assists and 62 points all represented league highs among rookies. At 20 years and nine months, he also became the second-youngest player in NHL history to lead his team in scoring. Richards finished second to San Jose Sharks goalie Evgeni Nabokov for rookie-of-the-year honors.

In 2002–03, Richards posted 74 points and 57 assists, helping the Lightning to their first post-season appearance in seven years. But he managed just five assists in 11 games and Tampa Bay was ousted in Round 2. In 2003–04, he scored 22 goals 60 points over the final 51 games and stormed into the playoffs. Richards stole the show in the post-season, setting an NHL record with seven game-winning goals, breaking the previous mark of six held by his boyhood idol Joe Sakic.

Richard's move to Dallas was big news for all concerned. He brought the Stars veteran savvy, while the Lightning gained depth players and a young talented goaltender in Smith, who might be ready for his shot. It also gave rookie co-GM's Brett Hull and Les Jackson a good test with their first bold managerial move. It paid off well as Richards posted 15 points in 18 post-season games, helping Dallas upset the defending champion Ducks and the heavily favored Sharks, before falling to the eventual Cup-champion Wings.

Daniel SEDIN 22

VANCOUVER CANUCKS – LW

Vancouver Canucks GM Brian Burke told everyone quite bluntly that the only team leaving the 1999 draft with both Sedin twins would be his. The trouble was he only held the third overall pick and that likely meant he would only get one of the brothers, who were hoping they could play together. Undeterred by this fact, Burke made a trade with the Chicago Blackhawks that saw him acquire the fourth overall selection by giving up defenseman Bryan McCabe and a first round draft choice (in 2000 or 2001). He then took that pick and sent it to Tampa Bay along with two other picks for the first overall selection in '99. To complete his dream scenario, Burke then sent the first overall choice to Atlanta in return for the Thrashers second overall spot. Now Burke had the second and third picks, and when the time came he took Daniel at No. 2 and Henrik at No. 3. Just as he predicted, the Canucks did indeed emerge with the coveted brother act. Burke made another prediction at the draft when he said it would take time for these two players to fully develop into legitimate NHL stars, but that it would indeed happen. The percipient GM was not actually around to see the full benefits of his deal, as Burke moved on to manage the Anaheim Ducks (winning the Stanley Cup in 2007), but he was ultimately proven right.

The twins were born in Ornskoldsvik, Sweden, a town that had a clearly established hockey tradition. They both went on to play for the local team, MoDo, which had produced such NHL stars as Markus Naslund, Peter Forsberg, Anders Hedberg and Tomas Gradin, a one-time star with the Canucks. The scouting report on Daniel leading up to his draft year was that he was a high-scoring, finesse-type of player with the maturity to handle the pressures of playing pro hockey. He scored 21 goals in 50 games in 1998–99 and recorded 45 points in 50 games the following year with MoDo. The twins joined the Canucks for the 2000–01 campaign, with Daniel scoring 20 goals in 75 games and notching 34 points to Henrik's 29. Those are not bad numbers for most first-year NHLers, but Canuck fans were anticipating so much more from the brothers given the buildup. Neither was especially fast or overly physical and they quickly became a focal point of derision for victory-starved Vancouver fans, some of whom wanted to see the brothers shipped out of town fast. The twins certainly did not appear to be first-line material as they entered the league, but they just needed time to develop a confidence that they could play at the NHL level. Luckily, team management gave them that opportunity.

In the case of Daniel, the road to stardom was especially tough in the first few years when his goal total read nine, 14 and 18, while his point totals were 32, 31 and then a more respectable 54 in 2003–04. He and his brother returned to MoDo for the lockout season of 2004–05 and seemed to comeback rejuvenated for the 2005–06 campaign. Daniel scored 22 times and totaled 71 points in 82 games, while Henrik had 75 points (including 57 assists) as they started to drive the Canucks' attack. That year the twins played on a line with Anson Carter (a 33-goal man that season) and a chemistry developed that saw the trio become one of the better lines in the league. Carter was gone a year later, but Daniel followed up with a 36-goal, 84-point season in 2006–07, while Henrik set a team record with 71 assists. A big part of the turn around for both players was that they were now getting prime minutes (both over 18 a game) while other players had their roles reduced for a variety of reasons.

The twins have developed an on-ice relationship that can be seen clearly in their puck movement and slick passing. Both have also become more physical and much more difficult to move off the puck or in front of the net. In 2007–08, Daniel kept up his fine play by scoring 29 goals and 74 points, while Henrik racked up 76 points.

Both will have to keep that up if the Canucks are to get back to the playoffs.

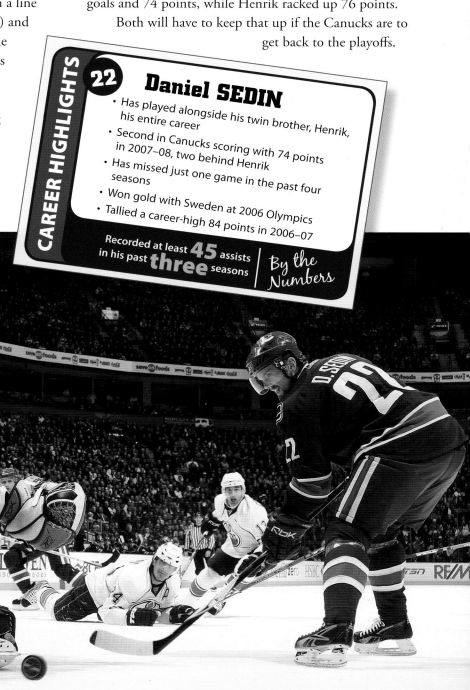

CAREER HIGHLIGHTS

22

Daniel SEDIN

- Has played alongside his twin brother, Henrik, his entire career
- Second in Canucks scoring with 74 points in 2007–08, two behind Henrik
- Has missed just one game in the past four seasons
- Won gold with Sweden at 2006 Olympics
- Tallied a career-high 84 points in 2006–07

Recorded at least **45** assists in his past **three** seasons | *By the Numbers*

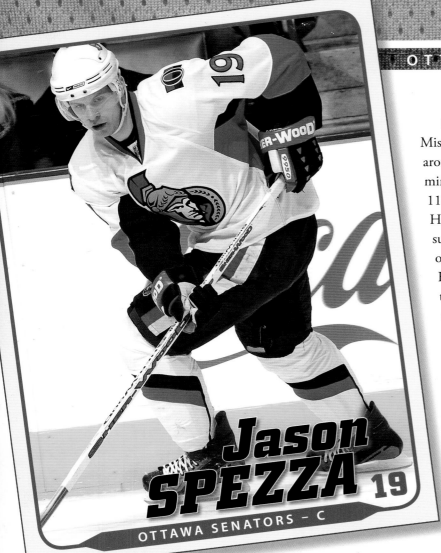

Jason
SPEZZA 19
OTTAWA SENATORS – C

Spezza, a 6-foot-3, 213-pound native of Mississauga, Ontario, has built most of his game around being a top attacker. As a youngster playing minor hockey for the Toronto Marlies, he recorded 114 points in 54 games in midget in 1997–98. He continued to be a prolific producer when he suited up for his hometown Mississauga IceDogs of the Ontario Hockey League the following year. However, the Dogs were one of the worst junior teams in Canada during Spezza's second season and he was traded to the Windsor Spitfires just 15 games into the year. Spezza was moved the following year as well, this time to the Belleville Bulls. There were whispers Spezza made life difficult for his coaches, but that did not stop the Ottawa Senators from drafting him second overall in 2001 after acquiring the pick from the New York Islanders in the Alexei Yashin deal. Spezza's agent, the legendary Bobby Orr, assured all who asked that his client would be a dominating player in the NHL, just as he was in junior. While Spezza was not as noticeable early on with a Senators club that had established players in most spots, he did record 21 points in 33 games as a rookie in 2002–03. His first full season saw the swift-skating Spezza play in 78 games and score 22 times, but he got little ice time in the playoffs under coach Jacques Martin. Two years later, with Bryan Murray as coach, Spezza started to fulfill Orr's prophecy by recording 90 points in just 68 games. He followed that up in 2006–07 with 87 points in just 67 games, helping the Sens become serious Cup contenders.

When Spezza has the puck, he immediately captures the attention of anyone watching the game because he has the ability to carry it the length of the ice, undressing defenders along the way . Once in close, the opposing goaltender has no idea what Spezza might do to score a goal. A bullet shot or a fancy deke are both equally possible and his highlight goals can be seen many times over on all the television sports reports at the end of a hockey night. Sometimes he can get into

N o one has ever questioned Jason Spezza's talent. But when the Ottawa Senators started to see a more driven Spezza in the 2007 playoffs, they realized one of the top young centers in the NHL was starting to mature. Blocking shots and paying attention to defense were just two of the things Ottawa management was seeing from its emerging star. Spezza's offensive game was still in high gear as he also tied for the team lead in points with 22 during Ottawa's run to the Stanley Cup final. As a result, the 25-year-old was given a seven-year $49-million deal during the 2007-08 season, locking him up until the 2014–15 campaign. Spezza's linemate, Dany Heatley, was also signed to a long-term deal by the Senators, ensuring the two stars will be leading the charge in Canada's capital city for years to come.

trouble by making one too many moves or passes, but he's learning to pick his spots better. His defensive decisions are becoming more noticeable not just to his teammates, but to the opposition and hockey observers as well. If there is one aspect of the game Spezza could work on it is his physical play. He typically needs a little room to make his plays and when that's taken away, Spezza struggles. He, along with many of his teammates, found it difficult to thrive against a tough Anaheim squad in the '07 final. A snarl in his style might get him involved in more of the heavy action, but it's difficult to see the perpetually smiling Spezza ever becoming a tough guy.

Even though Heatley missed six weeks with a shoulder injury during the 2007–08 season, Spezza was still able to produce 34 goals and a career-high 92 points.

19 Jason SPEZZA

ICE CHIPS

Spezza was still eligible top play in the American Hockey League during the 2004–05 NHL lockout. That season he was named AHL MVP with a league-leading 117 points while playing with the Binghamton Senators.

CAREER HIGHLIGHTS

- Posted back-to-back 34-goal seasons in 2006–07 and 2007–08
- Scored a career-high 92 points in 2007–08
- Played for Canada's world junior team as a 16-year-old
- Has 39 points in 40 career playoff games

But one year after making the Cup final, Ottawa was swept out of the playoffs in Round 1 by Pittsburgh. Spezza is now in the prime of his career and he needs to realize consistency will always be expected of him, especially in the playoffs.

Martin
ST-LOUIS 26
TAMPA BAY LIGHTNING – RW

L ong before the NHL made life easier for smaller players, 5-foot-9, 185-pound Martin St-Louis had learned to survive in a tough sport. People were always quick to tell him he was too small for the world's fastest league. St-Louis did not let all the negativity get to him and turned it into a motivational tool to prove his detractors wrong. It was a long journey for St-Louis, but at the end of the 2003–04 season he was named league MVP after leading the NHL in scoring — an incredible feat given he was never drafted by an NHL club!

The native of Laval, Quebec, was a good goal-scorer and point-producer during his development years in his home province, but St-Louis decided to try the U.S. college route and attended the University of Vermont for

four years. On three occasions he was a finalist for the Hobey Baker Award, given to the NCAA's best hockey player, but he never won the trophy. In 1995–96, St-Louis had 29 goals and 85 points for the Vermont club in just 35 games for his best college season. But no NHL team was willing to spend even a late-round draft choice on him. When he left Vermont, he had no immediate NHL option to pursue, so he signed to play in the International Hockey League and showed he could handle pro hockey, with 50 points in just 56 games.

His performance with Cleveland of the IHL caught the attention of the Calgary Flames, who signed the diminutive right winger as a free agent in 1998 and assigned him to their farm team in Saint John, New Brunswick. St-Louis played in the American Hockey League, getting 58 goals and 114 points in 95 games over three seasons, but he did not impress the Flames enough when he played 69 NHL games over the same time frame. They decided to let him go, making St-Louis a free agent once again.

Discouraged, but not willing to quit by any means, he signed a contract in 2000 with the Tampa Bay Lightning, which was hoping it might have found a diamond in the rough. Little did the Bolts know they had found a big piece of a larger puzzle that would one day land them the Stanley Cup.

Given the opportunity to play regularly, St-Louis started out with modest numbers in his first two years playing in the Sunshine State. But in 2002–03, he broke through with a 33-goal, 70-point season in 82 games. His play earned him a spot in the NHL All-Star Game, granting him proof, for the first time, he was considered among the league's best players. 2003–04 was a dream season for St-Louis, who won the Art Ross Trophy as the league's leading scorer with 38 goals and 94 points. His great play also earned him the Hart Trophy as league MVP and, perhaps more importantly, the Lester B. Pearson Award, which is given to the NHL's best player as voted by the players; St-Louis was now recognized as

the best player in the league by not only the opinion makers of the NHL, but his peers, making his journey to the top all the sweeter.

Tampa Bay went on to claim its first Stanley Cup with a seven-game win over St-Louis' old team, the Calgary Flames, in the 2004 final. St-Louis had 24 points, including a playoff-leading 15 assists, in 23 games. He also played for his country in the 2004 World Cup of Hockey and, with four points, helped Team Canada win the tournament. The young man with the big heart has accomplished just about everything a hockey player can ever dream of and is an inspiration to all those who hear the words, "You are too small to play."

St-Louis and the rest of the Lightning had great difficulty defending their championship in the 2005–06 season, but he scored 31 goals and totaled 61 points in 80 games. He followed that up with the best year of his career when he recorded 43 goals and 102 points in 2006–07 and then added 83 points in 2007–08. Signed to a long-term deal, St-Louis figures in the Tampa Bay plans for the foreseeable future and he is expected to play a major role in getting them back to the playoffs.

Henrik ZETTERBERG 40
DETROIT RED WINGS – LW/C

their dads expose them to. When Zetterberg was growing up in a town north of Stockholm, Sweden, his father, Goran, put a pair of skates on his two-year-old son and then watched the youngster make his way across a frozen body of water. The elder Zetterberg, who owned an appliance store, had been something of a hockey player in his youth and he wanted to share his passion for the game with his son. Henrik was soon playing hockey as much as he could, with his father giving him tips on how to play the game properly. He learned his lessons well and as he hit his teen years, Zetterberg was playing with boys of all ages for a variety of teams. He stands a fairly modest 5-foot-11 and 176 pounds now and Zetterberg was always one of the smaller boys growing up, which forced him to toughen up and emphasize skill over brawn.

The Detroit Red Wings have been excellent at unearthing gems late in the NHL draft over the years and selecting Zetterberg 210th overall in 1999 was another late coup for the scouting staff. The Red Wings were in no hurry to get Zetterberg over to North America and let him develop his skills further in Sweden. He scored just 15 to 20 goals a season playing for Timra IK in the Swedish Elite League, but impressed enough people to be selected for the Swedish Olympic team for the 2002 Games. He enjoyed the experience and felt he was now ready to play in the NHL.

Zetterberg joined the Red Wings for his first training camp in September, 2002 and was quickly tested by the veteran players and the coaches. The defending Stanley Cup champions wanted to see if he was worthy of making their roster. He passed one test by taking all the physical punishment thrown at him and got to play 79 games as a rookie in 2002–03, scoring 22 goals and 44 points. He was indeed ready for the NHL. Zetterberg's goal total dropped to 15 the next season in Detroit, but he did have six more assists than the previous year. He spent the lockout year recording 50 points in 50 games while playing in Sweden and made noise about not

Winning the Stanley Cup, the Conn Smythe Trophy and scoring the Cup-clinching goal has a way of convincing people you're one of the elite players in the NHL. In the 2008 playoffs, Henrik Zetterberg achieved all of the above and silenced any critics who did not believe he was a top playoff performer. Not only did he lead Detroit with 14 goals and 27 points in the post-season, he was at his absolute best in defensive situations. During one 5-on-3 penalty kill, he stopped a sure goal by Pittsburgh's Sidney Crosby to preserve a Red Wing victory in the final. Zetterberg, who scored 43 goals and 92 points in the regular season, showed teams with great two-way players have the best chance to win the championship.

Young boys are often influenced by what activities

returning to the NHL if he did not get the contract he wanted from the Red Wings.

Detroit GM Ken Holland handled the situation very adroitly and soon Zetterberg was back in the fold. He blossomed as a goal-scorer with a team-best 39 goals in 2005–06. The Red Wings had the best record in the NHL with 58 wins and 124 points, and Zetterberg dazzled with his great stickhandling and picturesque goals. He was very prominent on the power play, where he scored 17 goals, and on the penalty-killing unit, where he honed his shutdown game — his devotion to playing at both ends of the ice helped him finish the year plus-29. Zetterberg is perfectly suited to the post-lockout style of NHL play and will continue to produce for years to come.

As former stalwarts like Steve Yzerman and Brendan Shanahan retired or moved on from Detroit, the Red

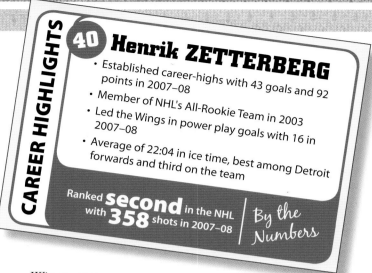

CAREER HIGHLIGHTS

40 Henrik ZETTERBERG

- Established career-highs with 43 goals and 92 points in 2007–08
- Member of NHL's All-Rookie Team in 2003
- Led the Wings in power play goals with 16 in 2007–08
- Average of 22:04 in ice time, best among Detroit forwards and third on the team

Ranked **second** in the NHL with **358** shots in 2007–08

By the Numbers

Wings came to count on a new wave of players like Zetterberg, Pavel Datsyuk and Niklas Kronwall. Winning the Stanley Cup in 2008 has elevated Zetterberg to the status of a truly great NHL player. And he may be just the guy to one day accept the Wings captaincy from countryman Nicklas Lidstrom when the time is right.

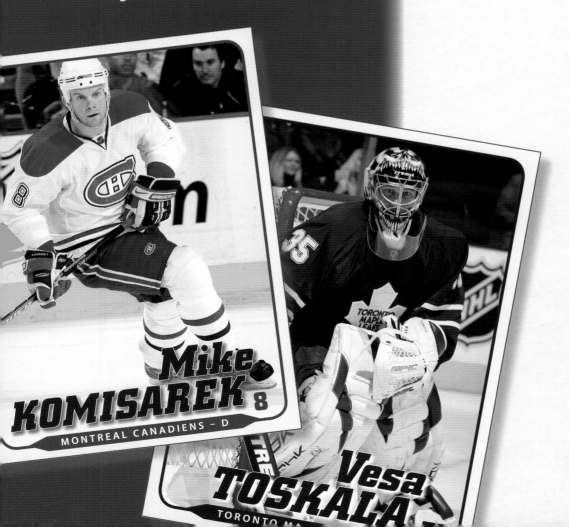

Mike
KOMISAREK 8
MONTREAL CANADIENS – D

Vesa
TOSKALA
TORONTO M

GAME
BREAKERS

*Players who will change
a game with a highlight goal,
a big hit or a fantastic save.*

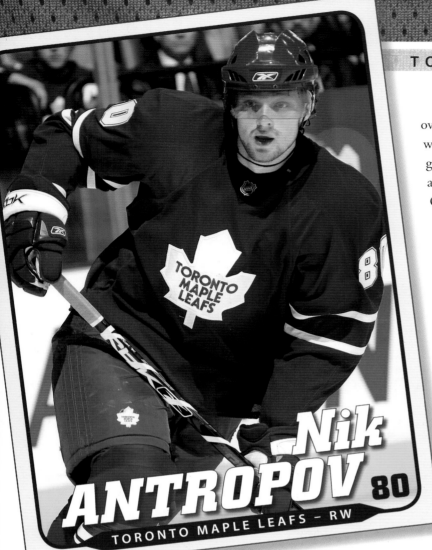

Nik ANTROPOV 80

TORONTO MAPLE LEAFS – RW

There were more than a few teams hoping 6-foot-6, 235-pound Nik Antropov was going to be available when it came their turn to select at the 1998 entry draft. Edmonton, selecting 13th overall, certainly had its eye on the kid from Kazakhstan, as did the Stanley Cup-champion Detroit Red Wings, who were in the 25th spot. Both teams felt Antropov might be available because he had not been heavily scouted and in addition, this center was going to be a project for any team that selected him. However, the Toronto Maple Leafs were also aware of Antropov and knew they could get the lumbering forward for certain at eighth overall, but they were also looking for more draft choices. Toronto peddled its No. 8 pick to Chicago, giving the Leafs additional picks while holding on to their tenth

overall pick as well. The Blackhawks took Mark Bell with their selection and when the New York Islanders grabbed Michael Rupp ninth, the Leafs happily announced Antropov's name with the next pick. The Oiler and Red Wing scouts threw their pens in the air — the big guy they were going to sneak through had just been taken!

Antropov started skating at the age of four and was soon playing the game in Ust-Kamenogorsk, Russia (now Kazakhstan): an area that became known as a place where athletes developed into good hockey players. He was playing in a second-tier league in the Russian system for the Ust-Kamenogorsk Torpedoes by the time he was 16. During his second season as a Torpedo he scored 15 goals and added 24 assists in just 42 games and some scouts started to take notice, especially since he played with an edge, racking up 62 penalty minutes. Noted as a poor skater, it was believed Antropov was going to be a big gamble for some team if it took him too early. He was projected as a second-rounder at best. The Leafs GM at the time was Mike Smith, a man known for his love of European-trained players. He was also encouraged by scout (and former NHL player) Anders Hedberg to take the risk.

The 1999–2000 season saw Antropov come to Toronto and he acquitted himself rather well as a rookie with 12 goals and 30 points in 66 games. The future looked bright for the young man.

Since that time Antropov has battled the injury bug season after season and has faced the wrath of Leaf fans who again believed a great shot to take a good player had been wasted. Although Antropov showed signs he could be a terrific player, it always seemed like every time he was going to make a major break though, the slow-footed Leaf would suffer another setback. In 2002–03, he got into 72 contests and recorded a very respectable 16 goals and 45 points. But other than that season, knee or ankle injuries always seemed to keep Antropov out of the lineup. Some suggested his injuries were directly related to his poor skating technique and at one point it made no sense that the hulking player was adding bulk to his frame instead of trying to lighten the load. When Antropov did play well he was the ultimate big tease, using his size and somewhat nasty demeanor to get his way on the ice. His hockey sense is very good and he is a load to deal with in front of the net. In the 2006–07 season, he played on a line with Mats Sundin and Alexei Ponikarovsky to form an effective and huge (all three are 6-foot-3 or taller) line for the Leafs, but he only got into 54 games (with 18 goals and 33 points). Many fans wanted him out of Toronto, but he re-signed and that proved to be one of the few good moves since-departed GM John Ferguson made before he was dismissed.

In 2007–08, Antropov produced his best year to date with 26 goals and 58 points while playing 72 games. He rediscovered his touch around the net and his size allowed him to dominate the crease area. Antropov has worked at the art of tipping shots around the net and it has paid off as many of his goals have come in this fashion. He has developed a quicker first step, enabling him to compete better and give Leaf fans hope this star in the making has finally arrived.

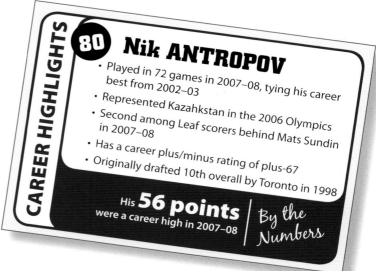

CAREER HIGHLIGHTS

80 Nik ANTROPOV

- Played in 72 games in 2007–08, tying his career best from 2002–03
- Represented Kazahkstan in the 2006 Olympics
- Second among Leaf scorers behind Mats Sundin in 2007–08
- Has a career plus/minus rating of plus-67
- Originally drafted 10th overall by Toronto in 1998

His **56 points** were a career high in 2007–08 | *By the Numbers*

Patrice BERGERON 37

BOSTON BRUINS – C

learner with superior skating, shooting and playmaking skills, and is becoming adept at shielding the puck with his increasingly muscular body.

Bergeron adjusted quickly to the NHL and registered 16 goals and 39 points in the final low-scoring season before the lockout, ranking fifth among all first-year players. He also finished at plus-5, indicating he has a strong two-way game. Had he not lost the last 11 games due to a shoulder injury, he would have been a Calder Trophy contender. The Bruins were upset by the Montreal Canadiens in the opening round of the 2004 playoffs, but Bergeron was solid with four points in seven games and continued to gain coach Mike Sullivan's confidence. His ice time went up nearly a minute to 17:13 minutes per game in the playoffs.

After the Bruins were eliminated, Bergeron flew to Prague in the Czech Republic and helped Canada win a gold medal at the World Championship. Still only 18, he was the third-youngest player ever to play for Canada at the worlds and the third-youngest to score a goal. He went home for the summer and dedicated himself to a regimen of weight training, running and skating for six days a week and returned a much stronger player for 2004–05.

While most NHL players were locked out, young Bergeron was still eligible to play in the American Hockey League and scored 23 goals and 73 points for Providence in 70 games, adding another 15 points in the playoffs. He also spent time with Brad Boyes, another promising youngster, whom the Bruins had obtained from San Jose the previous spring. In the middle of that season, Bergeron joined Team Canada for the World Junior Championship, where he not only won another gold medal, but also led the tournament in scoring while being named MVP of the event.

When NHL play resumed in the fall of 2005, Bergeron was playing extremely well, but the Bruins were not. As playoff possibilities grew more distant, the Bruins

Boston fans were surprised when Patrice Bergeron made the Bruins roster just two months after his 18th birthday. But nobody was more shocked than Bergeron. He had fully expected to return to the Quebec Major Junior League to hone his skills for another season. However, Bergeron makes a habit of accomplishing things earlier than anticipated.

The Bruins selected the center 45th overall in the 2003 draft after he showed promise with a 73-point season as a 17-year-old rookie playing for the Acadie-Bathurst Titan. He played so well in his first NHL training camp and his game was so mature that there was simply no sending him back. And there has been nothing since then to indicate the Bruins made even the slightest mistake in promoting Bergeron so rapidly. He is a quick

shocked the hockey world by trading star center Joe Thornton to San Jose in late November. For Bergeron, the Thornton trade meant two things: He stepped into Thornton's role as a top-line center and became a leader on the team at age 20. He also found a new winger among the three players who came to the Bruins from San Jose. Marco Sturm, a 26-year-old with a scoring touch, moved onto a line with Bergeron and Boyes. The exciting troika immediately became the Bruins' top unit, providing most of the offensive punch in an otherwise dismal season. Bergeron finished the year with 31 goals and 41 assists for 72 points, leading the Bruins in all three categories.

Even though Boyes was dealt away to St. Louis, Bergeron still flourished with 22 goals and 70 points in 2006–07. The Bruins did not make the playoffs, however, and a new coach was hired to replace Dave Lewis. Claude Julien was installed behind the Bruins bench and knew he would need Bergeron's offense if Boston was going to get back to the

playoffs. But Bergeron's season was cut to just ten games after he suffered a concussion when Randy Jones of the Philadelphia Flyers recklessly hit him into the boards from behind. NHL justice once again proved to be very inadequate as Jones was suspended for a mere two games! Bergeron was never able to resume his season, but everyone in hockey looks forward to seeing this very creative youngster getting back into the Bruins lineup starting in 2008–09.

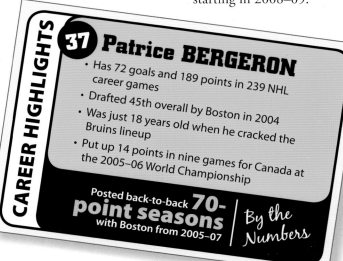

CAREER HIGHLIGHTS

37 Patrice BERGERON

- Has 72 goals and 189 points in 239 NHL career games
- Drafted 45th overall by Boston in 2004
- Was just 18 years old when he cracked the Bruins lineup
- Put up 14 points in nine games for Canada at the 2005–06 World Championship

Posted back-to-back **70-point seasons** with Boston from 2005–07

By the Numbers

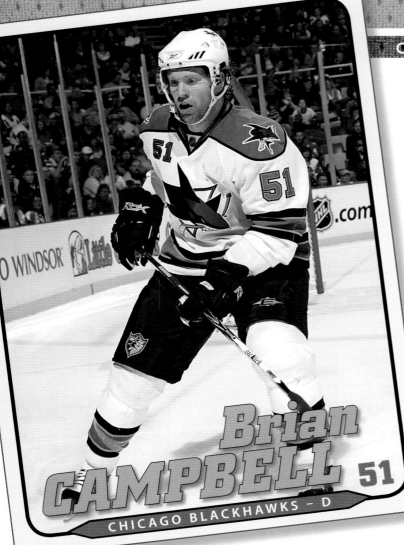

Brian
CAMPBELL 51
CHICAGO BLACKHAWKS – D

San Jose Sharks for winger Steve Bernier and a first round draft choice. At least the Sabres could say they got something of value for their asset, but Buffalo fans were left wondering how their team would replace its best offensive blueliner. It would seem the lockout accomplished little for loyal Sabre supporters. The Sharks paid a high price to be sure, but they were very happy to land a defender who gave their team a missing element that is very hard to find.

Not long ago, few fans even knew of Brian Campbell. It was a long, slow climb for the finesse-first defenseman, who was selected 156th overall by Buffalo in 1997. The 6-foot, 190-pound native of Strathroy, Ontario, played four seasons in the Ontario Hockey League with the Ottawa 67's and during his final season he recorded 75 assists and won a Memorial Cup. His lack of size and soft approach to the game did not endear him to most NHL scouts, but the Sabres invested a sixth round pick for the puck-mover. He toiled for the American Hockey League's Rochester Americans for three seasons, but also managed to get into 49 games with Buffalo.

He continued to hone his offensive game early in his pro career, recording 24-, 25-, and 35-assist years with the Americans. That earned him his first significant NHL playing time in 2002–03. Campbell's first two seasons as a Sabre were rather uneventful with 19 and 11 points, respectively. But after the lockout, he began his rise to prominence.

The new rules implemented by the NHL seemed to suit Campbell's style perfectly. His puck-moving skills became highly valued and his work on the power play gave the Sabres a strong identity. He played in 79 games in 2005–06 and scored 12 times while adding 32 assists. The revitalized Buffalo squad was one the best prepared for the post-lockout league and nearly made it to the Stanley Cup final before the Carolina Hurricanes ousted them in seven tough games during the Eastern Conference final. The next season saw Campbell score only six times, but he got his assist total up to 42 and

T he result of the NHL lockout of 2004–05 was supposed to ensure teams like the Buffalo Sabres could keep their best players and compete with the so-called 'large market' clubs. However, the reality is proving to be something entirely different. First the Sabres lost unrestricted free agents Chris Drury and Daniel Briere. Then they were forced to match a lucrative Edmonton Oiler offer sheet tendered to young sniper Tomas Vanek. Having learned these painful lessons in the summer of 2007, the Sabres were determined not to repeat the error of their ways. As the 2008 trade deadline approached, Buffalo management did its best to secure the services of highly valued defenseman Brian Campbell. But when the smooth-skating rearguard declined a contract offer, the Sabres shipped him to the

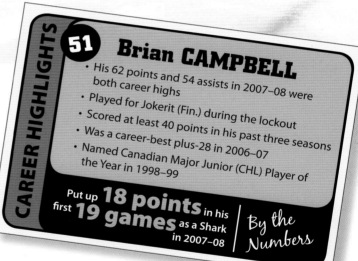

his team was the best in the NHL during the regular season. The playoffs were another matter, however, as the Sabres underperformed and dropped the conference final to Ottawa, four games to one. When Buffalo lost key players in the off-season, it only put more pressure on management to get Campbell under contract as he was destined for unrestricted free agency in the summer of 2008. When Buffalo offered only a three-year deal, Campbell knew his days as a Sabre were about to end.

He seemed sad to leave Buffalo, even though he was headed to a contending team in the Western Conference. Going to the Sharks reunited him with childhood pal Joe Thornton and the San Jose club was hopeful the new addition could ignite more offense — especially with his ability to quarterback the power play. Campbell wanted to blend in quietly, but a spectacular goal against the Montreal Canadiens at home sparked cries of 'Sign him, sign him' from the excited San Jose fans. With Campbell in the fold, the Sharks finished the season on a tear and

he produced a season total of 54 assists and 62 points.

The Sharks sank once again in the second round of the playoffs in 2008, but Campbell's value remains high because of the demand for puck-moving defensemen. As such, the Chicago Blackhawks swooped in and signed him to an eight-year deal worth $7.1 million per year. Campbell will be the main offensive threat from the Blackhawk blueline which now boasts four defensemen who recorded 30 or more points in 2007–08.

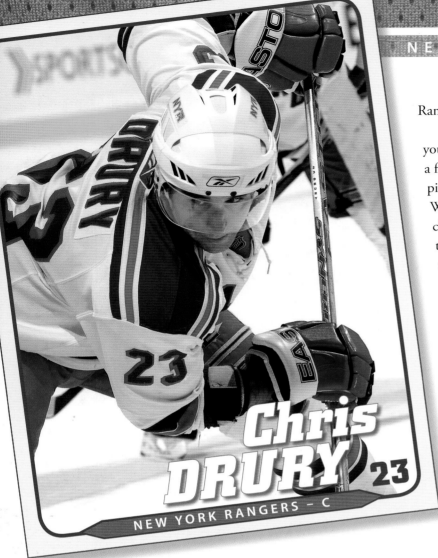

Chris
DRURY 23
NEW YORK RANGERS – C

Rangers sign him to a five-year, $35.25-million deal? Drury was actually a top baseball player in his youth. Born in Trumbull, Connecticut, he grew up a fan of the New York Yankees and was the winning pitcher when his team won the Little League World Series in 1989 against a powerful Taiwan club. Luckily, he also played hockey and advanced through the ranks to the point where he helped the Boston University Terriers win the NCAA title in 1995. He won the Hobey Baker Award as the best U.S. college hockey player in 1998. Drury scored a remarkable 101 goals and 187 points for the Terriers in his final three NCAA years. After four years at BU, he was clearly ready to give the NHL a shot. He was quite impressive, scoring 20 goals and totaling 44 points for Colorado while beating out Marian Hossa of Ottawa for top rookie honors. Colorado coach Bob Hartley noted Drury was very intense and competitive for a first-year player. He followed up his good start with 67 points in 1999–2000 and looked to have a secure place on the Avalanche for years to come.

When Colorado won its second Stanley Cup in '01, Drury racked up 24 goals and 65 points during the regular season and added 11 goals and 16 points in the playoffs. His overall production slipped a little the following season and Colorado really wanted to add Calgary blueliner Derek Morris to its team. Drury did not complain and had a good season with the Flames, scoring 23 goals and adding 30 assists in 2002–03. But like the Avs, Calgary had its eye on acquiring a blueliner and did just that when it sent Drury to Buffalo for the rugged Rhett Warrener in the summer of '03. Drury scored a career low in goals in 2003–04 when he managed just 18 tallies, but he did have 35 assists on a team not known for its goal-scoring.

Drury is all about being a consistent, versatile performer. He has scored 20 or more goals eight times in his career, including a career high of 37 in 2006–07, and can play wing or center. A very good skater, he

For a player as good as Chris Drury is, he sure has moved around the National Hockey League quite a bit in his nine seasons. Although he was originally drafted 72nd overall by Quebec in 1994, he began his career with the Colorado Avalanche, where he was named rookie of the year in 1998–99 and was a member of the Stanley Cup-winning team in 2001. He was dealt to Calgary in October, 2002, but was a Flame for just one season before being sent to the Buffalo Sabres in July, 2003. Both of the deals involved highly coveted defensemen — always prized commodities — going the other way, so it was hardly an insult when Drury was sought after as part of the trades. Despite the slew of deals, teams obviously value Drury's package of skills and intangibles. Why else would the New York knows the direct route to the net. Drury is certainly not the biggest player in the league at 5-foot-10 and 180 pounds, but he is sturdy and can take the rough going. With 304 career assists, he is more likely to be setting up a goal than scoring one, but he is a threat from just about anywhere in the offensive zone. Drury gives it his all every time he is out on the ice and that approach makes him a leader and revered member of any club he skates for. The Sabres took the right approach to building their roster for the 2005–06 season and won 52 games. Drury's 30 goals were the most on the Sabres, as were his 16 power play goals and he tied for the team lead with five game-winning goals. The Sabres advanced to the 2006 Eastern Conference final after beating Philadelphia and Ottawa in the playoffs. Drury scored a lightning-fast overtime winner just 18 seconds into extra time to give Buffalo a 7–6 win over Ottawa in Game 1 of that series. The Sabres were then defeated by Carolina in the third round.

CAREER HIGHLIGHTS

23 Chris DRURY

- Won the Stanley Cup with Colorado in 2001
- Took home the Hobey Baker as NCAA player of the year in 1998
- Has represented Team USA twice at the Olympics
- Won the Calder Trophy in 1999
- Is a career plus-29 in the post-season

Has recorded at least **30** assists in **five** straight seasons

By the Numbers

Buffalo had its sights on the Cup after recording the most points of any team during the 2006–07 season, but ultimately fell short of that goal. Adding insult to injury, Drury walked away from the team as an unrestricted free agent in July, 2007. Drury started slowly with the Rangers, but played better as the year went along. However the New York club did not last long once they played Pittsburgh in the playoffs.

Patrik ELIAS 26

NEW JERSEY DEVILS – LW/C

Team All-Star selection, an honor he richly deserved based on his 40-goal, 96-point season that placed him third in NHL scoring, behind only Jaromir Jagr and Sakic, during 2000–01.

There is certainly no reason to feel sorry about Elias missing out on a trophy since he has had a very successful career to date, including being on a Stanley Cup winner with the Devils in 2000 in just his fourth year in the league. He spent his first full year in the NHL in 1997–98, when he scored 18 goals and added 19 assists, earning All-Rookie Team honors. Elias produced a second good season in 1998–99, when he scored 17 times and upped his point total to 50. During the 1999–2000 campaign, he had 35 goals and 37 assists and then added 20 points in 23 post-season games, including a tie for the most assists (13) as the Devils won their second Cup in team history. The speedy winger was selected by the Devils 51st overall in 1994, but played a little with Albany of the American Hockey League, where New Jersey has wisely decided to groom its best prospects for the pro game. Elias learned his lessons well by producing 27 goals and 63 points for the River Rats in 1995–96.

For two-and-a-half seasons, Elias was on one of the top lines in the NHL, joining center Jason Arnott and right winger Petr Sykora. The line was a perfect blend of size, skill, toughness and determination. But at the trade deadline in 2002, Arnott was shipped to Dallas and that summer, Sykora was dealt to Anaheim. The players they got in return — Jamie Langenbrunner, Joe Nieuwendyk, Jeff Friesen and Oleg Tverdovsky — helped reshape the Devils for 2002–03. New Jersey won the Stanley Cup that season and, for the fourth year in a row, Elias was its leading scorer. Elias developed his will to succeed in his native Czech Republic, where he waited until he was 14 years of age before getting his older brother's skates — the first pair he ever actually owned. His father, Zdenek, was a truck driver in the construction industry and his mother, Zdena, had suffered a serious injury,

As the 2001 Stanley Cup final was drawing to a close, the experts began to discuss who might win the Conn Smythe Trophy as the playoffs' most valuable player. While it was hard to gain a consensus, many agreed New Jersey Devils left winger Patrik Elias was going to get major consideration. No European-born player had ever won the coveted award and Elias certainly would have been deserving of the trophy. His outstanding play throughout the playoffs helped the Devils get to the seventh game of the final. His was a performance that included nine goals and 23 points, second best only to Joe Sakic of Colorado. Avalanche goalie Patrick Roy ended up winning the Conn Smythe after his team claimed the Stanley Cup over Elias and New Jersey. Elias had to settle for a First

ironically enough at a hockey rink where she worked. These circumstances made Elias appreciate his lot in life.

Elias is one of the top skaters in hockey and is a very creative player. He can do everything at top speed and boasts a powerful shot. At 6-foot and 195 pounds, Elias is not big enough to be a power forward, but he will get his nose dirty to dig out a puck and can take the heavy slugging required to survive in the NHL as a goal-scorer and playmaker. Many have tried to intimidate the Devils winger, but Elias knows how to get himself into open space where he can be most effective. He played an integral part in the Devils' Cup win in the 2003 playoffs, scoring five goals and adding eight assists.

Elias had a superb season in 2003–04 with 38 goals and 81 points in 81 games and spent the lockout year playing in the Czech Republic and Russia. It was there Elias contracted hepatitis B, which kept him out of the Devils lineup in 2005–06 until early January. As soon as he was back playing, New Jersey went out on a nine-game winning streak and eventually knocked off the New York Rangers in the '06 playoffs. In the last two years Elias has managed to produce just 21 and 20 goals, respectively, but injuries have slowed him down.

CAREER HIGHLIGHTS

26 Patrik ELIAS

- Holds New Jersey record for overtime goals with 14
- His 60 career game-winning goals is also a franchise best
- Two-time Stanley Cup winner
- Represented the Czech Republic in past two Olympics

Has recorded **110** points in **126** playoff games. The only Devil in history to record more than **100** post-season points

By the Numbers

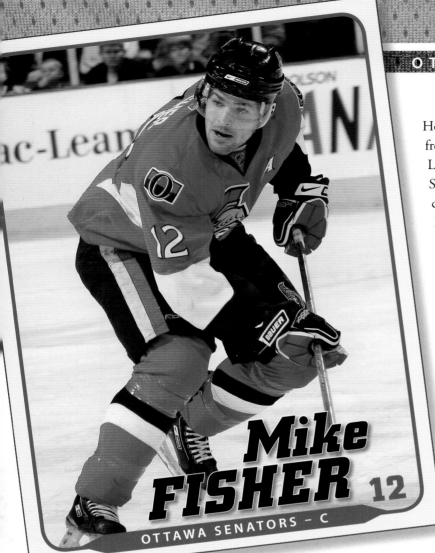

Mike FISHER 12

OTTAWA SENATORS – C

However, that sort of thing would never deter Fisher from dropping his gloves to defend a teammate. Later in the season, Fisher was trying to help out Shean Donovan in a tussle when Philadelphia Flyers cheap shot artist Steve Downie tried to intervene. Fisher quickly went with Downie and pounded out a decision, giving the fading Ottawa side some life. Lest anyone think Fisher is only a fighter, consider his third-period hat trick in an 8–6 loss to Washington during the 2007–08 campaign. He scored at even strength, shorthanded and on the power play, showing he can play the game in any manner. No wonder the Senators signed him up to a five-year deal worth $21 million.

A robust 6-foot-1, 213-pound center, Fisher was born in Peterborough, Ontario and played his major junior hockey in Sudbury. He scored 24 goals and 49 points in 1997–98 and that got him selected 44th overall by Ottawa during the 1998 entry draft. Fisher was very good at his first NHL training camp and nearly stuck with the Senators as an 18-year-old, but was sent back to junior for another season. The Ontario Hockey League's Sudbury Wolves were happy to have him back and he produced 41 goals and 106 points in 68 games. His confidence soared and he made the big team the next season, but an injury — the first of many in his career — restricted him to just 32 games. Fisher's next two years had him appearing in 60 and 58 games, respectively, and saw him score only 22 goals and never more than 24 points. Ottawa management was hoping for more out of Fisher since it had dealt away problem child Alexei Yashin, leaving a hole in the middle of the ice. In 2002–03, the stocky pivot upped his production with an 18-goal, 38-point season in 74 games played. However, an elbow injury held his 2003–04 season to only 24 games. But the rule changes which opened up the game after the lockout had a huge bearing on Fisher, who began to thrive.

With less obstruction and more emphasis on skating, the speedy Fisher started to produce better numbers.

T he Ottawa Senators had an up, then down regular season in 2007–08. They got off to a 15–2 start coming off an appearance in the Stanley Cup final and some began to foolishly compare them to the great Montreal Canadiens teams of the late 1970s. The Ottawa club, besieged with problems (in goal and later, behind the bench), began to lose with a high degree of frequency that challenged their supremacy atop the NHL's Eastern Conference. One player who constantly stood up for his team was rugged, two-way center Mike Fisher. When the Carolina Hurricanes ran over netminder Martin Gerber in the Senators goal, it was Fisher who stepped up and battled Scott Walker. Fisher quickly gained the upper hand in the fight, but Walker head-butted the Senator, causing a tooth to get damaged.

Even though another injury held him to just 68 games in 2005–06, he still managed 22 goals and 44 points and earned a nomination for the Selke Trophy, given to the NHL's top defensive forward. He produced virtually the same numbers the following year and was outstanding in the playoffs with 10 points in 20 games. Fisher was also one of the few Senator players who stood up well to the pounding the Anaheim Ducks dished out in the final, going head-to-head with the rather large Ryan Getzlaf in the process. In 2007–08, he once again suffered an injury early in the year, but still produced 23 goals and 47 points in 79 games. Fisher clearly understands offense can come from good defense and while he will likely never be a big-time goal-scorer, he is one of the most valuable players in the NHL.

Fisher thrives on being good at both ends of the ice and is highly respected for his grit, character and determination to succeed. The Senators missed him badly when an injury held him out of the 2008 playoffs. If Fisher uses his great skating stride to maximum effectiveness, he will be a player to be reckoned with every time the Senators hit the ice. It's too bad for Ottawa fans there aren't more players like Fisher on their team. They might have won a Stanley Cup by now!

12 Mike FISHER

ICE CHIPS

Considered a leader on and off the ice, Mike Fisher is honorary chair of Roger's House, a care home for families of sick children. It was named in tribute to former NHL mentor and Ottawa assistant coach Roger Neilson.

CAREER HIGHLIGHTS

- Led the 2007–08 Senators in hits with 234, good for seventh in the NHL
- Recoded career-bests in games (79) penalty minutes (82) and goals (23) in 2007–08
- Has posted three consecutive 20-goal seasons

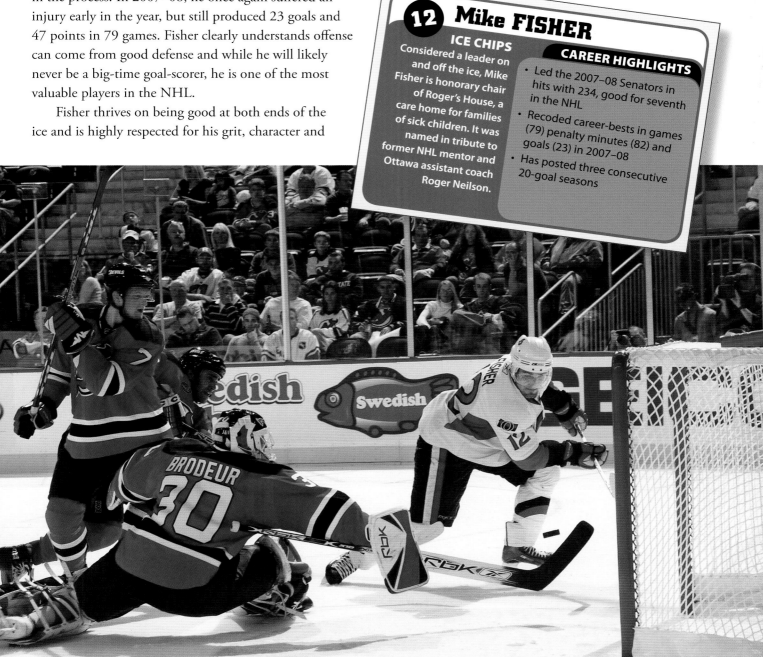

Tomas **HOLMSTROM** 96

DETROIT RED WINGS – LW

T omas Holmstrom is an old-fashioned hockey player, mostly because he is willing to pay the price in front of the net to get a goal. His choppy skating stride meant there was no chance of playing a finesse game, so Holmstrom decided he would make a living in the game by crashing to the crease and making goalies' lives miserable. He will never win a foot race, but when the puck is any where near the goalmouth, 'Homer' always gets the job done. Not many players are willing to stand just outside the crease and take the inevitable whacks from defenseman and goalies, but those hits just seem to bounce off Holmstrom. Sure, he's had his share of lost teeth and stitches, but it's all in a day's work for the Swedish left winger. Holmstrom has his act down pat; he plants his

6-foot, 202-pound body a couple of feet from the goalie and proceeds to cause havoc. On a couple of occasions during Detroit's run to the 2008 Stanley Cup, the agitating winger was called for goaltender interference penalties, though many argued those calls were made more on reputation than merit. Many an opponent has been frustrated trying to eradicate Holmstrom from the front of the net and few have been successful in their efforts. Even when they thwart his attempts, everyone knows he is going right back to his office.

Holmstrom's hockey career began in his hometown of Pitea, Sweden. He caught the eye of the Red Wings, who, as they've done with many Europeans, took a chance and drafted him 257th overall in 1994. He stayed in his native country until the 1996–97 season, when Holmstrom split the year between Detroit and Adirondack of the American Hockey League. He got into one playoff game as the Red Wings took home the Stanley Cup. Detroit coach Scotty Bowman took one look at Holmstrom and told him his job was to stay in front of the net and not move — even if the puck went into the corner. He was much more involved the next year, when Detroit repeated as champion, recording 19 points in 22 post-season games. For the next four seasons, Holmstrom never scored more than 16 goals, although he did have eight playoff tallies in 2002 when the Red Wings took their third Cup since his arrival. In 2002–03, Holmstrom scored 20 goals, but slipped back to 15 the next year. He spent the lockout season in Sweden, but came back to score a surprising 29 goals and a career-high 59 points for the Red Wings in 2005–06. He was also a member of Sweden's gold medal-winning team at the '06 Winter Olympics, collecting four points in eight games.

The 2006–07 campaign saw Holmstrom score a career-best 30 goals, but the Red Wings, for the fourth year in a row, came up short in their Cup quest. Detroit easily took out the Calgary Flames in the first round and

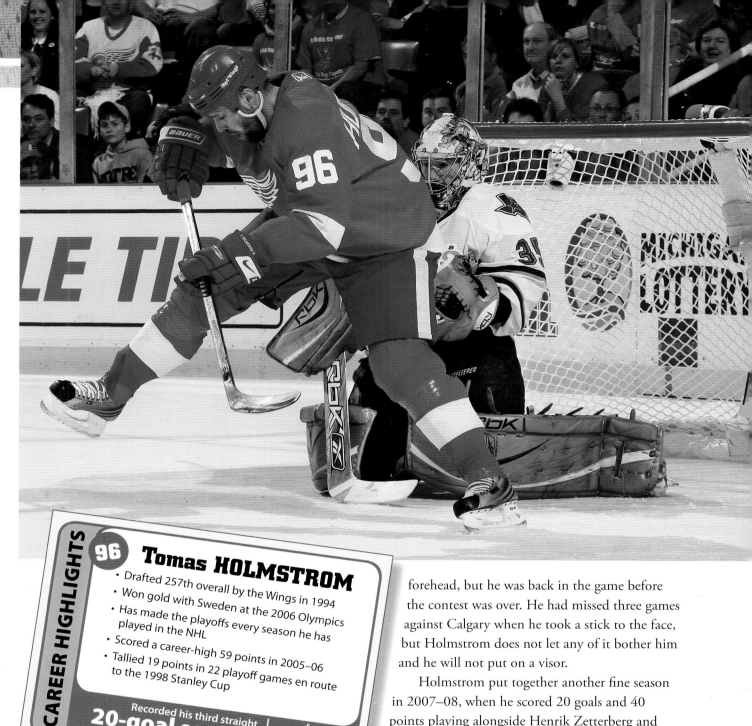

got by San Jose in six games before losing to the eventual-champions from Anaheim. Holmstrom did his best to get under the skin of the Ducks and two players, Rob Niedermayer and Chris Pronger, ran him viciously into the boards after he scored twice during Detroit's 5–0 victory in the third game of the series. The hit opened a nasty gash over Holmstrom's forehead, but he was back in the game before the contest was over. He had missed three games against Calgary when he took a stick to the face, but Holmstrom does not let any of it bother him and he will not put on a visor.

Holmstrom put together another fine season in 2007–08, when he scored 20 goals and 40 points playing alongside Henrik Zetterberg and Pavel Datsyuk. This time, the Red Wings dispatched Nashville, Colorado and Dallas to make it back to the Stanley Cup final. Holmstrom and the Wings then defeated the Pittsburgh Penguins in six games to capture their fourth Cup in 11 seasons. Holmstrom contributed 12 points in 21 playoff games, but not without controversy and much debate. Through it all Holmstrom took the scrutiny and goaltender interference calls the same way he takes the jabs — he didn't let them change his style one bit.

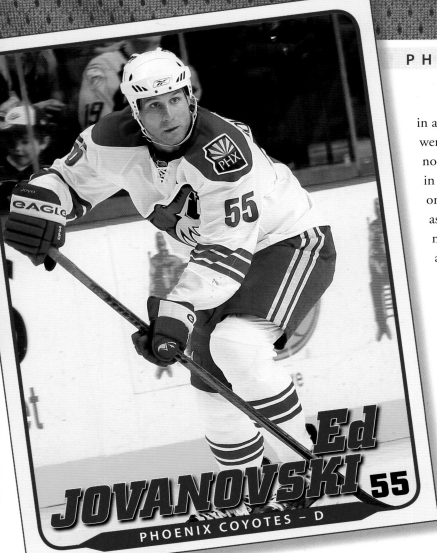

Ed
JOVANOVSKI 55
PHOENIX COYOTES – D

When a player gets selected first overall in the entry draft as Ed Jovanovski did in 1994 by the Florida Panthers, expectations are always high. Initially, Jovanovski lived up to the hype, stepping into the Panthers lineup for the 1995–96 season. It was a dream year for the young defenseman as he produced 10 goals and 21 points in 70 games and then helped the upstart Panthers get to the Stanley Cup final in just their third year in the NHL. The 6-foot-2, 210-pound rearguard was constantly in the face of key opponents like Mario Lemieux and Eric Lindros and he fared very well against such tough competition, posting nine points in the playoffs to go along with 52 penalty minutes. But the youngster soon came to learn success can be fleeting.

Before he knew what was happening, Jovanovski was

in a downward spiral. The next two-and-a-half seasons were not very good in Florida, as the Cats became a non-playoff team. Jovanovski put up decent numbers in that time span and he kept up his aggressive play on a poor team, but he was nowhere near as effective as he'd been in his rookie year. Changes had to be made and Florida management decided to go for a high-profile forward in the person of goal-scorer Pavel Bure from Vancouver. The Canucks wisely asked for Jovanovski to be added to the 1999 deal, which also included Kevin Weekes, Mike Brown, Dave Gagner and a first round draft choice in the 2000 entry draft. Considering Jovanovski was floundering along with the fortunes of the Panthers, the blockbuster trade could not have come at a better time for him.

Vancouver's GM at the time, Brian Burke, saw the potential in the young blueliner. Blessed with offensive instincts and tough to play against, Jovanovski needed to use his size to become truly effective. Maximizing all his assets could make Jovanovski a force to be reckoned with in the NHL. When Marc Crawford took over as coach of the Canucks, Jovanovski's career was rejuvenated. In 2000–01, the Canucks made it back to the playoffs and Jovanovski had a very good year with 12 goals and 47 points in 79 games. He followed that up with a career-best 17 goals and 48 points the next season. For four straight seasons he led all Canucks defensemen in scoring and, in 2002–03, he finished among the NHL's top 10 blueliners with 46 points.

Jovanovski's fine play has been recognized with three appearances in the NHL All-Star Game and his selection for Team Canada in 2002. He played well at the Salt Lake City Olympics, winning a gold medal, and had five points during a playoff series later that year versus Detroit, which the Canucks lost in six games. An injury cost him 15 games in the 2002–03 season and hurt his chances to win the Norris Trophy, but he had clearly established himself as the leader of the Canucks blueline as Vancouver won 45 games and established a new club record with 104 points. He played in only 56 games in 2003–04 and recorded just 23 points, but his open-ice hits kept the opposition honest at all times.

Jovanovski missed 44 games during the 2005–06 season due to abdominal surgery, but still managed 33 points. The Canucks missed his passionate play and leadership dearly, as did Team Canada at the Olympics in Turin, Italy. He returned late in the season, but it was too late for Vancouver to make the playoffs. He then signed with the Phoenix Coyotes as a free agent in July of 2006.

Jovanovski's play in Phoenix has been up and down and his name always seems to be involved in trade rumors. Perhaps that is to be expected when a team does not make the playoffs and a player gains a reputation as being injury prone. In 2006–07, the large defender got into only 54 games, recording 29 points, and the Coyotes won only 31 times. The 2007–08 season was much better with Jovanovski playing in 80 contests and recording 12 goals and 51 points — the best point total of his career. The Coyotes began to turn things around under coach Wayne Gretzky, winning 38 games and getting within sniffing distance of the post-season. Phoenix is a team clearly bent on building with youth, which means Jovanovski will either be a stabilizing force or act as trade bait to further strengthen the Coyotes' future.

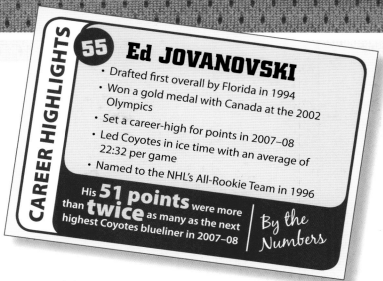

CAREER HIGHLIGHTS

55 Ed JOVANOVSKI

- Drafted first overall by Florida in 1994
- Won a gold medal with Canada at the 2002 Olympics
- Set a career-high for points in 2007–08
- Led Coyotes in ice time with an average of 22:32 per game
- Named to the NHL's All-Rookie Team in 1996

His **51 points** were more than **twice** as many as the next highest Coyotes blueliner in 2007–08 *By the Numbers*

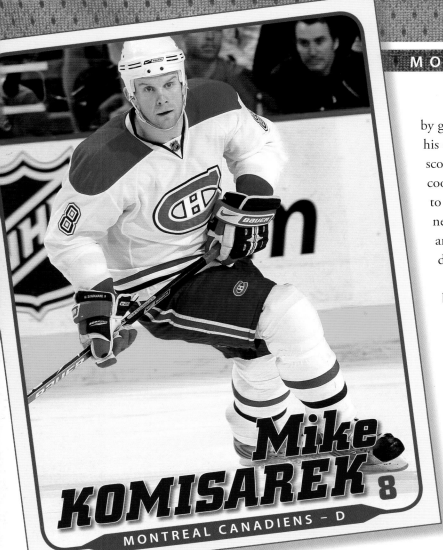

Mike KOMISAREK 8

MONTREAL CANADIENS – D

by goalie Andrew Raycroft. But with only one goal to his credit in the young season, Komisarek's chances of scoring seemed very slight. However, he showed the coolness of a seasoned sniper as he waited for Raycroft to make his move before depositing a shot into the net. The smiling hero was mobbed by his teammates and the Habs had an important 4–3 win over their division rival.

While the goal against the Leafs might have been an unusual moment for Komisarek, his smart and effective defensive play was getting noticed around the NHL during the 2007–08 campaign. It has been a slow rise to prominence for the 6-foot-4, 242-pound native of West Islip, New York. The Canadiens drafted Komisarek seventh overall in 2001 after he spent one season at the University of Michigan. Former NHL defenseman Gerry Hart is one of the coaches who deserves credit for molding Komisarek's raw skill when he was a youngster. Hart, who played 730 games with four teams, was a family friend who gave sound direction and guidance to the kid who loved many sports and was a good all-around athlete growing up. After completing a second season at Michigan in which he was named to the first All-American team, Komisarek played 21 games for Montreal in 2002–03 and 46 the following year. However, he spent plenty of time with Hamilton in the American Hockey League honing his game as a defensive specialist. By the 2005–06 season, Komisarek was ready for full-time employment with the big league team and has not looked back.

A big part of Komisarek's development as an NHL player is due to his pairing with highly skilled Andrei Markov, considered by many to be among the league's best defensemen. But Komisarek has also been very good for Markov and they seem to make a perfect 1–2 punch on the Canadiens blueline. Determined to make the opposition pay for everything they get, Komisarek has become the Montreal defender you seek to avoid. He takes great pride in handing out bone-rattling

T he Montreal Canadiens and the Toronto Maple Leafs had battled to a 3–3 tie at the Air Canada Center during a November, 2007 contest and were starting the five-minute overtime period playing 3-on-3 because of penalties assessed at the end of regulation play. The Leafs were looking to win the contest at home and put out two forwards along with defenseman Bryan McCabe. The Habs, on the other hand, had two defenders out along with one forward. One of the Montreal blueliners was Mike Komisarek, known much more for preventing goals than scoring them. Suddenly, McCabe attempted a cross-ice pass at the Montreal blueline and Komisarek smartly anticipated the play and picked off the puck. The rugged defender had a long, clean breakaway to the Leaf net, occupied

8 Mike KOMISAREK

CAREER HIGHLIGHTS

- His 60 takeaways in 2007–08 ranked third among NHL defensemen
- Ranked second in the league in hits with 266 in 2007–08
- Has recorded 95 or more penalty minutes three times
- Drafted seventh overall by Montreal in 2001

Posted **227** blocked shots in 2007–08, **first** in the NHL

By the Numbers

bodychecks and will fight to back up his physical play. Komisarek also gets in the way of pucks, as he led all NHLers with 227 blocked shots. He and Markov usually face the opposition's best line and his development is now a matter of being more consistent as he gains valuable experience. He also knows he is not nearly as talented as Markov and will not try to match his teammate in points. Komisarek is a good skater, but 20 to 25 points a season might be his offensive limit.

Komisarek makes the kind of contributions that get him named one of the game's three stars without ever showing up on the scoresheet. His physical domination is impossible to ignore, evidenced by the fact he threw 266 hits last year, second most in the league. As he learns to pick his spots more wisely, Komisarek will become more effective. He shows great passion and emotion as he patrols the blueline, recording 101 penalty minutes

in 2007–2008, and in many ways he reminds fans that a top defensive defenseman is crucial to the success of any winning hockey club. Komisarek had some epic run-ins with young Boston power forward Milan Lucic during Round 1 of the 2008 playoffs, restoring some hate to the old Bruins-Habs rivalry. However, the post-season was a bit of a learning experience for the 26-year-old, who still has room to improve.

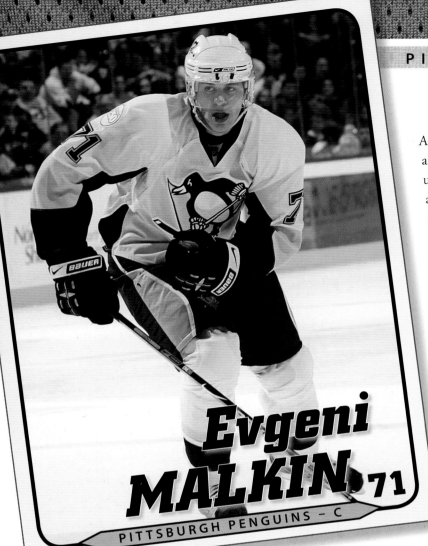

Evgeni MALKIN 71

PITTSBURGH PENGUINS – C

When the 2004 NHL draft was held at the RBC Center in Carolina, most agreed Alex Ovechkin was the prize catch and the Washington Capitals happily grabbed the rights to the flashy left winger with the No. 1 pick. It has often been said everyone remembers who was drafted first overall and all the other selections have to fight harder to get recognition. However, when the Pittsburgh Penguins took Russian Evgeni Malkin, a 6-foot-3 195-pound center, No. 2 overall, they were certain he would be a big star in the NHL. While Ovechkin joined the NHL for the 2005–06 season and won the Calder Trophy as the best rookie, Malkin stayed in Russia and played one more year in his hometown of Metallurg. He had 21 goals and 46 points in 47 games that year.

Malkin did not have an easy path to the NHL. After the 2005–06 campaign, he signed on to play another season in Russia. It was reported Malkin was under heavy pressure to remain in his homeland for an additional season. The youngster eventually had a change of heart and was forced to hide out for five days in Finland while acquiring a travel visa and working out a deal worth just under $3 million — including bonuses — with the Pens. Malkin's Russian team was not very pleased and eventually tried to get the U.S. District courts in New York to rule that he belonged to them, but the legal challenge failed. With both Malkin and Crosby in the fold, team management believed it now had two of the best young players in the game, reminiscent of the days when Mario Lemieux and Jaromir Jagr led the Pens to two Stanley Cups in the early 1990s.

Malkin showed what all the fuss was about when he came through with 33 goals and 85 points during his rookie season of 2006–07, good enough for Calder Trophy honors. He showed incredible athleticism — perhaps passed on to him by his father, Vladimir, who was a defenseman when he played hockey — as he ripped through the NHL. Despite suffering a shoulder injury in a pre-season contest, Malkin managed to score a goal in his first six NHL regular season games, tying a rookie record that dated back 89 years. Malkin can handle the puck with great ease and his skating skills show a burst of speed at just the right moment. Like many great players, he can do almost anything at full speed and knows when he has to go to the net to make a play. Still maturing, Malkin needs to add a little beef to his large frame, but he is not afraid of the heavy going as 80 penalty minutes in his first year indicate. However, Malkin's playoff performance in his first post-season was less than stellar. He lacked the intensity required to succeed in spring as the young Pens were dispatched in five games by the Ottawa Senators.

Malkin's disappointing playoff did not linger when

CAREER HIGHLIGHTS

71 **Evgeni MALKIN**

- His 15-game point streak in 2007–08 was the longest ever by a Russian in the NHL
- Also recorded 36 goals in his final 47 games of 2007–08
- Posted two four-point games in 2007–08, plus another in the playoffs
- Put up back-to-back 50 assist seasons to begin his NHL career

Ranked **second** in NHL scoring with **106 points** in just his second season (2007–08) | *By the Numbers*

He was the only Penguin to reach triple digits — he won the club's scoring race by a whopping 34 points. The slick skater showed he could score goals in a variety of ways and his ability to lead was also evident when Crosby was on the sidelines. All this earned Malkin a Hart Trophy nomination and a First Team All-Star selection.

The Penguins were better prepared for the 2008 playoffs and dropped only two games en route to advancing to the Stanley Cup final. Malkin finished with 22 points in 20 playoff games, but, like a few of his teammates, he struggled to get going versus a suffocating Detroit Red Wings team in the final. The Penguins run to the final got everybody excited in Pittsburgh. That joy was accentuated when Penguins management signed Malkin to a five-year contract extension, keeping both him and Crosby with the club through 2013.

the 2007–08 campaign began. Much more comfortable in his second season, he often played alongside Crosby in the first half of the year. A bad ankle sprain forced Crosby out of the lineup and that necessitated Malkin's return to his natural center position. He thrived in Crosby's absence and produced a season where he scored 47 goals and added 106 points.

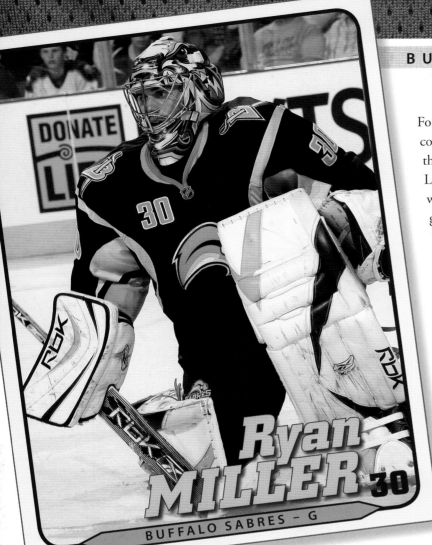

Ryan
MILLER 30
BUFFALO SABRES – G

For instance, Kevin worked Miller's glove hand by coming down the wing and ripping a slapshot, which the goalie would try to snare. Growing up in East Lansing, Michigan, allowed Miller to rub shoulders with Michigan State Spartan hockey players like goaltender Jason Muzzatti, who had a very brief NHL career after being drafted in the first round by the Calgary Flames in 1988. Muzzatti helped Miller with his footwork and showed him how to slide across the crease while maintaining the butterfly position. Miller eventually played at Michigan State himself — in 2000–01 he won 31 of 40 games, earning himself the Hobey Baker Award as the top NCAA hockey player.

The Buffalo Sabres had already drafted the lanky 6-foot-2, 170-pound Miller by that point. The Sabres scouts had gambled by taking Miller before he even got to college, based on what they saw of him when he played Jr. A hockey for Sault Ste. Marie of the North American Hockey League. The Sabres were not too worried about goalkeeping since they also had Martin Biron as their main backstopper, a good goalie in his own right. Miller got into 15 games for the Sabres in 2003–04 and was a rather ordinary 6-8-1 for a struggling team. He had bad outings against the New York Islanders, where he gave up six goals, and the Detroit Red Wings, who whipped seven pucks past him. Those numbers got him a ticket to the minors, but that was probably the best thing that happened to Miller. He got plenty of work with the Rochester Americans of the American Hockey League and became the top goalie prospect not playing in the NHL. During the lockout season he won 41 games to lead the AHL and was ready for the big league in 2005–06.

The Sabres revamped their team for the more open, post-lockout game. Part of the plan was to depend on Miller and many of his teammates who had played in Rochester the previous year. The confident netminder quickly showed he was ready for prime time. Miller

When Ryan Miller was a kid learning to play the very difficult position of goaltender, he was seldom seen as a star in the making. Other kids were supposedly better and some people took to feeling sorry for the smallish Ryan, who just sort of stood there and let his body block the shots while other goalies would try to steal the show with spectacular saves. Miller's father, Dean, told him to hang in there and just try to get better with each opportunity. Ryan listened to his dad's advice and stuck to mastering the fundamentals of netminding. Eventually, it paid off.

Miller had more people than just his father encouraging him. His second cousins, Kevin, Kelly and Kip, were NHL players who gave the aspiring goalie plenty of practice on how big-leaguers shoot.

is effective because he uses his entire frame to cover as much of the net as possible. He has great flexibility and likes to sit back in his crease and read the play. He has a tremendous work ethic and is determined to forget any bad goals. The Sabres' leading scorer in 2005–06 was Maxim Afinogenov, who finished 43rd overall in NHL scoring. That meant Buffalo relied heavily on Miller to make the big save at the right time. Miller came through with a record of 30–14–1 to help his team record a 110-point season. He then led the Sabres to playoff victories over Philadelphia and Ottawa. Only a seven-game loss to Carolina stopped the Sabres from advancing to the Stanley Cup final.

The 2006–07 season was one of the best in Sabres history, as Buffalo recorded a team-record 113 points and took the Presidents' Trophy. Miller won 40 of Buffalo's 53 regular season victories and then got his team past the Islanders and Rangers in the first two rounds of the playoffs before Ottawa overwhelmed a Sabres squad that was clearly struggling as the playoffs progressed. The Sabres may have blown their best chance to win the franchise's first Stanley Cup.

Many changes were made to the team before and during the 2007–08 campaign and Miller's play suffered as well — so much so that the Sabres missed the playoffs. Buffalo needs its star goalie to be at his best if the team is to turn things around.

30 **Ryan MILLER**

ICE CHIPS

Miller set a Buffalo Sabres record for most wins in one season with 40 in 2006–07. He surpassed Don Edwards' mark of 38 set in 1977–78. Dominik Hasek sits in third place with 37 wins in both 1996–97 and 2000–01.

CAREER HIGHLIGHTS

- Played a career-high 4,474 minutes in 2007–08
- Played in a career-best 76 games in 2007–08
- Has played in two outdoor games — one with Buffalo, one with Michigan State
- Has posted three straight 30-win seasons

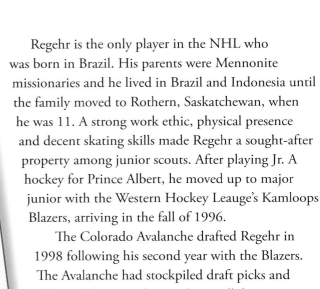

Robyn REGEHR 28

CALGARY FLAMES – D

Regehr is the only player in the NHL who was born in Brazil. His parents were Mennonite missionaries and he lived in Brazil and Indonesia until the family moved to Rothern, Saskatchewan, when he was 11. A strong work ethic, physical presence and decent skating skills made Regehr a sought-after property among junior scouts. After playing Jr. A hockey for Prince Albert, he moved up to major junior with the Western Hockey Leauge's Kamloops Blazers, arriving in the fall of 1996.

The Colorado Avalanche drafted Regehr in 1998 following his second year with the Blazers. The Avalanche had stockpiled draft picks and although he was taken 19th overall, he was Colorado's third choice of the first round. All that extra young talent made for attractive trade options, and in February, 1999, Regehr was swapped to Calgary with Rene Corbet, Wade Belak and two draft choices for Theoren Fleury and Chris Dingman. Five months later, he was involved in the horrible car crash. But the same work ethic that characterizes his on-ice play helped Regehr overcome his injuries faster than anyone predicted. By the first anniversary of the crash, he had played 57 games for the Flames.

Regehr scored his first NHL goal in his second week in the league and totaled five goals in his rookie season, the most he'd put up until his sixth year in Calgary. He was the Flames' nominee for the Masterton Trophy — the youngest nominee in the history of the award at the time — recognizing his perseverance and dedication to hockey. In Regehr's sophomore season, he finished fourth on the team in penalty minutes, second in hits and first in blocked shots. Although the Flames were in the midst of a seven-year stretch out of the playoffs, Regehr was gaining notice and in his third season he played in the Young Stars Game during the NHL all-star weekend. On March 18, 2003, he achieved what is referred to as a 'Gordie Howe Hat Trick,' recording a goal, an assist and a fight in a game against Los Angeles.

Regehr and his Flames really came into prominence

Robyn Regehr has developed into a premier defensemen, a hard hitter who makes opponents think twice before crossing to his side of the ice. But it's a minor miracle Regehr is in the NHL at all.

On July 4, 1999, just a few months after his junior career ended, Regehr's nearly lost his life. An oncoming vehicle crossed over to his side of the road and smashed head-on into his Chevy Nova. Two people in the other car were killed and Regehr broke the tibias in both his legs. With his hockey future in serious jeopardy, he put himself through such intensive rehabilitation that only a few months after the accident he had recovered enough to join the Calgary Flames' American Hockey League farm team in Saint John, New Brunswick. And by late October, after only five games there, he was in the NHL to stay.

in the magical year of 2003–04, when Calgary went to the seventh game of the Stanley Cup final before losing to Tampa Bay. It was the team's first appearance in the playoffs since 1996 and Regehr made the most of the exposure, finishing third in scoring among defensemen with nine post-season points. He got the underdog Flames heading in the right direction by scoring their first playoff goal in eight years, against Detroit, and he scored into an empty net for the clinching goal of the Western Conference final. Flames coach Darryl Sutter showed his confidence in Regehr by making him an assistant captain early in the 2003–04 season and the defenseman went on to record career highs with 14 assists, 18 points and 82 games played. He also finished the year as a plus player for the time in his career at plus-14.

His post-season play got him onto Canada's gold medal World Cup team that fall, before the NHL shut down for a year due to the lockout. In 2005–06, he increased his point total to a career-high 26 and was chosen for Canada's Olympic team. Regehr continues to be a physical presence and averages about 20 points a year. His value to the Flames was recognized with a new five-year $20-million dollar contract, signed during the summer of 2007. Calgary has now locked up Jarome Iginla, Dion Phaneuf, Miikka Kiprusoff and Regehr to new deals, giving the Flames a solid core of players to build around.

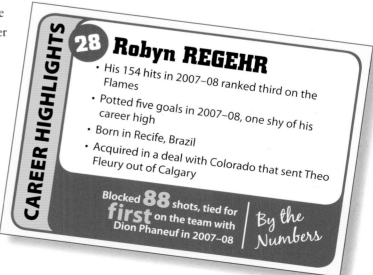

CAREER HIGHLIGHTS

28 Robyn REGEHR

- His 154 hits in 2007–08 ranked third on the Flames
- Potted five goals in 2007–08, one shy of his career high
- Born in Recife, Brazil
- Acquired in a deal with Colorado that sent Theo Fleury out of Calgary

Blocked **88** shots, tied for **first** on the team with Dion Phaneuf in 2007–08

By the Numbers

137

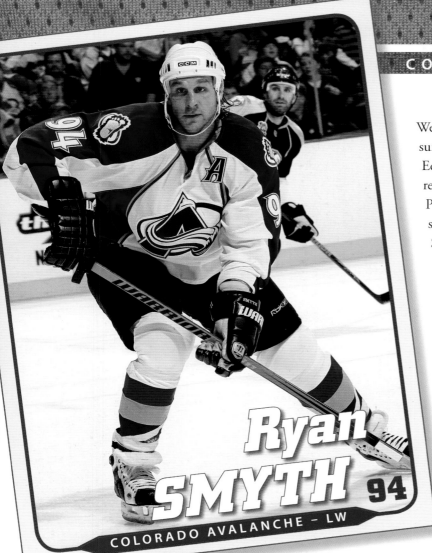

Ryan
SMYTH 94
COLORADO AVALANCHE – LW

Western Hockey League's Moose Jaw Warriors. That summer, Smyth was drafted sixth overall by the Edmonton Oilers, who were desperately looking to rebuild their reputation for selecting young talent. Previous Oiler drafts had produced precious little to sustain a team that enjoyed a dynasty in the 1980s. Smyth finally changed the draft woes of the Oilers, but not until the 1996–97 season when he scored 39 times and totaled 61 points in 82 games during his first full year in the NHL. He was motoring along the next season with 20 goals in 65 contests before sustaining a serious knee injury that put an end to his year and cast doubts on his career. Smyth did return to play 71 games in 1998–99, but scored only 13 goals and did not look like the same player.

The Oilers wanted a return to form from their young star because his style of play was so infectious. Smyth was fearless and his reckless approach was something Edmonton fans had not seen since kamikaze winger Glenn Anderson was driving the net in the club's glory days. Smyth plays a confident game when he is on,which usually means his helmet is coming off and his trademark hockey hair is waving all over the place. Smyth is no fighter, but he will battle very hard along the boards for the puck and for every inch of ice. He will irritate goalies to distraction with his willingness to charge the net and often gets netminders to take penalties on him. He gets into trouble only when he plays too recklessly; it often looks like he has no regard for his body on the ice.

Smyth's bull-in-a-china-shop approach works well for him because of his soft hands in close — that's why he has scored over 30 goals in a season four times in his career. Smyth scored the kind of goal that sums up his career during the 2001 playoffs in a series against Dallas, when he poked in a loose puck while down on the ice fighting off both a Stars defenseman and goalie Ed Belfour!

Being teamed with center Doug Weight worked well

At 6-foot-1 and 195 pounds, Ryan Smyth is really not big enough to be considered a power forward. And the Colorado Avalanche left winger cannot be called a true "hit man" in that his bodychecks are not especially noticeable. Yet whenever you watch a team with Smyth on it, you always notice him because he constantly crashes into something: often the other team's net or goaltender. Smyth carved out a niche playing the game this way — much to the dismay of opposing goalies — and by giving his all every time he was on the ice. Combine that heart with a scoring touch and you have a player many teams covet.

A native of Banff, Alberta, Smyth played in western Canada between 1990 and 2007. He had his best year in 1993–94, scoring 50 goals and 105 points for the for Smyth. The two developed a certain chemistry that was unmistakable. During the 1999–2000 season, Smyth bounced back with a 28-goal effort and followed that up with a 31-goal season in 2000–01. But Weight was traded to St. Louis in July, 2001 and Smyth became the team leader. In 2001–02, he missed 21 games with an ankle injury and scored only 15 times. He returned in time to win an Olympic gold with Team Canada.

The 2005–06 campaign saw Smyth score a career-best 36 goals as he played his usual robust game in front of the net. The Oilers were back in the playoffs and upset Detroit, San Jose and Anaheim, with Smyth racking up 14 of his 16 post-season points (including a four-point game against San Jose), before losing to Carolina in a thrilling seven-game Cup final. Smyth took a puck to the face, but kept playing — a typical performance by one of the grittiest players in the NHL.

Smyth was having another stellar year in 2006–07 with 31 tallies in 53 games for Edmonton, but they traded away their heart and soul to the New York Islanders at the trade deadline when a contract extension couldn't be worked out. He helped the Isles make the playoffs, but signed with Colorado for the 2007–08 season. His year was shortened to 55 games, which saw him score 14 goals and 37 points.

CAREER HIGHLIGHTS

94 **Ryan SMYTH**

- Recorded 37 points in just 55 games in 2007–08
- Ranked third on the Avs in 2007–08 with 168 shots on net
- Won Olympic gold with Canada in 2002
- Frequent member of Canada's World Championship team
- Drafted sixth overall by the Oilers in 1994

Has recorded at least **20** assists in **eight** straight seasons

By the Numbers

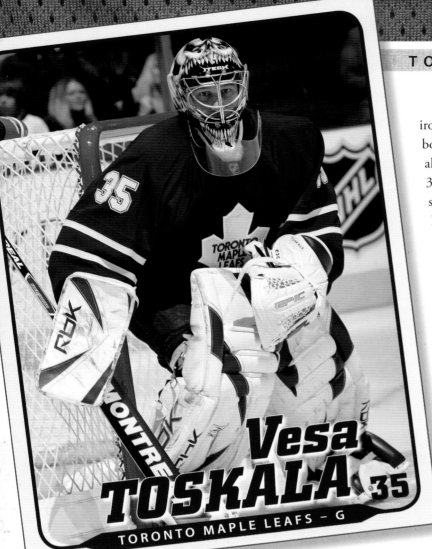

Vesa TOSKALA 35
TORONTO MAPLE LEAFS – G

ironic the Maple Leafs made the deal for the Finnish-born Toskala when they supposedly had a No. 1 goalie already in place in the person of Andrew Raycroft, a 37-game winner in 2006–07. Soon after the 2007–08 season began, Toskala showed the was the undisputed No. 1 netminder in a city that scrutinizes every goal scored against a Leafs goalie.

The opportunity to be the main backstopper for an NHL team was a long time coming for Toskala. He was drafted 90th overall by the Sharks in 1995 while playing junior hockey in Finland. He stayed home for a few more seasons before coming to North America in 2000. He was assigned to play in Kentucky of the American Hockey League for the 2000–01 campaign and recorded 22 wins in 44 games. He had a very tough task ahead of him if he was going to beat out the likes of Nabokov, Miikka Kiprusoff and Johan Hedberg, all of whom were goalies the Sharks owned at one point or another.

The next few years had Toskala going back and forth between the minors and San Jose, with the 2005–06 campaign being one of his best seasons with a 23–7–4 record. He played in 11 playoff games in 2006 (his only playoff experience to date) and won six of them. The 2006–07 season saw him play 38 games (26–10–1), but he could never quite unseat Nabokov for the starter's position.

However, Toskala proved to be a wise acquisition for the Maple Leafs. Once he settled in, the athletic stopper often became the only reason the Leafs were in any of their games and when he was out of the lineup with an injury, the team slipped badly and eventually missed the playoffs. Upon adjusting to Eastern Conference play, Toskala showed himself to be one of the most acrobatic netminders in the league. He has one of the fastest glove hands in the NHL and displays his dogged competitiveness every time he's on the ice. Toskala goes up and down easily to get to any shot and is usually good at getting back into position. He does have some difficulty when the puck is loose in the crease area or if

As he approached the age of 30, goaltender Vesa Toskala felt it was time to see if he could become a No. 1 goalie in the NHL. The longtime member of the San Jose Sharks was promised by team GM Doug Wilson that he would straighten out the club's crease cram. Wilson decided to retain Evgeni Nabokov and true to his word, he worked at dealing Toskala to give him his opportunity. Many teams were interested, but ultimately the Toronto Maple Leafs paid the price with a package of draft choices and the willingness to take on the contract of forward Mark Bell as part of the deal in the summer of 2007. Even though Toskala was under contract for one more year, the Maple Leafs quickly extended his pact for two more seasons (at $4 million per year) to protect their investment. It was

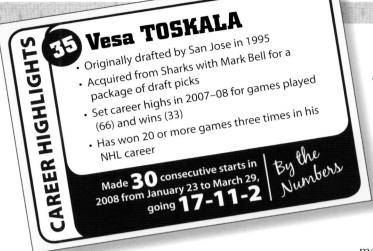
coverage of the Leafs was much different than what the Sharks received on a daily basis. He played 66 games for Toronto and somehow managed to win 33 contests with a .904 save percentage and 2.74 goals-against average.

The Leafs ended the reign of error that epitomized former GM John Ferguson's time with the club when they axed him during the 2007–08 season. The swap that brought Toskala to the Leafs may be the only move Toronto fans will remember with some fondness when they look back at Ferguson's tenure. The problem is that Toronto has little to offer other teams in potential deals, which might force it to deal Toskala in the not-too-distant future. However, it is just as likely the Leafs will try to hold on to the talented netminder and build a solid team from the crease out.

there is a scramble for the disk in the blue paint. The Leafs were not one of the strongest defensive clubs to say the least and they came to rely on Toskala to bail them out on many occasions. Playing in the spotlight did not seem to throw off Toskala in any way, although he would often comment on how

Marty TURCO 35

DALLAS STARS – G

NHL, was studying law at Michigan at that time and became Turco's unofficial goalie coach. Turco was replacing Steve Shields, who had graduated as the all-time winningest goalie in NCAA history. But the newcomer announced he would be a force himself when he stopped 68 shots in one game against the Maine Black Bears. Turco led the Wolverines into the NCAA Frozen Four tournament in each of his four years and he was named tournament MVP in 1998. By the end of his Michigan career, Turco had racked up 127 wins, surpassing Shields and every other goalie in the history of NCAA hockey.

Turco didn't even have to leave the state to begin his pro career, as the Stars assigned him to the Michigan K-Wings of the now-defunct International Hockey League. He registered a 2.61 goals-against average and was named the 1998–99 rookie of the year. The next season, he lowered his GAA to 2.45, was chosen top goalie in the All-Star Game and ran together a streak of four straight shutouts. When the Stars promoted Turco to the NHL in 1999, it was in the role of backup to Ed Belfour, who had led Dallas to a Stanley Cup in 1999 and the Cup final again in 2000. Turco learned focus and discipline by watching Belfour, who was breaking in his third backup in three years. Turco quickly showed he could handle NHL shooters. He played only 26 games, but led the entire league with a very solid .925 save percentage and a 1.90 GAA.

The Stars knew they'd found Belfour's future replacement. That future arrived sooner than expected when Dallas sputtered early in the 2001–02 season and Belfour had some off-ice problems. Eventually, coach Ken Hitchcock was fired, the Stars missed the playoffs and Belfour lost his No. 1 job. Turco's agility, quick glove and improved positioning carried him to a 15–6–2 record. His .921 save percentage was fourth highest in the league and his 2.09 GAA was the third-best mark. At the end of the season, Belfour signed with Toronto as a free agent and Turco had the Dallas netminding duties to himself.

When it came time for his draft year, Canadian major junior teams ignored Marty Turco because they thought he was too small. The problem is they never tallied the size of his determination. The goaltender with the lightning-quick glove hand has been a star at every level he's ever played at, including the NHL.

After every Canadian Hockey League team passed on Turco, the native of Sault Ste. Marie, Ontario, played Jr. B hockey. He fared well enough to entice the Dallas Stars to select him 124th overall in the 1994 entry draft. The next year he won the starting job at the University of Michigan, where coach and former NHL player Red Berenson became his mentor for four years.

Mike Liut, an all-star when he played goal in the

The easygoing Turco has a completely different personality in the dressing room than the prickly Belfour. He improved his work ethic when he became the No. 1 goaltender because he knew his teammates expected more from him in that role. His first full season as the starter was 2002–03 and he proved he could do the job with a 31–10–10 record in 55 games and set a modern-day NHL mark by recording a minuscule 1.72 GAA. Turco showed that was no fluke with a 37-win season in 2003–04 and then set a franchise record with 41 wins in 2005–06. Only New Jersey's Martin Brodeur and Calgary's Miikka Kiprusoff won more games during the regular season that year. Turco likes to play often and has appeared in 68, 67 and 62 games over the last three seasons, winning 41, 38 and 32 games, respectively. He is also not afraid to be a team leader who speaks his mind when necessary.

Turco's playoff performances had been less than stellar until the 2008 post-season, when he got his team past Anaheim and San Jose. He was not as good against Detroit, but his overall performance earned him some well-deserved praise. Turco's contract runs until 2010 and virtually assures he will be the Stars' main netminder for the foreseeable future, but they will continue to expect a top performance in the playoffs every year. Dallas surely believes Turco's $6-million price tag is worth every penny.

CAREER HIGHLIGHTS

35 Marty TURCO

- Stopped a franchise-record 61 shots in 4OT win over San Jose in the 2008 playoffs
- NCAA Championship MVP in 1998
- Led the NHL in goals-against average (1.72) and save percentage (.932) in 2002–03
- Also named an NHL Second-Team All-Star in 2003
- Won a career-best 41 games in 2005–06

Has put up **five** consecutive **30-win** campaigns | *By the Numbers*

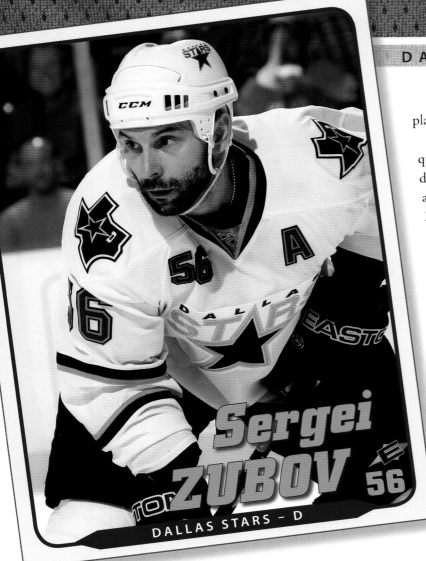

Sergei ZUBOV 56

DALLAS STARS – D

player in return.

Though not exactly a household name, Zubov has quietly built up a reputation as one of the top-scoring defensemen in the game. He reads the play very well and almost always finds the open man with a pass. Zubov is a great skater and exceptional at handling the puck, the two qualities most teams want from their offensive blueliners. He is not afraid to rush the puck out of his own end and he picks up a lot of loose pucks by positioning himself properly. At 6-foot-1 and 200 pounds, Zubov cannot be run over by opposing forwards, yet he is not an overly physical player. His penalty minutes are generally low, but Zubov's game is getting the puck and advancing it to the forwards as quickly as possible.

Selected 85th overall by the New York Rangers in 1990, Zubov played in the former Soviet Union before coming to the NHL and was a member of the Unified team that won the Olympic gold medal in 1992. He joined Binghamton of the American Hockey League for the 1992–93 season, before making the jump to the big club that same year. He played in 49 games in his debut season and had a very respectable 31 points. The following year was a big one for Zubov and the Rangers. He scored a club-high 89 points and then added 19 points in 22 playoff games as New York won the Stanley Cup for the first time since 1940. His play in the post-season earned Zubov some well-deserved acclaim. He had 36 points in 38 games during the shortened 1994–95 season, but the team became disenchanted with him for some reason and he was dealt to the Pittsburgh Penguins.

Zubov enjoyed a good season in Pittsburgh with 66 points in 64 games and recorded a career-high plus-28 rating. However, he was soon on the move again, this time to Dallas. The Stars were starting to stress a defensive game, but they still liked what Zubov could bring to the table. He seemed to find the right mix of offense and defense to suit the Dallas system and he led

Every championship hockey team needs a blueline brigade that can supply some attack in today's game. Without points from the defense corps, a team can pretty much forget about winning it all. That's why defensemen such as Sergei Zubov are especially valuable to their team. Players like Zubov can take some of the pressure off forwards by providing points from the back end. Zubov can also quarterback the power play, which is a big part of any NHL game since the lockout ended. Many penalties are now called, even in the playoffs, so an effective extra-man unit can win a team a lot of games. The Dallas Stars certainly recognized they were giving up a good power play specialist when they dealt away Kevin Hatcher to acquire Zubov from Pittsburgh, but they knew they were receiving a quality all NHL blueliners with 47 assists in 1997–98. He had 57 points in 73 games that season, then added 51 points in 81 contests during the 1998–99 campaign. During the 1999 playoffs, Zubov showed his previous experience was invaluable and he was one of the Stars' best players. Coach Ken Hitchcock gave him plenty of ice time and Zubov enjoyed a second Stanley Cup triumph.

He hasn't slowed his pace since then, consistently coming in around the 50-point mark. Zubov's 71 points in 2005–06 was the second-best total among all NHL defensemen.

The star blueliner has never been about self-promotion and does not seek the spotlight at all. If his personality warranted a greater profile, Zubov's chances of winning the Norris Trophy would increase greatly. But Stars coach Dave Tippett appreciates what he does in his own end and on the attack. When Zubov returned to the Stars lineup just in time for the 2008 playoffs, it was clear just how much Dallas had missed its superlative defenseman. Well rested after sitting out with an injury, Zubov was back to controlling the play and setting up his teammates for quality chances. His play helped the Stars beat Anaheim and San Jose, two teams considered Stanley Cup contenders prior to the start of the post-season.

56 Sergei ZUBOV

ICE CHIPS

Zubov's 545 regular season points make him the Stars' highest scoring defenseman; he also holds the franchise mark in playoff assists for defensemen with 72.

CAREER HIGHLIGHTS

- Two-time Stanley Cup winner, has played in the final three times
- Rang up a career-high 89 points for the Rangers in 1993–94
- Has tallied at least 30 assists in 12 straight seasons
- Put up 31 assists in just 46 games in 2007–08
- Second Team All-Star in 2006

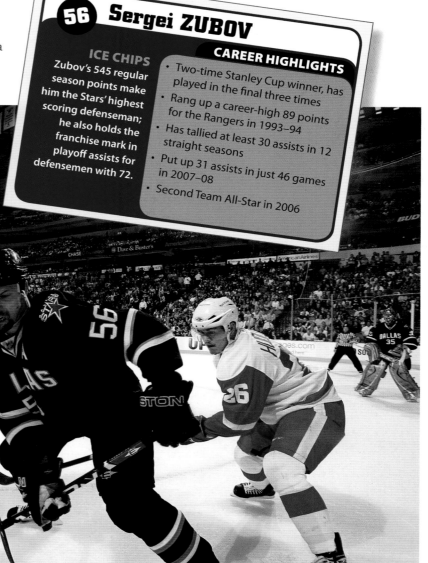

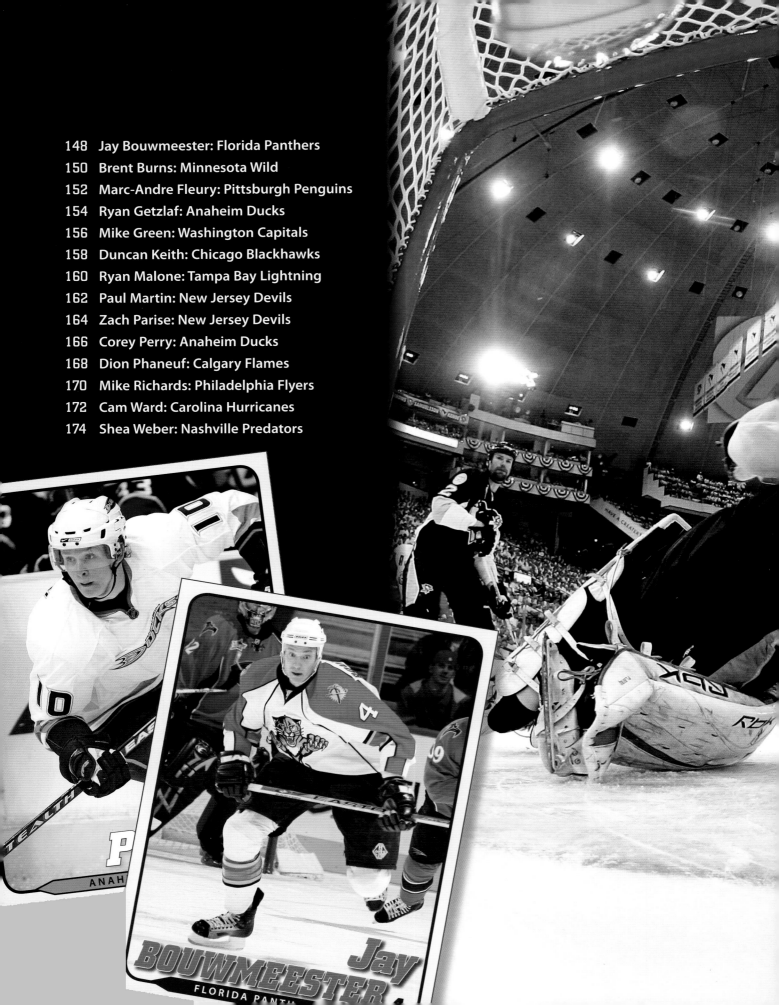

ON THE RISE
Young players ready to dominate.

Jay BOUWMEESTER 4

FLORIDA PANTHERS – D

impressive enough that Bouwmeester was considered by some to be the best player available in the 2002 NHL entry draft. It was anticipated the Florida Panthers would use the first overall selection to draft Bouwmeester, but a deal with Columbus allowed the Blue Jackets to select Rick Nash first while Atlanta took goalie Kari Lehtonen second. The Panthers got Bouwmeester with the third pick and were happy to have their 6-foot-4, 212-pound defenseman, plus the extra picks acquired in the deal with Columbus.

Since he had already completed three seasons of junior, Bouwmeester jumped straight to the NHL after being drafted and played all 82 games during his rookie season of 2002–03. He recorded 16 points, for a talent-starved Panthers team that won just 24 games all year. The following season was not much better as he played in just 61 games (recording 20 points), but the Florida club missed the playoffs again. The lockout season saw Bouwmeester assigned to San Antonio of the American Hockey League, but he was traded to the Chicago Wolves during the season in the hopes of getting him some playoff experience. He did play in 18 post-season games with the Wolves, but recorded no points. He returned to the Panthers for 2005–06 and played in all 82 contests, recording a very respectable 46 points, 41 of which were assists. For the first time in his career, Bouwmeester

Jay Bouwmeester was a typical Canadian kid who first learned to skate on a backyard rink in suburban Edmonton, Alberta. Just under two years of age at the time, young Jay pleaded with his father to let him stand alone on his skates. Bouwmeester took to skating naturally and was playing organized hockey by the time he was six years old. A natural athlete, Bouwmeester excelled at every sport he tried, but was especially good at hockey — one of the best minor hockey players in all of Edmonton, in fact. He got a taste of winning early while playing triple-A bantam hockey in 1997–98, helping lead his team to the provincial championship. At the age of 15, Bouwmeester was the first selection of the Western Hockey League's Medicine Hat Tigers and the gangly teenager felt he was ready for the rigors of one of the toughest development leagues in all of hockey.

Bouwmeester cracked the Tigers lineup at the age of 16 and that meant a move to Medicine Hat for the 1999–2000 season. Even though Bouwmeester was a superior skater and a very strong player when it came to handling the puck, the Tigers were a very average team during his three seasons there. His point totals increased every year (hitting a high of 61 in 61 games during 2001–02), but the team never made the playoffs during his tenure. Although his team failed to see post-season action, Bouwmeester did get some exposure to high-pressure situations by being named to Canada's World Junior Championship team on three occasions — the first when he was only 16 years old. His all-round performance in junior was

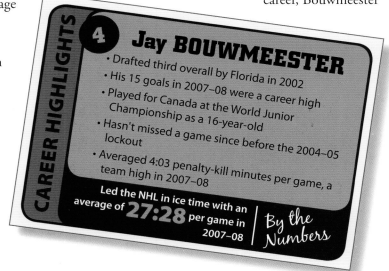

CAREER HIGHLIGHTS

4 Jay BOUWMEESTER

- Drafted third overall by Florida in 2002
- His 15 goals in 2007–08 were a career high
- Played for Canada at the World Junior Championship as a 16-year-old
- Hasn't missed a game since before the 2004–05 lockout
- Averaged 4:03 penalty-kill minutes per game, a team high in 2007–08

Led the NHL in ice time with an average of **27:28** per game in 2007–08

By the Numbers

finished on the positive side of the plus/minus rating, posting a plus-1. It appears his time in the minors was time well spent.

The first thing everyone notices about Bouwmeester's play is his great instincts for the game. He knows where to go and if he ever gets caught out of position, his long, galloping strides can get him back to where he needs to be. He has reached a point where he can be counted on at both ends of the ice and it's just as important for Bouwmeester to stop goals as it is to score them. Bouwmeester does possess a strong shot from the point

and is learning how to assert himself into the attack more as his experience level rises. He is not an overly aggressive player, a fact some use against him, and he is a quiet person by nature. Still, he looks destined for greatness thanks to his overwhelming natural ability.

In 2006–07, he scored 14 times and totaled 53 points while recording a plus-23 rating and playing over 26 minutes a game. Proving that season was no fluke, Bouwmeester recorded 15 goals and 37 points in 2007–08. As his play progresses steadily, a future as team captain is quite possible for the young rearguard.

campaign and scored 11 goals for the AHL club. Once the NHL lockout ended, he played 72 games for the Wild in 2005-06, picking up 16 points along the way. The next season saw Burns up his production to seven goals and 25 points, giving a glimpse of what the future might hold for the fast-moving defender. He had started the 2006–07 season at forward, but he blossomed upon being returned to the blueline and paired with veteran Keith Carney. Burns was learning how to maximize his effortless skating stride while demonstrating he could handle 1-on-1 battles by using his size and long reach. He also got into his first fight during the 2007 playoffs and acquitted himself rather well in taking on Chris Kunitz of Anaheim and then taking a decision against Corey Perry, also of the Ducks.

Minnesota Wild coach Jacques Lemaire is not the easiest man to please. The former NHL star and member of the Hall of Fame demands two-way play from all members of his team and woe to those who take the wrong risks and get caught out of position. Under Lemaire's system, it is not easy for a young player, especially a forward turned defenseman, to find the right mix of playing well in your own end while getting involved in the attack as well. Twenty-three-year-old Brent Burns often finds himself straddling a fine line as the blueliner seeks to establish himself as a legitimate NHL star. It has not been an easy process, but Burns has a relaxed approach to the game and life in general. His easygoing demeanor has likely helped him survive under the watchful eye of his head coach. If the last two NHL seasons are any indication, it appears Burns is well on his way to making a name for himself throughout the league.

Since drafting him 20th overall in 2003, the Wild have not been quite sure what to do with its highly prized prospect. A native of Ajax, Ontario, Burns initially developed his hockey skills in and around the Toronto area, and finished his junior career playing in nearby Brampton. The 2002–03 season saw the 6-foot-4, 207-pound Burns score 15 goals and add 25 assists while playing wing for the Ontario League's Brampton Battalion. He played 36 games for Minnesota the season after he was drafted, notching a modest one goal and six points. It was clear he needed more time to develop. Burns was assigned to San Antonio for the 2004–05

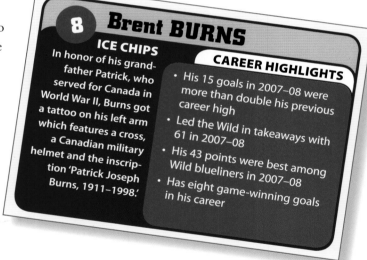

8 Brent BURNS

ICE CHIPS
In honor of his grandfather Patrick, who served for Canada in World War II, Burns got a tattoo on his left arm which features a cross, a Canadian military helmet and the inscription 'Patrick Joseph Burns, 1911–1998.'

CAREER HIGHLIGHTS
- His 15 goals in 2007–08 were more than double his previous career high
- Led the Wild in takeaways with 61 in 2007–08
- His 43 points were best among Wild blueliners in 2007–08
- Has eight game-winning goals in his career

By the time the 2007–08 season began, the Wild coaching staff had more and more confidence in the happy-go-lucky blueliner and his days on the wing were few and far between. Burns developed a strong sense of timing when it came to joining the attack and it translated to his best offensive numbers to date when he scored 15 goals and 43 points. He was even summoned to take part in a shootout and ended up scoring the winning goal! His energy level is quite noticeable, but the Wild still want him to select his spots a little better, which will come with more experience. Lemaire noticed Burns was not hitting the net often enough with his shot and pointed this out to the youngster. Burns quickly understood the need to get the puck to the net from his position on the point. During a mid-March game in 2008 against Colorado, Burns scored the opening goal of the game by using his quick release to beat former Avs goalie Jose Theodore from the blueline. Later in the same contest, Burns took a puck into the center of the ice during a Wild power play and sent a perfectly placed pass that teammate Branko Radivojevic re-directed into the net. Burns was also strong in front of his own net and the Wild took a close 3–1 contest, which it needed to help the club make the playoffs. There was no dispute when Burns was named the first star of the game!

Burns has worked on making a strong first pass out of the defensive zone and as such is being given more responsibility by the Wild coaches. If his career continues on its current trajectory, he's going to be a key player for years to come in Minnesota.

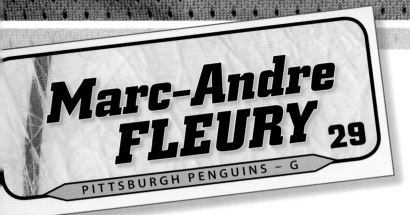

Marc-Andre FLEURY 29

PITTSBURGH PENGUINS – G

The Pittsburgh Penguins were a pretty bad hockey team during the 2002–03 season. They won just 27 games and earned a meager 65 points, and that was with Mario Lemieux recording 91 points in 67 games. Pittsburgh's goaltending that year was handled primarily by Johan Hedberg, J.S. Aubin and Sebastien Caron — which essentially meant the Penguins were using three netminders better suited to being backups than starters. Pittsburgh was scheduled to pick third at the 2003 draft, but the Pens sent forward Mikael Samuelsson and the third overall selection to the Florida Panthers in exchange for the No. 1 pick. Determined to shore up their club from the net out, the Penguins used the pick to take goaltender Marc-Andre Fleury, a native of Sorel, Quebec, who had starred with Cape Breton of the Quebec Major Junior Hockey League. The 2003 draft was one of the best in history, but for a while the Penguins were not sure they had made the right choice.

Fleury had great appeal to the Penguins because of his tremendous reflexes, especially with his legs. He is very athletic and coverss a good amount of the net at 6-foot-1 and 170 pounds. His classic butterfly style is augmented with an aggressive approach that's very easy to spot. Fleury is a great skater, but until recently he had major problems handling the puck. During the 2004 World Junior Championship, Fleury had a puck-playing mishap in the gold medal game that helped Team USA defeat his Canadian team. Except for the 2001–02 season, when he won 26 games and then

another nine in the playoffs, Fleury's record in Cape Breton was not exceptional. He was not ready for the rigors of the NHL in 2003–04, although he did get into 21 games, winning just four times for another poor edition of the Penguins. Fleury also played back in Cape Breton and then joined the Penguins farm team for a couple of playoff games. He spent the entire lockout season in Wilkes-Barre of the American Hockey League and posted a 26–19–4 record. It looked like he was finally ready for the next step.

The Penguins were still struggling after the lockout season ended, but by now they were starting to piece together a very talented team. Despite the addition of Sidney Crosby and other youngsters, Fleury won only 13 of 50 starts in 2005–06 and found himself back in the minors for 12 games. However, he improved the following year and posted an impressive 40–16–9 record. The Penguins finally made the playoffs, but were quickly dispatched by the Ottawa Senators.

It appeared Fleury

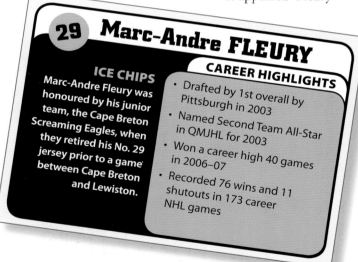

29 Marc-Andre FLEURY

ICE CHIPS
Marc-Andre Fleury was honoured by his junior team, the Cape Breton Screaming Eagles, when they retired his No. 29 jersey prior to a game between Cape Breton and Lewiston.

CAREER HIGHLIGHTS
- Drafted by 1st overall by Pittsburgh in 2003
- Named Second Team All-Star in QMJHL for 2003
- Won a career high 40 games in 2006–07
- Recorded 76 wins and 11 shutouts in 173 career NHL games

had gained the confidence required for a No. 1 goalie to shine.

Fleury was sailing along early in the 2007–08 season when a high-ankle sprain threatened his great season. He missed 28 games before he was able to get back in the Pittsburgh net, which had been occupied capably by Ty Conklin and Dany Sabourin. Upon his return, Fleury went 10–2–1, which helped him finish with a 19–10–2 record overall with four shutouts and a solid .921 save percentage. Fleury did a lot of learning while he was injured. He was advised to change his bright yellow goal pads to a white color, which blends easier with the ice and boards. He also pestered Conklin to help him with his puck-moving skills and he became more comfortable with that aspect of the game, forgetting the nightmare of his junior experience. Goaltending coach Gilles Meloche helped by getting Fleury to position himself differently as soon as opponents crossed the red line. He also improved his rebound control and got better at being in position to stop second shots. Fleury has discovered that, when tending goal, sometimes less is more. He lets the puck come to him now and this approach has kept things much calmer in the defensive zone.

Fleury really became an NHL star during the 2008 playoffs when he posted a 14–6 record as his team fell to the Detroit Red Wings in the Stanley Cup final. Fleury ended the playoffs with a fantastic 1.97 goals-against average and a very impressive .938 save percentage to go along with three shutouts. The Penguins net will be heavily protected as long as Fleury is in the crease.

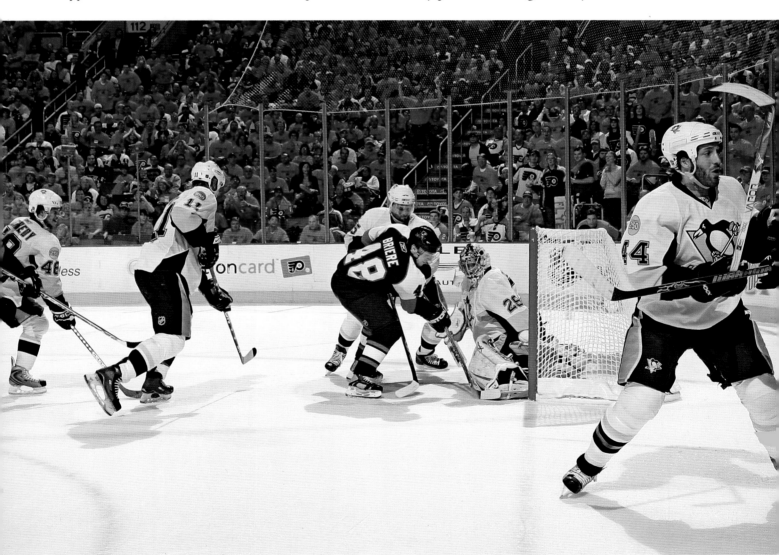

Ryan GETZLAF 15

ANAHEIM DUCKS – C

When the Anaheim Ducks drew up their NHL 2003 entry draft list, they had large power forward Ryan Getzlaf rated as the fifth-best player available. The Anaheim scouting staff did not expect the 6-foot-3, 211-pound center to still be in play when they selected 18th overall. Much to their amazement, Getzlaf was still there when the Washington Capitals selected just before the Ducks and the Anaheim staff fully expected him to be taken at that point. But the Capitals shocked them when they announced right winger Eric Fehr as their choice. The Anaheim people thought there might be a problem with Getzlaf, but quickly dismissed that notion and were more than happy to take Getzlaf's rights with their pick. It was a choice they would not regret.

Maybe it shouldn't come as a complete surprise Getzlaf's stock dropped down somewhat considering he never hit the 30-goal barrier in junior (he had 29 twice) during a three-year career with the Western Hockey League's Calgary Hitmen. By contrast, a player like Fehr scored 50 and 59 goals over his final two years in the WHL. Getzlaf played briefly in Cincinnati and Portland of the American Hockey League, but soon found himself a regular with the Ducks in 2005–06, scoring 14 goals and totaling 39 points in just 57 games. He showed that performance was no fluke by scoring 25 goals and adding 33 assists during the 2006–07 season. In the playoffs, he led the Ducks with 17 points en route to Anaheim winning its first-ever Stanley Cup championship.

If there was any great concern about Getzlaf it was

his consistency from game to game. The team was worried about the big center's ability to compete at a level that went beyond being merely a good player. Certainly Getzlaf has all the tools necessary to be a dominating player for a long time if he wants to do it. He has size, strength, skill and a long stride that would make every team envious. At times, he has flashed the type of brilliance usually reserved for true superstars in the league. One such moment came in Game 1 of the 2007 Stanley Cup final when he scored the game-tying goal after not even registering a shot on goal in the first two periods of the contest. Teammate Travis Moen then potted the winner and the Ducks were on their way to winning the Cup in just five games against an overmatched Ottawa Senators team. Getzlaf also help set up Andy McDonald for the opening goal in the last game of the series, a 6–2 win to capture the championship on home ice.

The trio of Getzlaf, Corey Perry and Dustin Penner in the '07 post-season gave the Ducks one of the youngest, most dangerous lines in hockey. Although Penner was lost as a free agent to the Edmonton Oilers, Getzlaf and Perry still form a dynamic duo and comprised two-thirds of Anaheim's top line in the 2007–08 season, which saw Getzlaf lead all Anaheim scorers with 24 goals and 58 assists in 77 games. He also kept up his aggressive play with 94 penalty minutes. Getzlaf shows excellent hands for a big man and he maneuvers the puck in high-traffic areas with the same deftness as a player who possesses a smaller, more agile frame. At times, his inexperience still is evident as he gambles a little too often, but Getzlaf's competitive nature and willingness to mix it up keeps the opposition honest and leery. Experiencing success at an early age has not seemed to hamper Getzlaf's development one bit. Ducks management believes it has a future captain in the feisty Getzlaf.

The Ducks got off to a bit of a rocky start in 2007–08, but came on strong once Scott Niedermayer and Teemu Selanne returned to the team after a brief "retirement." They made the playoffs easily, but were knocked off by a surprisingly determined Dallas Stars team that won an opening round series in six games. Getzlaf had five points in six games, but it was clear from the outset the Ducks were not as hungry as they had been the previous year when they won the Cup. Young players like Getzlaf should be able to keep Anaheim in contention for the foreseeable future.

15 Ryan GETZLAF

ICE CHIPS

Getzlaf brought the Cup home to Regina, Saskatchewan, in 2007 and played in a ball-hockey tournament that raised $18,000 for Ronald McDonald House. The team winning the tournament also got to hoist the Cup!

CAREER HIGHLIGHTS

- Set career highs in assists (58) and points (82) in 2007–08
- Scored three game-winners en route to the 2007 Cup
- Tops on the Ducks in regular season and playoff scoring in 2007–08
- Won gold with Canada at the 2005 World Junior Championship

Mike GREEN 52

WASHINGTON CAPITALS – D

Over the years, the Washington Capitals have had their share of defensemen who put up solid offensive numbers. Scott Stevens (in the early years of his Hall of Fame career), Kevin Hatcher, Al Iafrate, Sylvain Cote and Sergei Gonchar all come to mind when discussing prolific Washington rearguards. It might be time to add a new name to that illustrious list. Mike Green scored 18 goals and recorded 56 points during the 2007–08 season and his strong performance helped the Capitals get into the playoffs for the first time since 2003. Once there, he notched seven points during a seven-game loss to the Philadelphia Flyers.

At the start of the 2007–08 campaign, it appeared Green was not going to do much more than he had previously done since being drafted 29th overall by Washington in 2004. He played 70 games in 2006–07 and notched only two goals to go along with 10 assists. Prior to that, Green had some success in the American Hockey League playing with the Caps' farm team in Hershey, Pennsylvania. He scored 43 points in 53 games during the 2005–06 campaign before tacking on 18 more points in 21 playoff games as the Bears won the Calder Cup. That performance and a growing confidence as a result of being a champion got Green a long look with the big club. The 2007–08 season did not start well for Washington, which stumbled out of the gate with a 6–14–1 record. Green's game was restricted somewhat by former Caps coach Glen Hanlon and he only had

seven points in 21 games. But a coaching change saw Bruce Boudreau installed behind the Caps bench and suddenly the team, especially Green, started to take off.

Given the opportunity to play more under Boudreau, his old coach from Hershey, Green's game began to thrive as he was encouraged to initiate the attack. Paired with the defensively responsible Shaone Morrisonn, Green felt he could jump into the play and feel comfortable that his partner would be able to back him up. He was also able to contribute strongly to a power play that featured Alex Ovechkin, Victor Kozlov, rookie Nicklas Backstrom and later after the trade deadline, veteran Sergei Fedorov. Green realized if he was going to be effective as an NHL blueliner, he would have to do it with offensive flair. When he tried to do too much, Boudreau was there to remind the youngster

CAREER HIGHLIGHTS

52 Mike GREEN

- Led the NHL in goals by a defenseman in 2007–08
- Won the Calder Cup with Hershey (AHL) in 2006
- Tallied seven points in seven playoff games in 2007–08
- Drafted 29th overall by the Caps in 2004
- His 56 points were seventh-best among league defensemen in 2007–08

His **18 goals** in 2007–08 was **nine times** better than his previous high of two

By the Numbers

there's a time to attack and a time to sit back. Knowing his coach had faith in him and was going to continue to give him ice time despite any mistakes did wonders for Green's confidence. Just as important, Green is giving the opposition something more to worry about other than just watching Ovechkin and Backstrom.

Green's game is largely built around his superior skating skills. He has a smooth, balanced stride and can skate at full speed while carrying the puck. Once he gets into the offensive zone, he shows a great deal of creativity by either spotting an open man or getting into the right position for a bomb from the blueline. Green tends to get in trouble when he tries to force the issue, but that should improve with time and experience. He uses his 6-foot-1, 208-pound frame effectively and is not afraid to mix it up. Largely unknown until his breakout year, Green grew up in Calgary admiring Hall of Fame Flames defenseman Al MacInnis. He did not produce big numbers as a junior with the Western Hockey League's Saskatoon Blades until his draft year. In fact, he scored 14 goals in his last two years of junior and his final campaign in Saskatoon saw him record 66 points in 67 games while adding 105 penalty minutes.

Now that Green has established himself as a force with the Capitals, you can bet he will get more attention from opponents who will do their best to stop him from winding up and producing highlight-reel goals. However, with Boudreau having great faith in his stud defender, it's predictable Green will continue to thrive. His career shows proper coaching is just as important as it ever was if a team is to improve in the National Hockey League.

Duncan KEITH 2

CHICAGO BLACKHAWKS – D

The NHL All-Star Game does not have quite the luster it once did. Fans, except for those in the host city, are generally indifferent to the contest despite the fact the game usually features high-octane offensive action and plenty of goal-scoring. The game is now played in the middle of the season and many players (tired from a long regular season schedule) are not too disappointed to miss it at various times in their career. However, getting named to play in the All-Star Game for the first time is still very special and a career highlight for every player who gets the honor. Such was the case in 2008 when Chicago Blackhawks defenseman Duncan Keith was named to play in the match, held in Atlanta. He was the only Western Conference blueliner making his all-star debut and although Keith did not record a point in the 8–7 loss to the Eastern Conference, you can bet he enjoyed the unexpected pleasure of participating in the league showcase.

Few people outside of Chicago were aware Keith was performing at an all-star level. If those in the Blackhawks organization were completely honest, they would tell you it was not something they were expecting, either. Keith was born in Winnipeg, Manitoba, but spent much of his early years growing up in Fort Frances, Ontario. He started out playing both defense and forward, but eventually settled on the blueline because he felt he could be more involved and even control a game from that position. His father, David, had a strong influence on his development and coached his son in atom

hockey. Two other men, a pair of brothers named Gib and Bill Tucker, also coached young Keith in minor hockey and were very important to the defenseman's development. The family moved to British Columbia and the 1998–99 season saw Keith record a whopping 51 goals and 108 points in 44 games while playing bantam triple-A in Penticton. The next two seasons Keith played for the Jr. A Penticton Panthers of the British Columbia Hockey League before landing a spot at Michigan State University, where he played for two more seasons. It was during his second year at Michigan in 2002–03 that Keith realized he had a legitimate shot at being an NHL player, so he left school and joined Kelowna in the Western Hockey League in the hopes of fast tracking himself to the big league. Keith had 46 points in just 37 games while playing for the Kelowna Rockets to finish the season.

The Blackhawks had already noticed the swift-skating defender while he was at Michigan and made him their third choice, 54th overall, in the 2002 entry draft. After leaving junior, Keith played two seasons with the Norfolk Admirals of the American Hockey League and thrived under the tutelage of former NHL defenseman Trent Yawney. He did not put up spectacular numbers by any means (25 and 26 points, respectively), but Yawney took the time to teach him the finer points he would need to learn if he was to play in the NHL. Not only did Keith listen to his coach, he also

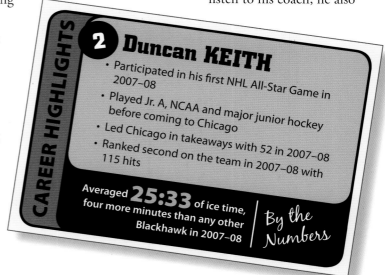

CAREER HIGHLIGHTS

2 Duncan KEITH

- Participated in his first NHL All-Star Game in 2007–08
- Played Jr. A, NCAA and major junior hockey before coming to Chicago
- Led Chicago in takeaways with 52 in 2007–08
- Ranked second on the team in 2007–08 with 115 hits

Averaged **25:33** of ice time, four more minutes than any other Blackhawk in 2007–08

By the Numbers

grew a little. He was drafted at 5-foot-11 and 160 pounds, but was now a sturdier 6-foot and close to 190 pounds.

Keith has been a Blackhawk since the 2005–06 season and has improved with each passing year. He had 21 points in 2005–06 and then 31 the next year while playing over 23 minutes per game. Keith is a fluid skater who displays incredible athleticism on a nightly basis. He handles the puck well and competes strongly at both ends of the ice, responding well to the enthusiastic, up-beat style of Hawks coach Denis Savard. Along with Brian Campbell, Keith is one of the go-to defenseman

on a Chicago club that is on the rise largely based on the youth the team has acquired over many years of drafting high. Keith is smart enough to lead his team from the blueline, but he must learn to handle the big forwards in his own end and in front of the Blackhawks net. His performance in 2007–08 saw him score 12 goals and record a career-high 32 points.

Chicago management loves how Keith works and stays humble even though he is starting to get some recognition around the league. Everyone senses a star in the making on the Blackhawks blueline.

Ryan MALONE 12

TAMPA BAY LIGHTNING – LW

When Greg Malone was playing for the Pittsburgh Penguins from 1976 to 1983, the talented center was one of the few NHLers who came from Canada's Maritime provinces. The native of Fredricton, New Brunswick, was selected 19th overall by the Penguins in 1976 after a good career with the Oshawa Generals of the Ontario Hockey League. Malone usually was around the 20-goal mark and posted a career-best 35 in 1978–79. He would go on to record 501 points in 704 career games, which included playing for Quebec and Hartford, before leaving hockey in 1987 and joining the Penguins as director of scouting. While he was playing in Pittsburgh, he had a son named Ryan, who was born December 1, 1979. The youngster developed into a hockey player and eventually became the first Pittsburgh-area native to make it to the NHL. Naturally, Ryan made his debut with the Penguins — a very fitting place, all things considered.

While he was in a scouting position with the Penguins, Greg Malone, who now scouts for Tampa Bay, would get updates on how his young son's career was progressing. Ryan played high school hockey in Minnesota and then Jr. A hockey for the Omaha Lancers of the United States Hockey League. The late and legendary Herb Brooks was scouting for the Penguins and told Greg that Ryan was scoring some great goals and the Penguins should make sure they picked this kid at some point during the 1999 draft. Brooks, coach of the famous 1980 U.S. Olympic hockey team, had a sharp eye for talent and thought it likely young Ryan

had inherited some of his dad's quality hockey genes. The Penguins drafted Ryan 115th overall and then watched as he developed while attending St. Cloud University for four seasons. Ryan had played high school hockey in the Pittsburgh area, but never really distinguished himself in any way until he attended the famous Shattuck-St.Mary's prep school in Minnesota. He got the needed training there and learned to round out his game rather than depend solely on goal-scoring ability.

As the years past, Malone filled out his 6-foot-4 frame to 224 pounds and made his start with an awful Penguins team in 2003–04, scoring 22 goals and totaling 43 points in 81 games. He displayed a strong nose for the net with a nice soft touch around the crease. Malone went to Europe for the lockout season, scoring 12 goals in just 26 games. He scored 22 times and added 22 assists in 2005–06, as the Penguins were starting to rebuild their team by adding Sidney Crosby and other talented youngsters to their lineup. Although the Penguins kept improving, the 2006–07 season saw his production dip to just 16 goals after he was limited to 64 games due to an arm injury. That led to rumors of Malone being available in a trade. The Penguins wisely kept the left winger on their team and it proved to be a great move as the 2007–08 season unfolded.

Serious injuries to Crosby and veteran Gary Roberts gave Malone more responsibility than ever and he responded to the challenge. He got time on the power play and some action as a penalty-killer, and was given the opportunity to play along side rising star Evgeni Malkin. He scored 27 goals and 51 points as the Penguins became one of the best teams in the NHL. His game continued to improve and a quicker shot release resulted in a higher goal total. Malone is certainly not afraid to drop his gloves and challengers need to be aware he can handle himself with his fists. Toronto's Mark Bell found that out the hard way when a Malone punch broke his orbital bone during a 2007–08 game in Pittsburgh. Like many other players in the NHL, the motivation of unrestricted free agency helped Malone to

become a more consistent player, with some believing he can be a first-liner. His six goals and 16 points in 20 playoff games during the Pens' run to the 2008 Cup final back that theory up.

Malone's big payday came shortly after the Penguins remarkable playoff run when the rugged winger inked a $31.5 million, seven-year contract with the Tampa Bay Lightning. Malone was one of many off-season acquisitions by the Lightning, which look again to be a serious contender.

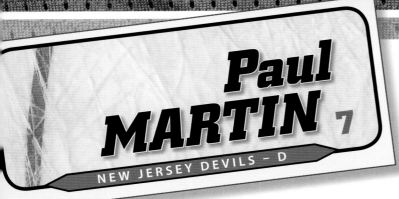

Paul MARTIN 7
NEW JERSEY DEVILS – D

The New Jersey Devils club that won the Stanley Cup in 2003 has certainly changed drastically over the last four seasons. The most obvious change is on the Devils blueline, where little remains from the championship team. One defender who remains with the team is Colin White, but gone are longtime stalwarts Scott Stevens (retired), Ken Daneyko (retired), Tommy Albelin (retired), Scott Niedermayer (signed as a free agent by Anaheim) and Brian Rafalski (signed as free agent by Detroit). Many of the forwards are also no longer in New Jersey, the most notable of which is Scott Gomez, who signed with the rival New York Rangers in 2007. Considering the loss of such talent, it would be understandable if the Devils slid down the Eastern Conference standings and began a long rebuilding process. Luckily, GM Lou Lamoriello is always prepared and New Jersey has remained a perennial playoff team. A big part of why the Devils have not slipped is the stability of having Martin Brodeur in goal and an influx of new talent that joins the club in a seamless manner year after year. One of the new additions is defenseman Paul Martin, a third round draft choice in 2000 who surprised everyone by making the team for the 2003–04 campaign.

Martin joined the Devils as a 23-year-old straight out of the University of Minnesota. The native of Minneapolis, Minnesota, played high school hockey in his home state and had a very good year in the 1999–2000 season, when he scored 15 goals and totaled 50 points in just 24 games. The Devils took a chance and

selected him right out of high school, but he played three NCAA seasons before even considering a move to the NHL. He earned many honors during his college career and learned to play on championship teams as the Golden Gophers took back-to-back NCAA titles in 2002 and 2003. He was nearly a point-per-game player, recording 77 points in 89 games over his last two years in college. It was assumed he would need some seasoning with Albany of the American Hockey League, but injuries on the blueline gave Martin a chance to play in the big league sooner than expected. He attended training camp not quite sure what to expect, but getting paired with an all-star like Niedermayer sent the rookie's confidence soaring. He got into 70 games and recorded six goals and 24 points, not a bad mark for a first-year player in New Jersey.

He played briefly in the Swiss League during the NHL lockout and got his point total to 37 in 80 games during 2005–06 with New Jersey. However, the next season saw the Devils install the rather conservative Claude Julien behind the bench. Martin played in all 82 games, but the restrictive style of play brought his point total down to 26 in 2006–07. Julien did not finish the year in New Jersey and Martin did not thrive under his coaching, posting a minus-9 rating — a surprising mark considering the Devils' ultra-defensive style of play. However, the Devils liked what they saw from the young rearguard (Martin played over 25 minutes per game) and re-signed him to a new contract prior to the start of the 2007–08 season. Lamoriello wanted to keep a defenseman he believed could play in all situations and rewarded the young rearguard a three-year deal worth a reported total $11.5 million dollars. For his part, Martin was excited about working with new coach Brent Sutter and about taking on more of a leadership role. He was also pleased to see New Jersey bring back former head coach Larry Robinson as an assistant coach for the purpose of working very closely with the team's defense corps.

Although the Devils still think defense first (they surround Brodeur around the crease with a military-like precision), Martin still gets the opportunity to show his offensive skills. He has good hands for a big man (6-foot-1, 190 pounds) and although he's not always smooth, he's a deceptively strong skater. Martin can handle the point on the power play and is getting better at dealing with big forwards in front of his own net. He scored five goals and had 32 points in 2007–08. There is little doubt the New Jersey club will continue to be a contender and Martin's contributions will be a big part of that.

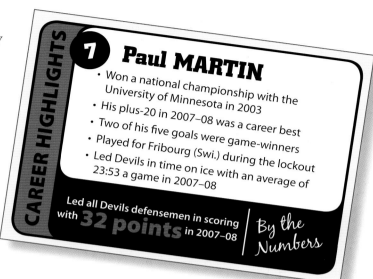

CAREER HIGHLIGHTS

7 Paul MARTIN

- Won a national championship with the University of Minnesota in 2003
- His plus-20 in 2007–08 was a career best
- Two of his five goals were game-winners
- Played for Fribourg (Swi.) during the lockout
- Led Devils in time on ice with an average of 23:53 a game in 2007–08

Led all Devils defensemen in scoring with **32 points** in 2007–08

By the Numbers

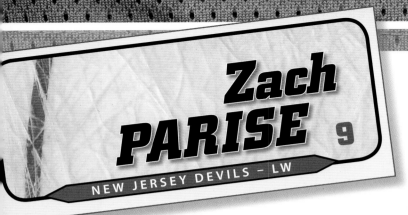

Zach PARISE 9

NEW JERSEY DEVILS – LW

The New Jersey Devils won their third Stanley Cup in franchise history in 2003 and were selecting 17th overall at the NHL entry draft. Somehow, left winger Zach Parise, who was anticipating being drafted around tenth overall, was still available when the champions were ready to select. Even the New York Islanders, the team his famous dad J.P. Parise had played for in the 1970s, passed on the youngster who had starred at the University of North Dakota. While he was somewhat disappointed his stock had dropped a little, Parise was still very happy to go to a winning team where he could develop properly before being inserted into an NHL lineup. The Devils, needless to say, were thrilled to see Parise available as they continued one of their most valued traditions of selecting and developing players who play in the U.S. college hockey system.

Considering his father was a top-notch NHL player and represented Canada in the famous 1972 Summit Series against the Soviet Union, it's little wonder Zach followed in his footsteps. Born and raised in Minnesota (where his father starred for the North Stars between 1968 and 1975), Zach and his older brother, Jordan, took to hockey at an early age, although their dad never pushed them. Skating by the time he was two, Zach and his brother (now a goalie in the Devils system) played some form of hockey just about every day of the year. To get more playing time, Zach decided to attend Shattuck-St. Mary's, a well known prep school in Minnesota that has helped produce many NHL players.

During his second season there in 2001–02, Parise produced an astounding 77 goals and 178 points in 67 games. He did this against players one year older than him while finding time to be a top student as well. Recruited by North Dakota, he spent two seasons there notching 116 points in 106 games. By this point it was obvious Parise was destined for an NHL career — it was just a matter of time.

Parise is not a large player at 5-foot-11 and 190 pounds, and the Devils, like many good organizations, like to give even their best prospects some time to adjust to the professional game. Assigned to the Albany River Rats of the American Hockey League for the entire 2004–05 season, he scored 18 times and totaled 58 points in 73 games. Although those were not overwhelming numbers, Parise made the Devils for the 2005–06 campaign and connected for 14 goals and 32 points in 81 contests.

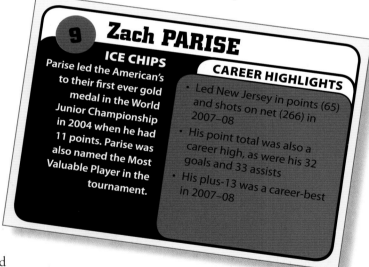

9 Zach PARISE

ICE CHIPS

Parise led the American's to their first ever gold medal in the World Junior Championship in 2004 when he had 11 points. Parise was also named the Most Valuable Player in the tournament.

CAREER HIGHLIGHTS

- Led New Jersey in points (65) and shots on net (266) in 2007–08
- His point total was also a career high, as were his 32 goals and 33 assists
- His plus-13 was a career-best in 2007–08

However, he came on strong in 2006–07 by scoring 31 times and adding 31 assists while playing in all 82 games. He also had a good playoff with 10 points in 11 games and was easily the Devils best forward in the post-season, although they were ousted in the second round. His solid performance did not go unnoticed by Devils management, which rewarded its rising star by giving him a four-year contract worth $12.5 million. Parise's

signing came right on the heels of the Devils losing Scott Gomez via free agency. By inking young Parise, New Jersey subtly let it be known the left winger was going to be counted on to be a consistent producer.

Parise is not nearly as stocky as his father, but he is getting stronger as he matures. He is deceptively fast and his quick release gets him plenty of goals. Take a look at the highlights of Devils games and Parise is likely to be one of their goal-getters — usually by hanging around the net. He shows no fear in going to the danger spots around the net – the kind of approach that gets you a

nasty introduction to the NHL's best defensemen. Parise manages to keep his stick clear of checkers and loves setting up just to the side of the net. His defensive play will develop, especially as he works under coach Brent Sutter, who will demand nothing less.

In 2007–08, Parise continued his terrific play with 32 goals and 33 assists, helping the Devils to their usual high standing in the Eastern Conference. He added five points in five playoff games, but New Jersey was eliminated in the first round. Parise has a tremendous future, but needs some goal-scoring support in New Jersey.

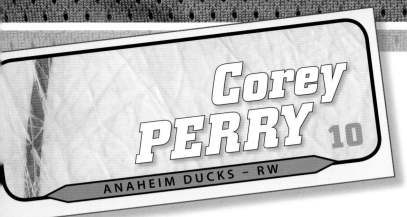

Corey PERRY 10

ANAHEIM DUCKS – RW

beat them in the opener and then easily took the final contest to cap a great year with a championship. Perry was named MVP of the tournament and finished the playoffs with a remarkable 38 points in 18 games. For Perry, it was the second major triumph of the year since he was part of the gold medal-winning Canadian team at the 2005 World Junior Championship.

Even though Perry enjoyed a great deal of success on the way to the NHL, he was only a late first round pick of the Anaheim Ducks, going 28th overall in the 2003 entry draft. He was picked lower than his junior play would merit because he was considered a marginal skater. The Ducks scouting staff were very aware of his skating deficiencies, but loved his character and skill level. They felt strongly Perry would work hard to get better and although he started the 2005–06 season with the big league team, he was assigned to the American Hockey League for some seasoning. He dominated while playing for the Portland Pirates, notching 34 points in 19 games, and he returned to the NHL to finish his rookie year with 13 goals and 25 points in 56 games.

Perry's main strength is that he competes hard every shift and even though he is a lean 202 pounds at 6-foot-3, he is a very intense player who can get under the skin of opponents. He shows great hockey sense and is not afraid to handle the puck in tight situations. Perry has a good wrist shot and will take the

Considering Corey Perry is just 23 years of age, he has done a great deal of winning during his still-developing hockey career. He was playing organized hockey at five years old while growing up in the town of Haileybury, near Peterborough, Ontario. He was so good with the puck that he scored more than 200 goals in one season when he was eight years old. It was great to be growing up in a cold-weather place like Haileybury, where Perry could play on a backyard rink with his brother. But ultimately the town's small size meant the best players had to go to larger centers if they were going to get better. The competition in Peterborough was much stronger, and Perry continued to excel as he scored 73 goals and totaled 119 points in the 2000–01 season for the bantam triple-A Peterborough Petes. It was hoped the local Petes of the Ontario Hockey League would draft Perry, but the London Knights snapped him up instead.

The Knights were under the control of the Hunter brothers — Dale and Mark — both former NHL players. Getting tutelage from such experienced pros could only help Perry become a better player and the results were there for all to see. Perry's point total went from 59 in 2001–02 to a league-best 113 by the 2004–05 campaign. London became a league power, rarely losing during the 2004–05 season and then playing host to the Memorial Cup. The Sidney Crosby-led Rimouski Oceanic were the Knights' main concern during the tournament, but they quickly gained the upper hand by coming back to

10 Corey PERRY

ICE CHIPS

Perry took the Stanley Cup back to Peterborough, Ontario, in 2007 for a public celebration. He then took the Cup west to London. A traffic jam gave Perry the opportunity to show the trophy to others stuck on the road.

CAREER HIGHLIGHTS

- Led the Ducks in goals in 2007–08 with 29, a career high
- His 2007–08 total points (54) and shots (200) were also career highs
- Registered 12 multi-point games in 2007–08
- His four game-winning goals in 2007–08 were a career-best

physical pounding that comes with driving to the net. While he lacks top-notch speed, Perry has worked hard to become an adequate skater. His second NHL season was a little up and down, as Perry endured a stretch of 22 games where he didn't register a goal. His ultimate redemption came in the playoffs, when he scored six times and totaled 15 points in 21 post-season games. The Ducks won their first-ever Stanley Cup, adding another championship trophy to Perry's already impressive list of victories.

The 2007–08 season saw Perry score a career-best 29 goals and 54 points in 70 games, as he became a more consistent player while still playing an agitating role for the team. Perry missed the first three games of the playoffs recovering from a serious leg cut before returning for the final three contests. Although he scored two goals, the Ducks were ousted by the Dallas Stars in the first round. Anaheim will do well in the future if it keeps a proven winner like Perry in the fold along with other young stars like Ryan Getzlaf.

Dion PHANEUF 3
CALGARY FLAMES – D

he would bring that aggressive personality to the NHL. Phaneuf has a sort of quiet confidence about him and while he will not brag, he knows he belongs among the best players in the world.

When the NHL players were locked out during the 2004–05 season, it meant one more year of major junior for top prospects like Phaneuf. It also gave Phaneuf an opportunity to play for Canada at the World Junior Championship, where he excelled as the squad went undefeated to take the gold medal. The robust defender also had his best offensive year with the Rebels in 2004–05 by scoring 24 goals and 56 points in just 55 games. His fine play continued when he arrived at the Flames training camp. Even though Calgary had just come off a Stanley Cup final appearance and was deep in defensemen, there was no doubt Phaneuf was going to make the team. In fact, Calgary sent a couple of extra defensemen — Toni Lydman and Denis Gauthier — away in trades to make room for Phaneuf. That's how sure they were about the youngster.

Phaneuf plays like a seasoned veteran at both ends of the ice. He displays excellent timing in delivering his smash-mouth bodychecks, making opposing forwards aware of his presence very quickly. Phaneuf loves dolling out open-ice hits, he clears the front of the net well and he'll even drop the gloves when necessary. With his bomb from the point Phaneuf has racked up 54 goals in his first three seasons in the

When hockey legends and luminaries take the time to comment on an NHL rookie, you know he must be pretty special. Such is the case for Calgary Flames defenseman Dion Phaneuf, who took the league by storm during the 2005–06 season. Wayne Gretzky saw a lot of Phaneuf as coach of the Phoenix Coyotes and was effusive in his praise of the youngster. Phrases like "a tremendous hockey player" and "going to be a force for a long time" were just two of the accolades tossed Phaneuf's way by 'The Great One.' Even *Hockey Night in Canada* broadcaster Don Cherry got in on the act, saying Phaneuf was the best rookie defenseman in the NHL since Bobby Orr! The high praise did not seem to faze the youngster, who took it all in stride and turned in one of the best freshman seasons in NHL history.

The Calgary Flames were thrilled to take the 6-foot-3, 213-pound defenseman as their first pick, ninth overall, in the 2003 entry draft. Flames GM Darryl Sutter was well aware of Phaneuf, since the youngster had played for his brother, Brent, who coached the Western Hockey League's Red Deer Rebels. A native of Edmonton, Alberta, the large defenseman professed to liking the way hard-rock rearguard Scott Stevens played the game and molded his approach around the style of the three-time Stanley Cup champion, who retired prior to the 2005–06 season. Phaneuf racked up more than his share of penalty minutes in Red Deer and the Flames were certainly hoping

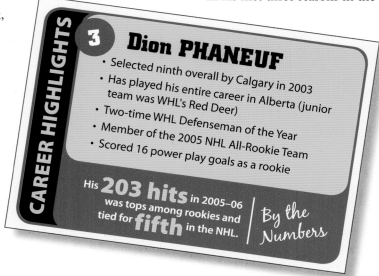

CAREER HIGHLIGHTS
3 Dion PHANEUF
- Selected ninth overall by Calgary in 2003
- Has played his entire career in Alberta (junior team was WHL's Red Deer)
- Two-time WHL Defenseman of the Year
- Member of the 2005 NHL All-Rookie Team
- Scored 16 power play goals as a rookie

His **203 hits** in 2005–06 was tops among rookies and tied for **fifth** in the NHL. *By the Numbers*

NHL, and has the distinction of holding the club record for goals by a rookie defenseman with 20, eclipsing Gary Suter's 1985–86 mark of 18. Phaneuf is also an excellent passer and likes getting into the middle of the action.

The 2007–08 season proved to be Phaneuf's coming out party as he tallied 60 points in the regular season and seven points in as many playoff games, both career highs. Phaneuf also ratcheted up his physical play, recording 182 penalty minutes, almost double his previous high

of 98 minutes in 2006–07. His dominance on the blue line garnered him his first-ever selection as an All-Star Game starter and put him in the company of greats such as Nicklas Lidstrom and Chris Pronger as he earned his first nomination as a Norris Trophy finalist. The young rearguard was named a 2008 First Team All-Star and also gained a substantial raise as he signed a six-year, $39 million contract extension that will keep him a Flame through the 2012–13 season.

When the news broke in December of 2007 that the Philadelphia Flyers had signed center Mike Richards to a 12-year contract extension for $69 million, many in the hockey world were incredulous, to say the least. After all, young Richards was only in the third year of his NHL career and had scored 11 and 10 goals, respectively, in his first two campaigns. Yet the 22-year-old was already seen as the long-term leader of the Flyers. Some observers compared him to legendary Flyer Bobby Clarke, who inspired teammates with his endless tenacity in the 1970s. The team didn't want to risk losing that combination of leadership and talent, so Richards is locked up until 2019–20. Time will tell if the Flyers made a wise investment, but if the 28 goals and 75 points he scored in 2007–08 are any indication, Philadelphia fans and management will be happy for a long time.

Richards was born in the northern Ontario town of Kenora and learned to play hockey on outdoor rinks in his youth. His family helped run the local outdoor facility and he was playing hockey by the time he was five years old. Even though the play was unstructured and without any formal coaching, Richards was able to develop his hockey skills in a care-free environment that stressed fun. He eventually played triple-A hockey in the Northern Ontario Hockey Association, where 10-hour bus rides were not uncommon. But it was worth it when Richards produced 76 goals and 149 points in 85 games while playing for the Kenora Stars in 2000–01. The

numbers got him noticed by the Kitchener Rangers of the Ontario Hockey League, who selected him fourth overall in 2001. He played four years for the Rangers, recording 85 or more points on two occasions, and won the Memorial Cup in 2003. During one Memorial Cup tournament game against Kelowna, the Rangers were down by two goals to a Rockets team that lost just once in 51 games when leading after two periods. Richards scored a pair of goals and his team won the game and earned a bye in the tournament final. The Flyers liked what they saw in the talented and feisty Richards, prompting his selection with the 24th pick in the talent-rich 2003 NHL draft.

After completing his major junior career during the 2004–05 season, Richards was assigned to the Philadelphia Phantoms of the American Hockey League for the playoffs and produced seven goals and 15 points in 14 games, helping the Phantoms win the Calder Cup championship. As an NHL rookie in 2005–06, Richards totaled 34 points in 79 games and his second year saw him record 32 points in 59 games during a season cut short by a sports hernia and a shoulder separation.

Richards will not overwhelm anyone with his skill level, but he has great instincts for the game and doesn't back down from anybody despite a modest 5-foot-11, 190-pound frame. His calmness with the puck is very noticeable and earned him power play time on the point. Richards leads by example and, as a result, when he speaks, teammates tend to listen. A game versus the Washington Capitals in November of 2007 might serve as an indication. Richards scored a goal and was bloodied in a fight and he led his team to a victory with his energetic efforts. He may never be a 50-goal man, but his two-way play will make him a valuable player for years to come. And the 'A' on his sweater will surely turn into a 'C' sometime in the near future.

His new contract creates big expectations, but the good news for Richards is he's the type of player who thrives under those conditions — which his career numbers in 2007–08 proved. The other good news for Richards is he's playing for a Philadelphia team that's

clearly on the rise. The Flyers made the playoffs in 2008 and won two rounds after finishing last overall the year before. Richards was at his feisty best in the post-season, scoring seven goals and totaling 14 points in 17 games. That the Flyers are now contenders should help Richards fulfill his leadership role more easily, much like the days when Clarke was taking his team to two Stanley Cups over 30 years ago.

18 Mike RICHARDS

ICE CHIPS

In Round 1 of the 2005–06 post-season Richards was awarded a penalty shot and scored his first-ever playoff goal. He was the second player ever to accomplish the feat. Wayne Connolly of the 1968 Minnesota North Stars was the first.

CAREER HIGHLIGHTS

- His 16-game home point streak in 2007–08 tied Bobby Clarke for the Flyers record
- His 75 points were more than double his previous career high
- Won the Memorial Cup with the Kitchener Rangers in 2003
- Won the Calder Cup with the Philadelphia Phantoms in 2005

Cam WARD 30

CAROLINA HURRICANES – G

Goaltender Cam Ward was born in Saskatoon, Saskatchewan, but spent his early childhood in Winnipeg, Manitoba. His family moved again and he developed as a teenage hockey player in Sherwood Park, Alberta, a suburb of Edmonton. He therefore had some mixed emotions when, as an unheralded rookie, he helped the Carolina Hurricanes defeat the Edmonton Oilers in seven games during the 2006 Stanley Cup final. Not only did Ward get to hoist the shinny silver trophy, he also won one of the most coveted awards of all — the Conn Smythe Trophy, given to the MVP of the playoffs. The irony was not lost on Ward, who brought the Cup to Sherwood Park for his day of celebration with the fabled trophy. He spent more than three hours signing autographs and posing for photos before he had to leave for other destinations. Before he left, Ward acknowledged the Edmonton area had been vital to his development as a netminder and appreciated how much support he received from the region, even though most of them were Oiler fans!

It is quite likely Ward became a goaltender because his father, Ken, had been a netminder during his playing days. When Cam began playing minor hockey as a young lad with the Saskatoon Flyers, he actually started out as a defenseman because the team he played on used a rotating system for the goaltender position. The good part about playing on the blueline was he developed strong skating (a very important and underrated part of the game for netminders) and puckhandling skills. When the

family moved to Winnipeg, Cam made it a commitment to play between the pipes. It was there Ward was first seen as having the potential to be an NHL puckstopper. However, when the family first settled in Sherwood Park, Ward at first had to play a level below his talent because the best team in his age group (a double-A squad) had already picked its goalie for the season. Undaunted by that minor set back, Ward continued his development and later posted a 14–6–3 record with the midget triple-A Sherwood Park team in 2000–01 before joining the Red Deer Rebels of the WHL.

Ward's first year in Red Deer saw him earn 30 wins in 46 games and that got him selected 25th overall by the Hurricanes at the 2002 entry draft. He played two more years with the Rebels and posted 40– and 31–win seasons for a club that was

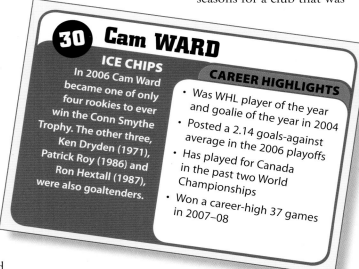

30 Cam WARD

ICE CHIPS
In 2006 Cam Ward became one of only four rookies to ever win the Conn Smythe Trophy. The other three, Ken Dryden (1971), Patrick Roy (1986) and Ron Hextall (1987), were also goaltenders.

CAREER HIGHLIGHTS
- Was WHL player of the year and goalie of the year in 2004
- Posted a 2.14 goals-against average in the 2006 playoffs
- Has played for Canada in the past two World Championships
- Won a career-high 37 games in 2007–08

always in contention for the Memorial Cup. Ward was named an all-star on more than one occasion and took home his share of awards, including being named the Canadian Hockey League's goaltender of the year in 2004. He then went to Lowell of the American Hockey League in 2004–05 and posted a 27–17–3 record in 50 games while playing for Carolina's farm club. He only played two games for Lowell the next year and was promoted to the big league for 28 games (going 14–8–2) in the 2005–06 season. That spring Ward found himself thrust into the starting role early on after the Canes' No. 1 man, Martin Gerber, faltered. Ward posted 15 wins and recorded two shutouts while notching a 2.14 goals-against average to give the Hurricanes their first ever Cup.

It had all gone so easy for the understated Ward, but the 2006–07 season brought him back down to earth. While he posted a winning mark of 30–21–6, his save percentage was only .897 and the Hurricanes shockingly missed the playoffs. He regrouped that summer by shedding roughly 20 pounds thanks to a renewed focus on diet and conditioning. It proved to be worth the

effort with Ward winning 37 games (tied for the fourth-best mark in the league) in 2007–08, even though the Carolina club lost out on a playoff spot by losing its last game of the season. Ward showed once again that he is a strong fundamental goalie with great reflexes. His calm demeanor was as evident as it had been in the '06 playoffs and he flashed a terrific glove hand, which has always been one of his trademarks.

Carolina needs to help Ward by adding younger defenders who can move the puck quickly, but the Canes look to be set in net for a long time.

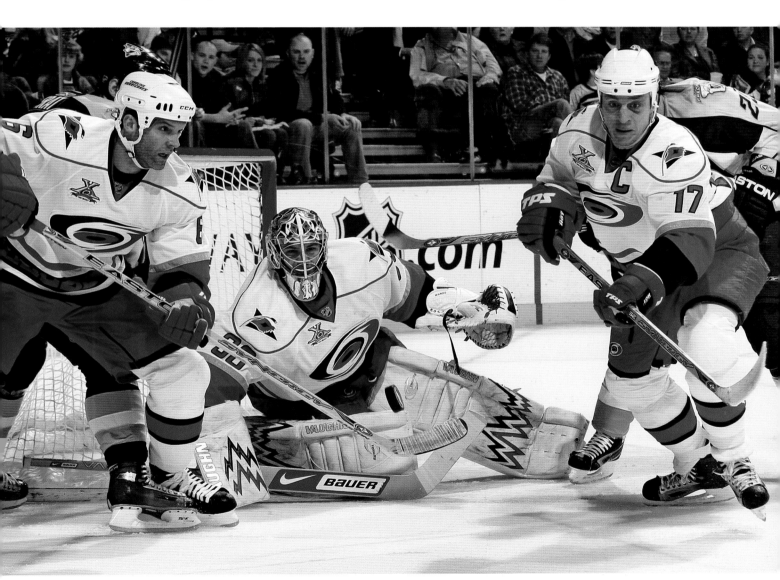

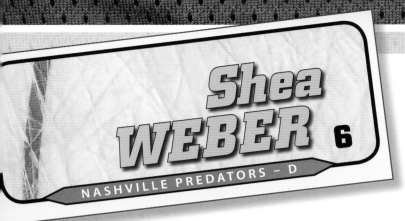

Shea WEBER 6

NASHVILLE PREDATORS – D

the eye of the Nashville Predators, who selected him 49th overall in 2003, the same year the team took another defenseman, Ryan Sutter, fifth overall.

Weber split the 2005–06 season between Nashville, where he played 28 games, and the Predators' American Hockey League farm team in Milwaukee, where he popped 12 goals and 27 points in 46 contests. He was one of Nashville's better players in the 2006 playoffs, scoring two goals in four games before returning to Milwaukee to help the Admirals in their post-season drive. The Admirals made it to the AHL final with Weber contributing six goals and 11 points in 14 games. The 2006–07 season was a break through for Weber, who scored 17 times and notched 40 points in 79 games while averaging just over 19 minutes a game. He also asserted himself physically with 165 hits. The Predators made the playoffs once again, but suffered another first round loss, although Weber had three assists in five games played.

The Predators were on the verge of great accomplishments when the team was forced to move out certain players (the most prominent being Paul Kariya, Kimmo Timonen and goaltender Tomas Vokoun) to reduce costs as ownership was in a state of flux. Although it took quite awhile, the ownership issue was finally resolved and the Predators, hoping to keep their fans interested in the

Shea Weber grew up in the small town of Sicamous, British Columbia, and found plenty of time to play hockey with his brother and their friends. His mother had a difficult time getting the brothers in the house for lunch or dinner and they would play out at the rink until it was too dark to see anymore. Summertime simply meant the hockey playing was shifted to the backyard of the house, where Shea would get to practice his shot. His father worked at a saw mill and that meant he could get plywood which the Weber brothers would use as a launching pad to fire the puck. It paid off as Shea's shot was timed at 78 miles per hour when he was just 13 years old!

Weber was not the biggest kid when it came time to play junior hockey, a fact that concerned teams in the Western Hockey League. He played most of 2001–02 with the Sicamous Eagles in a Jr. B loop (recording 42 points in 47 games) before he got to play in five games for the Kelowna Rockets of the WHL that same year. He then played three seasons for the Rockets and produced good statistics, but certainly not overwhelming numbers on the blueline. Weber got a taste of winning when the Rockets won the Memorial Cup in 2004 and he was a big-time contributor, netting 17 points in 17 playoff games. He also won a gold medal playing for Canada at the 2005 World Junior Championship, where he played alongside Dion Phaneuf, who plays a similar style to Weber's. His 6-foot-3, 213-pound frame and good play caught

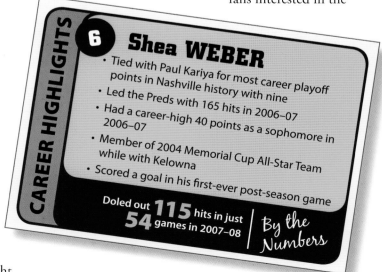

CAREER HIGHLIGHTS

6 Shea WEBER

- Tied with Paul Kariya for most career playoff points in Nashville history with nine
- Led the Preds with 165 hits in 2006–07
- Had a career-high 40 points as a sophomore in 2006–07
- Member of 2004 Memorial Cup All-Star Team while with Kelowna
- Scored a goal in his first-ever post-season game

Doled out **115** hits in just **54** games in 2007–08

By the Numbers

club, went about the business of trying to make the playoffs again. Weber was now feeling more comfortable as a pro player and looked forward to his continued development. However, a knee injury in the opening game of the 2007–08 season was a major setback for the young rearguard. Weber was out for 18 games and then he lost another 11 games with a leg injury. The injuries were part of the reason Weber scored just six goals and 20 points in 54 games that season, but the Predators did make the playoffs once again.

Weber is sure to rebound and realize the potential he's flashed in just three years of playing in the NHL. Nashville coach Barry Trotz views Weber as a young version of Rob Blake, a dominating defenseman for the Los Angeles Kings and Colorado Avalanche in recent years. Trotz thinks the Predators blueliner has the shot to be dangerous on the attack and the physical presence needed to keep opposing forwards honest with his heavy hits. The Predators and Weber shouldn't be surprised if his name is as prominent as Phaneuf's in the near future.

PROFILE INDEX

ACKNOWLEDGMENTS

The author would like to thank the contributions of the following sources that were consulted while writing this book:

NEWSPAPERS

Toronto Star, *Toronto Sun*, *The Globe and Mail*, *Calgary Sun*, *Ottawa Sun*, *Edmonton Journal*, *Dallas Daily News*, *Montreal Gazette*, *Minnesota Star Tribune*, *Vancouver Sun*.
Articles from the *Canadian Press* and the *Associated Press* that appeared in these newspapers were also consulted.

WEBSITES

HockeyBuzz.com, TheFourthPeriod.com, Faceoff.com, HockeyDraft.ca, CBCSports.ca, ESPN.com, TheHockeyNews.com, Hockey-Reference.com, HHOF.com, Canoe.ca, TSN.ca, Sportsnet.ca, NHLPA.com, as well as NHL.com and its network of websites.

MAGAZINES

The Hockey News, 2007–08; *McKeen's Hockey Yearbook*, 2007–08; *The Score Sports Forecaster*, 2007–08; *Hockey Yearbook*; *Powerplay Magazine*; *Hockey Life*; *Hockey Digest*; *Sports Illustrated*; *Maclean's Magazine*; 2007–08 Toronto Maple Leafs Programs.

RECORD BOOKS

NHL Official Guide and Record Book 2007–2008; *NHL Stanley Cup Playoff Guide*; *Total Hockey*; *Total NHL*; *World Cup of Hockey Media Guide*.

BOOKS

Hockey's Young Guns by Ryan Dixon and Ryan Kennedy; *Hockey's Young Superstars* by Jeff Rud; *Hockey Superstars* by Paul Romanik.

TELEVISION

CBC's Hockey Night in Canada; The NHL on TSN; The NHL on NBC; The NHL on Sportsnet; That's Hockey.

The author also wishes to thank Steve Cameron, Barbara Campbell, Lionel Koffler, and Michael Worek from Firefly Books for their assistance and support in producing this book. Thanks also to designer Kimberley Young for her great work.

A special thank you as always to my wife Maria and my son David for their constant encouragement and understanding.